Notes from a Big Country

Notes from a Big Country

NOTES ON RETURNING TO AMERICA AFTER TWENTY YEARS AWAY

BILL BRYSON

Chivers Press • Bath, England

This Large Print edition is published by Thorndike Press, USA and by Chivers Press, England.

I'm a Stranger Here Myself published in 1999 in the U.S. by arrangement with Bantam Books, a division of Random House, Inc.

Notes from a Big Country published in 1999 in the U.K. by arrangement with Transworld Publishers Ltd.

U.S.	Hardcover	0-7862-2002-3	(Basic Series Edition)
U.S.	Softcover	0-7862-2003-1	
U.K.	Hardcover	0-7540-1332-4	(Windsor Large Print)
U.K.	Softcover	0-7540-2247-1	(Paragon Large Print)

The text of this Large Print edition is unabridged.
Other aspects of the book may vary from the original edition.

Set in 16 pt. Plantin.

Printed in the United States on permanent paper.

British Library Cataloguing in Publication Data available

Library of Congress Cataloging-in-Publication Data

Bryson, Bill.
  I'm a stranger here myself : notes on returning to America after 20 years away / Bill Bryson.
    p.   cm.
   ISBN 0-7862-2002-3 (lg. print : hc. : alk. paper)
   ISBN 0-7862-2003-1 (lg. print : sc. : alk. paper)
    1. United States — Description and travel — Anecdotes.
  2. United States — Social life and customs — 1971-   —
  Anecdotes. 3. Bryson, Bill — Anecdotes. 4. Large type books.
  I. Title.
  [E169.04.B778   1999]
   973.92—dc21
                                                    99-27388

*To
Cynthia,
David,
Felicity,
Catherine,
and Sam*

Contents

Introduction

In the late summer of 1996, an old journalist friend from London named Simon Kelner called me in New Hampshire, to where I had lately moved after living for twenty-some years in Britain. Simon had recently been made editor of *Night & Day* magazine, a supplement of the *Mail on Sunday* newspaper, and it was his idea that I should write a weekly column for him on America.

At various times over the years Simon had persuaded me to do all kinds of work that I didn't have time to do, but this was way out of the question.

"No," I said. "I can't. I'm sorry. It's just not possible. I've got too much on."

"So can you start next week?"

"Simon, you don't seem to understand. I can't do it."

"We thought we'd call it 'Notes from a Big Country.' "

"Simon, you'll have to call it 'Big Blank Space in the Magazine' because I cannot do it."

"Splendid, splendid," he said, but a trifle absently. I had the impression that he was doing something else at the same time — reviewing models for a swimsuit issue would be my guess. In any case, he kept covering up the phone and issuing important editor-type instructions to other people in the vicinity.

"So we'll send you a contract," he went on when he came back to me.

"No, Simon, don't do that. I can't write a weekly column for you. It's as simple as that. Are you taking this in? Tell me you are taking this in."

"Excellent. I'm absolutely delighted. We're all delighted. Well, must run."

"Simon, please listen to me. I can't take on a weekly column. Just not possible. Simon, are you hearing this? Simon? Hello? Simon, are you there? Hello? Bugger."

And that is how I became a newspaper columnist, a pursuit I followed for the next two years, from September 1996 to September 1998. The thing about a weekly column, I discovered, is that it comes up weekly. Now this may seem a self-evident fact, but in two years there never came a week when it did not strike me as both profound and startling. Another column?

Already? But I just *did* one.

I mention this to make the point that what follows was not intended to be — could not be — a systematic portrait of America. Mostly I wrote about whatever little things had lately filled my days — a trip to the post office, the joy of having a garbage disposal for the first time, the glories of the American motel. Even so, I would like to think that they chart a sort of progress, from being bewildered and often actively appalled in the early days of my return to being bewildered and generally charmed, impressed, and gratified now. (Bewilderment, you'll note, is something of a constant in my life, wherever I live.) The upshot is that I am very glad to be here. I hope that what follows makes that abundantly clear.

These pieces were written in the first instance for a British readership and of necessity included chunks of explication that an American would find unnecessary — what a drive-through window is exactly, how the postseason playoffs work in base-ball, who Herbert Hoover was, that sort of thing. I have endeavored to excise these intrusions discreetly throughout, though just occasionally the drift of the text made such adjustments impossible. I apologize

13

for that, and for any other oversights that may have slipped through.

In addition to Simon Kelner, I wish to express my sincere and lasting thanks to Bill Shinker, Patrick Janson-Smith, John Sterling, Luke Dempsey, and Jed Mattes, to each of whom I am variously and deeply indebted, and, above all — way above all — to my dear, long-suffering wife and children for so graciously and sportingly letting me drag them into all this.

And a special thanks to little Jimmy, whoever he may be.

Coming Home

I once joked in a book that there are three things you can't do in life. You can't beat the phone company, you can't make a waiter see you until he is ready to see you, and you can't go home again. Since the spring of 1995, I have been quietly, even gamely, reassessing point number three.

In May of that year, after nearly two decades in England, I moved back to the United States with my English wife and four children. We settled in Hanover, New Hampshire, for no other reason than that it seemed an awfully nice place. Founded in 1761, it is a friendly, well-ordered, prettily steepled community with a big central green, an old-fashioned Main Street, and a rich and prestigious university, Dartmouth College, whose benignly dominant presence gives the town a backdrop of graceful buildings, an air of privileged endeavor, and the presence of five thousand students, not one of whom can be trusted to cross a road in safety. With this came other attrac-

15

tions — good schools, an excellent bookstore and library, a venerable movie theater (The Nugget, founded in 1916), a good choice of restaurants, and a convivial bar called Murphy's. Helplessly beguiled, we bought a house near the center of town and moved in.

Coming back to your native land after an absence of many years is a surprisingly unsettling business, a little like waking from a long coma. Time, you discover, has wrought changes that leave you feeling mildly foolish and out of touch. You proffer hopelessly inadequate sums when making small purchases. You puzzle over ATM machines and automated gas pumps and pay phones, and are astounded to discover, by means of a stern grip on your elbow, that gas station road maps are no longer free.

In my case, the problem was intensified by the fact that I had left as a youth and was returning in middle age. All those things that you do as an adult — take out mortgages, have children, accumulate pension plans, take an interest in the state of your guttering — I had only ever done in England. Things like furnaces and storm windows were, in an American context, the preserve of my father. So finding myself suddenly in charge of an old New England house, with its mysterious pipes and thermostats, its temperamental garbage disposal and life-threatening automatic garage door, was both unnerving and rather exhilarating.

It is disconcerting to find yourself so simultaneously in your element and out of it. I can enumerate all manner of minutiae that mark me out as an American — which of the fifty states has a unicameral legislature, what a squeeze play is in baseball, who played Captain Kangaroo on TV. I even know about two-thirds of the words to "The Star-Spangled Banner," which is more than some people know who have sung it publicly.

But send me to the hardware store and even now I am totally lost. For months I had conversations with the clerk at our local True-Value that went something like this:

"Hi. I need some of that goopy stuff you fill nail holes in walls with. My wife's people call it Pollyfilla."

"Ah, you mean spackle."

"Very possibly. And I need some of those little plastic things that you use to hold screws in the wall when you put shelves up.

I know them as rawl plugs."

"We call them anchors."

"I shall make a mental note of it."

Really, I could hardly have felt more foreign if I had stood there dressed in lederhosen. All this was a shock to me. Although I was always very happy in Britain, I never stopped thinking of America as home, in the fundamental sense of the term. It was where I came from, what I really understood, the base against which all else was measured.

In a funny way nothing makes you feel more like a native of your own country than to live where nearly everyone is not. For twenty years, being an American was my defining quality. It was how I was identified, differentiated. I even got a job on the strength of it once when, in a moment of youthful audacity, I asserted to a managing editor of the *London Times* that I would be the only person on his staff who could reliably spell Cincinnati. (And it was so.)

Happily, there is a flipside to this. The many good things about America also took on a bewitching air of novelty. I was as dazzled as any newcomer by the famous ease and convenience of daily life, the giddying abundance of absolutely everything, the boundless friendliness of strangers, the wondrous unfillable vastness of an American basement, the delight of encountering waitresses and other service providers who actually seemed to enjoy their work, the curiously giddying notion that ice is not a luxury item and that rooms can have more than one electrical socket.

As well, there has been the constant, unexpected joy of reencountering all those things I grew up with but had largely forgotten: baseball on the radio, the deeply satisfying *whoing-bang* slam of a screen door in summer, insects that glow, sudden run-for-your-life thunderstorms, really big snowfalls, Thanksgiving and the Fourth of July, the smell of a skunk from just the distance that you have to sniff the air quizzically and say: "Is that a skunk?", Jell-O with stuff in it, the pleasingly comical sight of oneself in shorts. All that counts for a lot, in a strange way.

So, on balance, I was wrong. You can go home again. Just bring extra money for road maps and remember to ask for spackle.

Mail Call

One of the pleasures of living in a small, old-fashioned New England town is that it generally includes a small, old-fashioned post office. Ours is particularly agreeable. It's in an attractive Federal-style brick building, confident but not flashy, that looks like a post office ought to. It even smells nice — a combination of gum adhesive and old central heating turned up a little too high.

The counter employees are always cheerful, helpful and efficient, and pleased to give you an extra piece of tape if it looks as if your envelope flap might peel open. Moreover, post offices here by and large deal only with postal matters. They don't concern themselves with pension payments, car tax, TV licenses, lottery tickets, savings accounts, or any of the hundred and one other things that make a visit to any British post office such a popular, all-day event and provide a fulfilling and reliable diversion for chatty people who enjoy nothing so much as a good long hunt in their purses and handbags for exact change. Here there are never any long lines and you are in and out in minutes.

Best of all, once a year every American post office has a Customer Appreciation Day. Ours was yesterday. I had never heard of this engaging custom, but I was taken with it immediately. The employees had hung up banners, put out a long table with a nice checkered cloth, and laid on a generous spread of doughnuts, pastries, and hot coffee — all of it free.

After twenty years in Britain, this seemed a delightfully improbable notion, the idea of a faceless government bureaucracy thanking me and my fellow townspeople for our patronage, but I was impressed and grateful — and, I must say, it was good to be reminded that postal employees are not just mindless automatons who spend their days mangling letters and whimsically sending my royalty checks to a guy in Vermont named Bill Bubba but rather are dedicated, highly trained individuals who spend their days mangling letters and sending my royalty checks to a guy in Vermont named Bill Bubba.

Anyway, I was won over utterly. Now I would hate for you to think that my loyalty with respect to postal delivery systems can be cheaply bought with a chocolate twirl doughnut and a Styrofoam cup of coffee, but in fact it can. Much as I admire Britain's Royal Mail, it has never once offered me a morning snack, so I have to tell you that as I strolled home from my errand, wiping crumbs from my face, my thoughts toward American life in general and the U.S. Postal Service in particular were pretty incomparably favorable.

But, as nearly always with government services, it couldn't last. When I got home, the day's mail was on the mat. There among the usual copious invitations to acquire new credit cards, save a rain forest, become a life member of the National Incontinence Foundation, add my name (for a small fee) to the Who's Who of People Named Bill in New England, help the National Rifle Association with its Arm-a-Toddler campaign, and the scores of other unsought inducements, special offers, and solicitations that arrive each day at every American home — well, there among this mass was a forlorn and mangled letter that I had sent forty-one days earlier to a friend in California care of his place of employment and that was now being returned to me marked "Insufficient

22

Address — Get Real and Try Again" or words to that effect.

At the sight of this I issued a small, despairing sigh, and not merely because I had just sold the U.S. Postal Service my soul for a doughnut. It happens that I had recently read an article on wordplay in the Smithsonian magazine in which the author asserted that some puckish soul had once sent a letter addressed, with playful ambiguity, to

HILL
JOHN
MASS

and it had gotten there after the postal authorities had worked out that it was to be read as "John Underhill, Andover, Mass." (Get it?)

It's a nice story, and I would truly like to believe it, but the fate of my letter to California seemed to suggest a need for caution with regard to the postal service and its sleuthing abilities. The problem with my letter was that I had addressed it to my friend merely "c/o Black Oak Books, Berkeley, California," without a street name or number because I didn't know either. I appreciate that that is not a complete address, but it is a lot more explicit than "Hill John Mass" and anyway Black

Oak Books is a Berkeley institution. Anyone who knows the city — and I had assumed in my quaintly naive way that that would include Berkeley postal authorities — would know Black Oak Books. But evidently not. (Goodness knows, incidentally, what my letter had been *doing* in California for nearly six weeks, though it came back with a nice tan and an urge to get in touch with its inner feelings.)

Now just to give this plaintive tale a little heartwarming perspective, let me tell you that not long before I departed from England, the Royal Mail had brought me, within forty-eight hours of its posting in London, a letter addressed to "Bill Bryson, Writer, Yorkshire Dales," which is a pretty impressive bit of sleuthing. (And never mind that the correspondent was a trifle off his head.)

So here I am, my affections torn between a postal service that never feeds me but can tackle a challenge and one that gives me free tape and prompt service but won't help me out when I can't remember a street name. The lesson to draw from this, of course, is that when you move from one country to another you have to accept that there are some things that are better and some things that are worse, and there is nothing you can do about it. That may not be the profoundest of insights to take away from a morning's outing, but I did get a free doughnut as well, so on balance I guess I'm happy.

Now if you will excuse me I have to drive to Vermont and collect some mail from a Mr. Bubba.

(Some months after this piece was written, I received a letter from England addressed to "Mr. Bill Bryson, Author of 'A Walk in the Woods,' Lives Somewhere in New Hampshire, America." It arrived without comment or emendation just five days after it was mailed. My congratulations to the U.S. Postal Service for an unassailable triumph.)

Drug Culture

Do you know what I really miss about Britain now that I live in America? I miss coming in from the pub about midnight in a blurry frame of mind and watching *Open University* on TV.

Now *Open University*, I should perhaps explain, is a wonderful, wholly commendable institution the British set up some years ago to provide the chance of a college education to anyone who wants it. Coursework is done partly at home, partly on campuses, and partly through lectures broadcast on television, mostly at odd hours like very early on a Sunday morning or late at night when normal programming has finished.

The television lectures, which nearly all appear to have been filmed in the early 1970s, typically involve a geeky-looking academic with lively hair and a curiously misguided dress sense (even by the accommodating standards of that hallucinogenic age) standing before a blackboard, with

26

perhaps a large plastic model of a molecule on a table in front of him, saying something totally incomprehensible like: "However, according to Mersault's theorem, if we apply a small positive charge to the neutrino, the two free isotopes will be thrown into a reverse gradient orbit, while the captive positive becomes a negative positron, and vice versa, as we can see in this formula." And then he scribbles one of those complex, meaningless blackboard formulas of the sort that used to feature regularly in *New Yorker* cartoons.

The reason that *Open University* lectures traditionally are so popular with postpub crowds is not because they are interesting, which patently they are not, but because for a long time they were the only thing on British TV after midnight.

If I were to come in about midnight now mostly what I would find on the TV would be Peter Graves standing in a trenchcoat talking about unsolved mysteries, the Weather Channel, the fourth hour of an *I Love Lucy* extravaganza, at least three channels showing old *M*A*S*H* episodes, and a small selection of movies on the premium movie channels mainly involving nubile actresses disporting in the altogether. All of which is diverting enough in its way, I grant you, but it doesn't begin to compare with the hypnotic fascination of *Open University* after six pints of beer. I am quite serious about this.

I'm not at all sure why, but I always found it strangely compelling to turn on the TV late at night and find a guy who looked as if he had bought all the clothes he would ever need during one shopping trip in 1973 (so that, presumably, he would be free to spend the rest of his waking hours around oscilloscopes) saying in an oddly characterless voice, "And so we can see, adding two fixed-end solutions gives us another fixed-end solution."

Most of the time, I had no idea what these people were talking about — that was a big part of what made it so compelling somehow — but very occasionally the topic was something I could actually follow and enjoy. I'm thinking of an unexpectedly diverting lecture I chanced upon some years ago for people working toward a degree in marketing. The lecture compared the selling of proprietary healthcare products in Britain and the United States.

The gist of the program was that the same product had to be sold in entirely different ways in the two markets. An advertisement in Britain for a cold relief capsule, for instance, would promise no more than that it might make you feel a little better. You would still have a red nose and be in your pajamas, but you would be smiling again, if wanly. A commercial for the self-same product in America, however, would guarantee total, instantaneous relief. A person on the American side of the Atlantic who took this miracle compound would not only throw off his pj's and get back to work at once, he would feel better than he had for years and finish the day having the time of his life at a bowling alley.

The drift of all this was that the British don't expect over-the-counter drugs to change their lives, whereas we Americans will settle for nothing less. The passing of the years has not, it appears, dulled the notion. You have only to watch any television channel for a few minutes, flip through a magazine, or stroll along the groaning shelves of any drugstore to realize that people in this counry expect to feel more or less perfect all the time. Even our household shampoo, I notice, promises to "change the way you feel."

It is an odd thing about us. We expend huge efforts exhorting ourselves to "Say No to Drugs," then go to the drugstore and buy them by the armloads. Almost $75 billion is spent each year in the United States on medicines of all types, and pharmaceutical products are marketed with a vehemence and forthrightness that can take a little getting used to.

In one commercial running on television at the moment, a pleasant-looking middle-aged lady turns to the camera and says in a candid tone: "When I get diarrhea I like a little comfort" (to which I always say: "Why wait for diarrhea?").

In another, a man at a bowling alley (men are pretty generally at bowling alleys in these things) grimaces after a poor shot and mutters to his partner, "It's these hemorrhoids again." And here's the thing. The buddy has some hemorrhoid cream in his pocket! Not in his gym bag, you understand, not in the glove compartment of his car, but in his shirt pocket, where he can whip it out at a moment's notice and call the gang around. Extraordinary.

But the really amazing change that occurred while I was away is that now even prescription drugs are advertised. I have before me a popular magazine called *Health* that is chock full of ads with bold headlines saying things like "Why take two tablets when you can take one? Prempro is the only prescription tablet that combines Premarin and a progestin in one tablet."

Another more intriguingly asks, "Have you ever treated a vaginal yeast infection in the middle of nowhere?" (Not knowingly!) A third goes straight to the economic heart of the matter and declares, "The doctor told me I'd probably be taking blood pressure pills for the rest of my life. The good news is how much I might save since he switched me to Adalat CC (nifedipine) from Procardia XL (nifedipine)."

The idea is that you read the advertisement, then badger your "healthcare professional" to prescribe it for you. It seems a curious concept to me, the idea of magazine readers deciding what medications are best for them, but then Americans appear to know a great deal about drugs. Nearly all the advertisements assume an impressively high level of biochemical familiarity. The vaginal yeast ad confidently assures the reader that Diflucan is "comparable to seven days of Monistat 7, Gyne-Lotrimin, or Mycelex-7," while the ad for Prempro promises that it is "as effective as taking Premarin and a progestin separately."

When you realize that these are meaningful statements for thousands and thousands of people, the idea of your bowling

31

buddy carrying a tube of hemorrhoid unguent in his shirt pocket perhaps doesn't seem quite so ridiculous.

I don't know whether this national obsession with health is actually worth it. What I do know is that there is a much more agreeable way to achieve perfect inner harmony. Drink six pints of beer and watch *Open University* for ninety minutes before retiring. It has never failed me.

What's Cooking?

Going to a restaurant is generally a discouraging experience for me because I always manage somehow to antagonize the waitress. This, of course, is something you never want to do because waitresses are among the relatively small group of people who have the opportunity to sabotage items that you will shortly be putting into your mouth.

My particular problem is being unable to take in all the food options that are presented to me. If you order, say, a salad, the waitress reels off sixteen dressings, and I am not quick enough to take in that many concepts at once.

"Can you run those past me again?" I say with a simpleton smile of the sort that I hope will inspire compassion.

So the waitress sighs lightly and rolls her eyes a trifle, the way you would if you had to recite sixteen salad dressings over and over all day long for a succession of half-wits, and reels off the list again. This time I

listen with the greatest gravity and atten-
tiveness, nodding at each, and then unfail-
ingly I choose one that she didn't mention.

"We don't do Thousand Island," she
says flatly.

I can't possibly ask her to recite the list
again, so I ask for the only one I can
remember, which I am able to remember
only because it sounded so awful —
Gruyère and goat's milk vinaigrette or
something. Lately I have hit on the expe-
dient of saying: "I'll have whichever one is
pink and doesn't smell like the bottom of a
gym bag." They can usually relate to that, I
find.

In fancy restaurants it is even worse
because the server has to take you through
the evening's specials, which are described
with a sumptuousness and panache that
are seldom less than breathtaking and
always incomprehensible. My wife and I
went to a fancy restaurant in Vermont for
our anniversary the other week and I swear
I didn't understand a single thing the
waiter described to us.

"Tonight," he began with enthusiasm,
"we have a crêpe galette of sea chortle and
kelp in a rich *mal de mer* sauce, seasoned
with disheveled herbs grown in our own
herbarium. This is baked in an inverted

Prussian helmet for seventeen minutes and four seconds precisely, then layered with steamed wattle and woozle leaves. Very delicious; very audacious. We are also offering this evening a double rack of Rio Ròcho cutlets, tenderized at your table by our own flamenco dancers, then baked in a clay *dong* for twenty-seven minutes under a lattice of guava peel and sun-ripened stucco. For vegetarians this evening we have a medley of forest floor sweetmeats gathered from our very own woodland dell. . . ."

And so it goes for anything up to half an hour. My wife, who is more sophisticated than I, is not fazed by the ornate terminology. Her problem is trying to keep straight the bewilderment of options. She will listen carefully, then say: "I'm sorry, is it the squib that's pan-seared and presented on a bed of organic spoletto?"

"No, that's the baked donkling," says the serving person. "The squib comes as a quarter-cut hank, lightly rolled in paya-paya, then tossed with oil of olay and calamine, and presented on a bed of chaff beans and snoose noodles."

I don't know why she bothers because, apart from being much too complicated to take in, none of the dishes sounds like anything you would want to eat anyway, except maybe on a bet after drinking way too much.

Now all this is of particular moment to me because I have just been reading the excellent *Diversity of Life* by the eminent Harvard naturalist Edward O. Wilson, in which he makes the startling and discordant assertion that the foods we in the Western world eat actually are not very adventurous at all.

Wilson notes that of the thirty thousand species of edible plants on earth, only about twenty are eaten in any quantity. Of these, three species alone — wheat, corn, and rice — account for over half of what the temperate world shovels into its collective gullet. Of the three thousand fruits known to botany, all but about two dozen are essentially ignored. The situation with vegetables is a little better, but only a little.

And why do we eat the few meager foods we do? Because, according to Wilson, those were the foods that were cultivated by our neolithic ancestors ten thousand or so years ago when they first got the hang of agriculture.

The very same is true of husbandry. The animals we raise for food today are not eaten because they are especially nutritious or delectable but because they were the ones first domesticated in the Stone Age.

In other words, in dietary terms we are veritable troglodytes (which, speaking personally, is all right by me). I think this explains a lot, not least my expanding sense of dismay as the waiter bombarded us with ecstatic descriptions of roulades, ratatouilles, empanadas, langostinos, tagliolinis, confits, filos, quenelles, and goodness knows what else.

"Just bring me something that's been clubbed," I wanted to say, but of course I held my tongue.

Eventually, he concluded his presentation with what sounded to me like "an oven-baked *futilité* of pumpkin rind and kumquats."

"It's *feuilleté*," my wife explained to me.

"And what's that when you take it out of the box?" I asked unhappily.

"Something you wouldn't like, dear."

I turned to the waiter with a plaintive look. "Do you have anything that once belonged to a cow?" I asked.

He gave a stiff nod. "Certainly, sir. We can offer you a 16-ounce *suprême de boeuf*, incised by our own butcher from the fore flank of a corn-fed Holstein raised on our own Montana ranch, then slow-grilled over palmetto and buffalo chips at a temperature of . . ."

"Are you describing a steak?" I asked, perking up.

"Not a term we care to use, sir, but yes."

Of course. It was all becoming clear now. There was real food to be had here if you just knew the lingo. "Well, I'll have that," I said. "And I'll have it with, shall we say, a *depravité* of potatoes, hand cut and fried till golden in a medley of vegetable oils from the Imperial Valley, accompanied by a *quantité de bière,* flash-chilled in your own coolers and conveyed to my table in a cylinder of glass."

The man nodded, impressed that I had cracked the code. "Very good, sir," he said. He clicked his heels and withdrew.

"And no *feuilleté,*" I called after him. I may not know much about food, but I am certain of this: If there is one thing you don't want with steak it's *feuilleté*.

Well, Doctor, I Was Just Trying to Lie Down . . .

Here's a fact for you: According to the latest *Statistical Abstract of the United States*, every year more than 400,000 Americans suffer injuries involving beds, mattresses, or pillows. Think about that for a minute. That is almost 2,000 bed, mattress, or pillow injuries a day. In the time it takes you to read this article, four of my fellow citizens will somehow manage to be wounded by their bedding.

My point in raising this is not to suggest that we are somehow more inept than the rest of the world when it comes to lying down for the night (though clearly there are thousands of us who could do with additional practice), but rather to observe that there is scarcely a statistic to do with this vast and scattered nation that doesn't in some way give one pause.

I had this brought home to me the other day when I was in the local library looking up something else altogether in the afore-

39

said *Abstract* and happened across "Table No. 206: Injuries Associated with Consumer Products." I have seldom passed a more diverting half hour.

Consider this intriguing fact: Almost 50,000 people in the United States are injured each year by pencils, pens, and other desk accessories. How *do* they do it? I have spent many long hours seated at desks where I would have greeted almost any kind of injury as a welcome diversion, but never once have I come close to achieving actual bodily harm.

So I ask again: How *do* they do it? These are, bear in mind, injuries severe enough to warrant a trip to an emergency room. Putting a staple in the tip of your index finger (which I have done quite a lot, sometimes only semi-accidentally) doesn't count. I am looking around my desk now and unless I put my head in the laser printer or stab myself with the scissors I cannot see a single source of potential harm within ten feet.

But then that's the thing about household injuries if Table No. 206 is any guide — they can come at you from almost anywhere. Consider this one. In 1992 (the latest year for which figures are available) more than 400,000 people in the United

States were injured by chairs, sofas, and sofa beds. What are we to make of this? Does it tell us something trenchant about the design of modern furniture or merely that we have become exceptionally careless sitters? What is certain is that the problem is worsening. The number of chair, sofa, and sofa bed injuries showed an increase of 30,000 over the previous year, which is quite a worrying trend even for those of us who are frankly fearless with regard to soft furnishings. (That may, of course, be the nub of the problem — overconfidence.)

Predictably, "stairs, ramps, and landings" was the most lively category, with almost two million startled victims, but in other respects dangerous objects were far more benign than their reputations might lead you to predict. More people were injured by sound-recording equipment (46,022) than by skateboards (44,068), trampolines (43,655), or even razors and razor blades (43,365). A mere 16,670 overexuberant choppers ended up injured by hatchets and axes, and even saws and chainsaws claimed a relatively modest 38,692 victims.

Paper money and coins (30,274) claimed nearly as many victims as did scissors (34,062). I can just about conceive of how you might swallow a dime and then wish you hadn't ("You guys want to see a neat trick?"), but I cannot for the life of me construct hypothetical circumstances involving folding money and a subsequent trip to the ER. It would be interesting to meet some of these people.

I would also welcome a meeting with almost any of the 263,000 people injured by ceilings, walls, and inside panels. I can't imagine being hurt by a ceiling and not having a story worth hearing. Likewise, I could find time for any of the 31,000 people injured by their "grooming devices."

But the people I would really like to meet are the 142,000 hapless souls who received emergency room treatment for injuries inflicted by their clothing. What can they be suffering from? Compound pajama fracture? Sweatpants hematoma? I am powerless to speculate.

I have a friend who is an orthopedic surgeon, and he told me the other day that one of the incidental occupational hazards of his job is that you get a skewed sense of everyday risks since you are constantly repairing people who have come a cropper in unlikely and unpredictable ways. (Only that day he had treated a man who had

had a moose come through the windshield of his car, to the consternation of both.) Suddenly, thanks to Table No. 206, I began to see what he meant.

Interestingly, what had brought me to the Statistical Abstract in the first place was the wish to look up crime figures for the state of New Hampshire, where I now live. I had heard that it is one of the safest places in America, and indeed the Abstract bore this out. There were just four murders in the state in the latest reporting year — compared with over 23,000 for the country as a whole — and very little serious crime.

All that this means, of course, is that statistically in New Hampshire I am far more likely to be hurt by my ceiling or underpants — to cite just two potentially lethal examples — than by a stranger, and, frankly, I don't find that comforting at all.

Rule Number 1: Follow All Rules

I did a foolish thing the other afternoon. I went into one of our local cafés and seated myself without permission. You don't do this in America, but I had just had what seemed like a salient and important thought (namely, "There is always a little more toothpaste in the tube — always. Think about it") and I wanted to jot it down before it left my head. Anyway, the place was practically empty, so I just took a table near the door.

After a couple of minutes, the hostess — the Customer Seating Manager — came up to me and said in a level tone, "I see you've seated yourself."

"Yup," I replied proudly. "Dressed myself too."

"Didn't you see the sign?" She tilted her head at a big sign that said "Please Wait to Be Seated."

I have been in this café about 150 times. I have seen the sign from every angle but supine.

"Oh!" I said innocently, and then: "Gosh, I didn't notice it."

She sighed. "Well, the server in this section is very busy, so you may have to wait a while for her to get to you."

There was no other customer within fifty feet, but that wasn't the point. The point was that I had disregarded a posted notice and would have to serve a small sentence in purgatory in consequence.

It would be entirely wrong to say that Americans love rules any more than it would be correct to say that the British love queuing. These things are done not with enthusiasm or affection but out of a more or less instinctive recognition that these are useful ways of helping to achieve and maintain a civilized and orderly society.

Generally this is a very good thing. There are times, I have to say, when a little Teutonic order wouldn't go amiss in England — for instance, when people take two spaces in a parking lot because they can't be bothered to park correctly (the one offense for which, if I may speak freely here, I would support capital punishment).

Sometimes, however, the American devotion to order goes too far. Our local public swimming pool, for example, has twenty-seven written rules — twenty-seven! — of which my favorite is "One Bounce Per Dive on Diving Board." And they're enforced.

What is frustrating is that it seldom matters whether these rules make any sense or not. A year or so ago, as a way of dealing with the increased threat of terrorism, America's airlines began requiring passengers to present photographic identification when checking in for a flight. The first I heard of this was when I showed up to catch a plane at an airport 120 miles from my home.

"I need to see some picture ID," said the clerk, who had the charm and boundless motivation you would expect to find in someone whose primary employment perk is a nylon tie.

"Really? I don't think I have any," I said and began patting my pockets, as if that would make a difference, and then pulling cards from my wallet. I had all kinds of identification — library card, credit cards, social security card, health insurance card, airline ticket — all with my name on them, but nothing with a picture. Finally, at the back of the wallet I found an old Iowa driver's license that I had forgotten I even had.

"This is expired," he sniffed.

"Then I won't ask to drive the plane," I replied.

"Anyway, it's fifteen years old. I need something more up to date."

I sighed and rooted through my belongings. Finally it occurred to me that I was carrying one of my books with my picture on the jacket. I handed it to him proudly and with some relief.

He looked at the book and then hard at me and then at a printed list. "That's not on our list of Permissible Visual Cognitive Imagings," he said, or something similarly vacuous.

"I'm sure it isn't, but it's still me. It couldn't *be* more me." I lowered my voice and leaned closer to him. "Are you seriously suggesting that I had this book specially printed so I could sneak on to a flight to Buffalo?"

He stared hard at me for another minute, then called in for consultation another clerk. They conferred and summoned a third party. Eventually we ended up with a crowd scene involving three check-in clerks, their supervisor, the supervisor's surpervisor, two baggage handlers, several inquisitive bystanders straining to get a better view, and a guy selling jewelry out of an aluminum case. My flight was due to take off in minutes and froth was starting to form at the corners of my mouth. "What is the point of all this anyway?" I said to the head supervisor. "Why do you need a picture ID?"

"FAA rule," he said, staring unhappily at my book, my invalid driver's license, and the list of permissible photo options.

"But *why* is it the rule? Do you honestly believe that you are going to thwart a terrorist by requiring him to show you a laminated photograph of himself? Do you think a person who could plan and execute a sophisticated hijacking or other illegal airborne event would be unable to contrive some form of convincing artificial identification? Has it occurred to you that it might be more productive, vis-à-vis terrorism, if you employed someone who was actually awake, and perhaps with an IQ above that of a small mollusk, to monitor the TV screens on your X-ray machines?" I may not have said all this in exactly those words, but that was the drift of my sentiment.

But the requirement, you see, is not simply to identify yourself but to identify yourself in a way that precisely matches a written instruction.

Anyway, I changed tack and begged. I promised never again to turn up at an airport without adequate ID. I took on an attitude of complete contrition. I don't suppose anyone has ever shown such earnest, remorseful desire to be allowed to proceed to Buffalo.

Eventually, with reluctance, the supervisor nodded at the clerk and told him to check me in, but he warned me not to try anything as slippery as this again and then departed with his colleagues.

The check-in clerk issued me a boarding pass and I started toward the gate, then turned back, and in a low, confidential tone shared with him a helpful afterthought.

"There is always a little more toothpaste in the tube," I said. "Think about it."

Take Me Out to the Ballpark

People sometimes ask me, "What is the difference between baseball and cricket?"

The answer is simple. Both are games of great skill involving balls and bats but with this crucial difference: Baseball is exciting, and when you go home at the end of the day you know who won.

I'm joking, of course. Cricket is a wonderful sport, full of deliciously scattered micromoments of real action. If a doctor ever instructs me to take a complete rest and not get overexcited, I shall become a fan at once. In the meantime, my heart belongs to baseball.

It's what I grew up with, what I played as a boy, and that of course is vital to any meaningful appreciation of a sport. I had this brought home to me many years ago in England when I went out on a soccer ground with a couple of English friends to knock a ball around.

I had watched soccer on television and

thought I had a fair idea of what was required, so when one of them lofted a ball in my direction, I decided to flick it casually into the net with my head, the way I had seen Kevin Keegan do it on TV. I thought that it would be like heading a beachball — that there would be a gentle, airy *ponk* sound and that the ball would lightly leave my brow and drift in a pleasing arc into the net. But of course it was like heading a bowling ball. I have never felt anything so startlingly not like I expected it to feel. I walked around for four hours on wobbly legs with a big red circle and the word "MITRE" imprinted on my forehead and vowed never again to do anything so foolish and painful.

I bring this up here because the World Series has just started, and I want you to know why I am very excited about it. The World Series, I should perhaps explain, is the annual baseball contest between the champion of the American League and the champion of the National League.

Actually, that's not quite true because they changed the system some years ago. The trouble with the old way of doing things was that it involved only two teams. Now, you don't have to be a brain surgeon to work out that if you could somehow

51

contrive to include more teams there would be a lot more money in the thing.

So each league divided itself into three divisions of four or five teams each. So now the World Series is not a contest between the two best teams in baseball — at least not necessarily — but rather between the winners of a series of playoff games involving the Western, Eastern, and Central divisional champions of each league, plus (and this was particuarly inspired, I think) a pair of "wild card" teams that didn't win anything at all.

It is all immensely complicated, but essentially it means that practically every team in baseball except the Chicago Cubs gets a chance to go to the World Series.

The Chicago Cubs don't get to go because they never manage to qualify even under a system as magnificently accommodating as this. Often they *almost* qualify, and sometimes they are in such a commanding position that you cannot believe they won't qualify, but always in the end they doggedly manage to come up short. Whatever it takes — losing seventeen games in a row, letting easy balls go through their legs, crashing comically into each other in the outfield — you can be certain the Cubs will manage it.

They have been doing this, reliably and efficiently, for over half a century. They haven't been in a World Series since 1945. Stalin had good years more recently than that. This heartwarming annual failure by the Cubs is almost the only thing in baseball that hasn't changed in my lifetime, and I appreciate that very much.

It's not easy being a baseball fan because baseball fans are a hopelessly sentimental bunch, and there is no room for sentiment in something as wildly lucrative as an American sport. For anyone from outside America, one of the most remarkable aspects of American sports is how casually franchises abandon their loyal fans and move to a new city. In English soccer, it would be unthinkable for, say, Manchester United to move to London or Everton to find a new home in Portsmouth, or anyone to go anywhere really, but here that sort of thing happens all the time, sometimes more than once. The Braves began life in Boston, then moved to Milwaukee, then moved to Atlanta. The A's started in Philadelphia, then switched to Kansas City, then pushed on to Oakland.

Meanwhile, the Major Leagues have repeatedly expanded to where they have reached the point where it is deucedly hard, for me at any rate, to keep track of it all. Of the thirty teams in Major League baseball, just eleven are where they were when I was a kid. There are teams out there now that I know nothing about. Without looking at the standings, I couldn't tell you whether the Arizona Diamondbacks are in the National League or the American League. That's a terrifying confession for someone who loves the game.

Even when teams stay put, they don't actually stay put. I mean by this that they are constantly tearing down old stadiums to build new ones. Call me eccentric, call me fastidious, but I truly believe that baseball should only be watched in an old stadium. It used to be that every big American city had a venerable ballpark. Generally these were dank and creaky, but they had character. You would get splinters from the seats, the soles of your shoes would congeal to the floor from all the years of sticky stuff that had been spilled during exciting moments, and your view would inevitably be obscured by a cast-iron column supporting the roof. But that was all part of the glory.

Only four of these old parks are left, and two of them — Yankee Stadium in New

York and Fenway Park in Boston — are under threat. I won't say that Fenway's relative nearness was the decisive consideration in our settling in New Hampshire, but it was certainly a factor. Now the owners want to tear it down and build a new stadium.

In fairness it must be said that the new ballparks of the 1990s, as opposed to the multipurpose arenas built in the previous thirty years, do strive to keep the character and intimacy of the old ballparks — sometimes even improve on them — but they have one inescapable, irremediable flaw. They are new. They have no history, no connection with a glorious and continuous past. No matter how scrupulous a new Fenway they build, it won't be the place where Ted Williams batted. It won't make your feet stick. It won't echo in the same way. It won't smell funny. It won't be Fenway.

I keep saying that I won't go to the new park when they finally raze Fenway, but I know I'm lying because I am hopelessly addicted to the game. All of which increases my almost boundless respect and admiration for the hapless Chicago Cubs. To their credit, the Cubs have never threatened to leave Chicago and continue to play at Wrigley Field. They even still play mostly day games — the way God intended baseball to be played. A day game at Wrigley Field is one of the great American experiences.

And here's the problem. Nobody deserves to go to the World Series more than the Chicago Cubs. But they can't go because that would spoil their custom of never going. It is an irreconcilable paradox.

You see what I mean when I say that it is not easy being a baseball fan?

Help!

The other day I called my computer helpline, because I needed to be made to feel ignorant by someone much younger than me, and the boyish-sounding person who answered told me he required the serial number on my computer before he could deal with me.

"And where do I find that?" I asked warily.

"It's on the bottom of the CPU functional dysequilibrium unit," he said, or words of a similarly confounding nature.

This, you see, is why I don't call my computer helpline very often. We haven't been talking four seconds and already I can feel a riptide of ignorance and shame pulling me out into the icy depths of Humiliation Bay. Any minute now, I know with a sense of doom, he's going to ask me how much RAM I have.

"Is that anywhere near the TV-screen thingy?" I ask helplessly.

"Depends. Is your model the Z-40LX

Multimedia HPii or the ZX46/2Y Chromium B-BOP?"

And so it goes. The upshot is that the serial number for my computer is engraved on a little metal plate on the bottom of the main control box — the one with the CD drawer that is kind of fun to open and shut. Now call me an idealistic fool, but if I were going to put an identifying number on every computer I sold and then require people to regurgitate that number each time they wanted to communicate with me, I don't believe I would put it in a place that required the user to move furniture and get the help of a neighbor each time he wished to consult it. However, that is not my point.

My model number was something like CQ124765900-03312-DiP/22/4. So here is my point: *Why?* Why does my computer need a number of such breathtaking complexity? If every neutrino in the universe, every particle of matter between here and the farthest wisp of receding Big Bang gas somehow acquired a computer from this company there would still be plenty of spare numbers under such a system.

Intrigued, I began to look at all the numbers in my life, and nearly every one of them was absurdly excessive. My Visa card number, for instance, has thirteen digits. That's enough for almost two trillion potential customers. Who are they trying to kid? My Budget Rent-a-Car card has no fewer than seventeen digits. Even my local video store appears to have 1.9 billion customers on its rolls (which may explain why *L.A. Confidential* is always out).

The most impressive by far is my Blue Cross/Blue Shield medical card, which not only identifies me as No. YGH475907018 00 but also as a member of Group 02368. Presumably, then, each group has a person in it with the same number as mine. You can almost imagine us having reunions.

Now all this is a long way of getting around to the main point of this discussion, which is that one of the great, great improvements in American life in the last twenty years is the advent of phone numbers that any fool can remember.

A long time ago people realized that you could remember numbers more easily if you relied on the letters rather than the numbers. In my hometown of Des Moines, for instance, if you wanted to call time, the official number was 244-5646, which of course no one could handily recall. But if you dialed BIG JOHN you got the same number, and *everybody* could remember

BIG JOHN (except, curiously, my mother, who was a bit hazy on the Christian name part, and so generally ended up asking the time of complete strangers whom she had just woken, but that's another story).

Now, of course, every business has a 1-800 number — 1-800-FLY TWA or 244-GET PIZZA or whatever. Not many changes in the past two decades have made life immeasurably better for simple folk like me, but this unquestionably has.

Now here is my big idea. I think we should all have one number for everything. Mine naturally would be 1-800-BILL. This number would do for everything — it would make my phone ring, it would appear on my checks and credit cards, it would adorn my passport, it would get me a video.

Of course, it would mean rewriting a lot of computer programs, but I'm sure it could be done. I intend to take it up with my own computer company, just as soon as I can get at that serial number again.

A Visit
to the Barbershop

I have very happy hair. No matter how serene and composed the rest of me is, no matter how grave and formal the situation, my hair is always having a party. In any group photograph you can spot me at once because I am the person at the back whose hair seems to be listening, in some private way, to a disco album called "Dance Craze '97."

Every few months, with a sense of foreboding, I take this hair of mine uptown to the barbershop and allow one of the men there to amuse himself with it for a bit. I don't know why, but going to the barber always brings out the wimp in me. There is something about being enshrouded in a cape and having my glasses taken away, then being set about the head with sharp cutting tools, that leaves me feeling helpless and insecure.

I mean, there you are, armless and squinting, and some guy you don't know is

61

doing serious, almost certainly regrettable, things to the top of your head. I must have had 250 haircuts in my life by now, and if there is one thing I have learned it is that a barber will give you the haircut he wants to give you and there is not a thing you can do about it. So the whole experience is filled with trauma for me. This is particularly so as I always get the barber I was hoping not to get — usually the new guy they call "Thumbs." I especially dread the moment when he sits you in the chair and the two of you stare together at the hopeless catastrophe that is the top of your head, and he says, in a worryingly eager way, "So what would you like me to do with this?"

"Just a simple tidy-up," I say, looking at him with touching hopefulness but knowing that already he is thinking in terms of extravagant bouffants and mousse-stiffened swirls, possibly a fringe of bouncy ringlets. "You know, something anonymous and respectable — like a banker or an accountant."

"See any styles up there you like?" he says and indicates a wall of old black-and-white photographs of smiling men whose hairstyles seem to have been modeled on Thunderbirds characters.

"Actually, I was hoping for something a bit less emphatic."

"A more natural look, in other words?"

"Exactly."

"Like mine, for instance?"

I glance at the barber. His hairstyle brings to mind an aircraft carrier advancing through choppy seas, or perhaps an extravagant piece of topiary.

"Even more subdued than that," I suggest nervously.

He nods thoughtfully, in a way that makes me realize we are not even in the same universe taste-in-hairwise, and says in a sudden, decisive tone: "I know just what you want. We call it the Wayne Newton."

"That's really not quite what I had in mind," I start to protest, but already he is pushing my chin into my chest and seizing his shears.

"It's a very popular look," he adds. "Everyone on the bowling team has it." And with a buzz of motors he starts taking hair off my head as if stripping wallpaper.

"I really don't want the Wayne Newton look," I murmur with feeling, but my chin is buried in my chest and in any case my voice is drowned in the hum of his dancing clippers.

And so I sit for a small, tortured eternity, staring at my lap, under strict instructions not to move, listening to terrifying cutting machinery trundling across my scalp. Out of the corner of my eye I can see large quantities of shorn hair tumbling onto my shoulders.

"Not too much off," I bleat from time to time, but he is engaged in a lively conversation with the barber and customer at the next chair about the prospects for the Boston Celtics and only occasionally turns his attention to me and my head, generally to mutter, "Oh, dang," or "Whoopsie."

Eventually he jerks my head up and says: "How's that for length?"

I squint at the mirror, but without my glasses all I can see is what looks like a pink balloon in the distance. "I don't know," I say uncertainly. "It looks awfully short."

I notice he is looking unhappily at everything above my eyebrows. "Did we decide on a Paul Anka or a Wayne Newton?" he asks.

"Well, neither, as a matter of fact," I say, pleased to have an opportunity to get this sorted out at last. "I just wanted a modest tidy-up."

"Let me ask you this," he says, "how fast

does your hair grow?"

"Not very," I say and squint harder at the mirror, but I still can't see a thing. "Why, is there a problem?"

"Oh, no," he says, but in that way that means, "Oh, yes." "No, it's fine," he goes on. "It's just that I seem to have done the left side of your head in a Paul Anka and the right in a Wayne Newton. Let me ask you this then: Do you have a big hat?"

"What have you done?" I ask in a rising tone of alarm, but he has gone off to his colleagues for a consultation. They talk in whispers and look at me the way you might look at a road-accident victim.

"I think it must be these antihistamines I'm taking," I hear Thumbs say to them sadly.

One of the colleagues comes up for a closer look and decides it's not as disastrous as it looks. "If you take some of this hair here from behind the left ear," he says, "and take it around the back of his head and hook it over the other ear, and maybe reattach some of this from here, then you can make it into a modified Barney Rubble." He turns to me. "Will you be going out much over the next few weeks, sir?"

"Did you say 'Barney Rubble'?" I

whimper in dismay.

"Unless you go for a Hercule Poirot," suggests the other barber.

"Hercule Poirot?" I whimper anew.

They leave Thumbs to do what he can. After another ten minutes, he hands me my glasses and lets me raise my head. In the mirror I am confronted with an image that brings to mind a lemon meringue pie with ears. Over my shoulder, Thumbs is smiling proudly.

"Turned out pretty good after all, eh?" he says.

I am unable to speak. I hand him a large sum of money and stumble from the shop. I walk home with my collar up and my head sunk into my shoulders.

At the house, my wife takes one look at me. "Did you say something to upset them?" she asks in sincere wonder.

I shrug helplessly. "I told him I wanted to look like a banker."

She gives one of those sighs that come to all wives eventually. "Well, at least you rhyme," she mutters in that odd, enigmatic way of hers, and goes off to get the big hat.

On the Hotline

I came across something in our bathroom the other day that has occupied my thoughts off and on ever since. It was a little dispenser of dental floss.

It isn't the floss itself that is of interest to me but that the container has a toll-free number printed on it. You can call the company's Floss Hotline twenty-four hours a day. But here is the question: Why would you need to? I keep imagining some guy calling up and saying in an anxious voice, "OK, I've got the floss. Now what?"

As a rule of thumb, I would submit that if you need to call your floss provider, for any reason, you are probably not ready for this level of oral hygiene.

My curiosity aroused, I had a look through all our cupboards and discovered with interest that nearly all household products these days carry a hotline number. You can, it appears, call up for guidance on how to use soap and shampoo, gain helpful tips on where to store ice cream so that it doesn't melt and run out of the bottom of the container, and receive professional advice on parts of your body to which you can most successfully and stylishly apply nail polish. ("So let me get this straight. You're saying *not* on my forehead?")

For those who do not have access to a telephone, or who perhaps have a telephone but have not yet mastered its use, most products also carry helpful printed tips such as "Remove Shells Before Eating" (on peanuts) and "Caution: Do Not Re-Use as Beverage Container" (on a bleach bottle). We recently bought an electric iron that admonished us, among other things, not to use it in conjunction with explosive materials. In a broadly similar vein, I read a couple of weeks ago that computer software companies are considering rewriting the instruction "Strike Any Key When Ready" because so many people have been calling in to say they cannot find the "Any" key.

Until a few days ago, my instinct would have been to chortle richly at people who need this sort of elemental guidance, but then three things happened that made me modify my views.

First, I read in the paper how John

Smoltz, the Atlanta Braves star, showed up at a training session one day with a painful-looking welt across his chest and, when pressed for an explanation, sheepishly admitted that he had tried to iron a shirt while he was wearing it.

Second, it occurred to me that although I have never done anything quite so foolish as that, it was only because I had not thought of it.

Third, and perhaps most conclusively, two nights ago I went out to run two small errands — specifically, to buy some pipe tobacco and mail some letters. I bought the tobacco, carried it straight across the street to a mailbox, opened the lid, and deposited it. I won't tell you how far I walked before it dawned on me that this was not a 100 percent correct execution of my original plans.

You see my problem. People who need labels on mailboxes saying "Not for Deposit of Tobacco or Other Personal Items" can't very well smirk at others, even those who iron their chests or have to seek lathering guidance from a shampoo hot-line.

I mentioned all this at dinner the other night and was appalled to see the enthu-siasm and alacrity with which all the members of the family began suggesting labels that would be particularly suitable for me, like "Caution: When Door Says 'Pull' It's Absolutely No Use Pushing" and "Warning: Do Not Attempt to Remove Sweater Over Head While Walking Among Chairs and Tables." A particular favorite was "Caution: Ensure That Shirt Buttons Are in Correct Holes Before Leaving House." This went on for some hours.

I concede that I am somewhat inept with regard to memory, personal grooming, walking through low doorways, and much else, but the thing is, it's my genes. Allow me to explain.

I recently tore out of the newspaper an article concerning a study at the University of Michigan, or perhaps it was the University of Minnesota (at any rate it was somewhere cold starting with "M"), that found that absentmindedness is a genetically inherited trait. I put it in a file marked "Absentmindedness" and, of course, mislaid the file.

However, in searching for it this morning I found another file intriguingly marked "Genes and So On," which is just as interesting and — here was the lucky part — not altogether irrelevant. In it I found a copy of a report from the November 29,

1996, issue of the journal *Science* entitled "Association of Anxiety-Related Traits with a Polymorphism in the Serotonin Transporter Gene Regulatory Region."

Now to be perfectly candid, I don't follow polymorphism in serotonin transporters as closely as I ought, at least not during the basketball season, but when I saw the sentence "By regulating the magnitude and duration of serotonergic responses, the 5-HT transporter (5-HTT) is central to the fine-tuning of brain serotonergic neurotransmission," I thought, as almost anyone would, "Gosh, these fellows may be on to something."

The upshot of the study is that scientists have located a gene (specifically, gene number SLC6A4 on chromosome 17q12, in case you want to experiment at home) that determines whether you are a born worrier or not. To be absolutely precise, if you have a long version of the SLC6A4 gene, you are very probably easygoing and serene, whereas if you have the short version you can't leave home without saying at some point, "Stop the car. I think I left the bathwater running."

What this means in practice is that if you are not a born worrier you have nothing to worry about (though of course you wouldn't be worrying anyway), whereas if you *are* a worrier by nature there is absolutely nothing you can do about it, so you may as well stop worrying, except of course you can't. Now put this together with the aforementioned findings about absentmindedness at the University of Somewhere Cold, and I think you can see that our genes have a great deal to answer for.

Here's another interesting fact from my "Genes and So On" file. According to Richard Dawkins in *The Blind Watchmaker*, each one of the ten trillion cells in the human body contains more genetic information than the entire *Encyclopaedia Britannica* (and without sending a salesman to your door), yet it appears that 90 percent of all our genetic material doesn't do anything at all. It just sits there, like Uncle Fred and Aunt Mabel when they drop by on a Sunday.

From this I believe we can draw four important conclusions, namely: (1) Even though your genes don't do much, they can let you down in a lot of embarrassing ways; (2) always mail your letters first, then buy the tobacco; (3) never promise a list of four things if you can't remember the fourth one; and (4).

Design Flaws

I have a teenage son who is a runner. He has, at a conservative estimate, sixty-one hundred pairs of running shoes, and every one of them represents a greater investment of cumulative design effort than, say, the Verrazano Narrows Bridge. These shoes are amazing. I was just reading a review in one of his running magazines of the latest in "Sport Utility Sneakers," as they are evidently called, and it was full of passages like this: "A dual density EVA midsole with air units fore and aft provides stability while a gel heel-insert absorbs shock, but the shoe makes a narrow footprint, a characteristic that typically suits only the biomechanically efficient runner." Alan Shepard went into space with less science at his disposal than that.

So here is my question. If my son can have his choice of a seemingly limitless range of scrupulously engineered, bio-mechanically efficient footwear, why does my computer keyboard suck? This is a serious inquiry.

My computer keyboard has 102 keys, almost double what my old manual typewriter had, which on the face of it seems awfully generous. Among other typographical luxuries, I can choose between three styles of bracket and two kinds of colon. I can dress my text with carets (^) and cedillas (~). I can have slashes that fall to the left or to the right, and goodness knows what else.

I have so many keys, in fact, that over on the right-hand side of the keyboard there are whole communities of buttons of whose function I haven't the tiniest inkling. Occasionally I hit one by accident and subsequently discover that several paragraphs of my w9rk n+w look l*ke th?s, or that I have written the last page and a half in an interesting but unfortunately nonalphabetic font called Wingdings, but otherwise I haven't the faintest idea what those buttons are there for.

Never mind that many of these keys duplicate the functions of other keys, while others apparently do nothing at all (my favorite in this respect is one marked "Pause," which when pressed does absolutely nothing, raising the interesting metaphysical question of whether it is therefore doing its job), or that several keys are

74

arrayed in slightly imbecilic places. The delete key, for instance, is right beside the overprint key so that often I discover, with a trill of gay laughter, that my most recent thoughts have been devouring, PacMan-like, everything I had previously written. Quite often, I somehow hit a combination of keys that summons a box that says, in effect, "This Is a Pointless Box. Do You Want It?" which is followed by another that says "Are You *Sure* You Don't Want the Pointless Box?" Never mind all that. I have known for a long time that the computer is not my friend.

But here is what gets me. Out of all the 102 keys at my disposal, there is no key for the fraction ½. Typewriter keyboards always used to have a key for ½. Now, however, if I wish to write ½, I have to bring down the font menu and call up a directory called "WP Characters," then hunt through a number of subdirectories until I remember, or more often blunder on, the particular one, "Typographic Symbols," in which hides the furtive ½ sign. This is irksome and pointless, and it doesn't seem right to me.

But then most things in the world don't seem right to me. On the dashboard of our family car is a shallow indentation about the size of a paperback book. If you are looking for somewhere to put your sunglasses or spare change, it is the obvious place, and it works extremely well, I must say, so long as the car is not actually moving. However, as soon as you put the car in motion, and particularly when you touch the brakes, turn a corner, or go up a gentle slope, everything slides off. There is, you see, no lip around this dashboard tray. It is just a flat space with a dimpled bottom. It can hold nothing that has not been nailed to it.

So I ask you: What then is it *for?* Somebody had to design it. It didn't just appear spontaneously. Some person — perhaps, for all I know, a whole committee of people in the Dashboard Stowage Division — had to invest time and thought in incorporating into the design of this vehicle (it's a Dodge Excreta, if you're wondering) a storage tray that will actually hold nothing. That is really quite an achievement.

But it is nothing, of course, compared with the manifold design achievements of those responsible for the modern video recorder. Now I am not going to prattle on about how impossible it is to program the typical VCR because you know that already. Nor will I observe how irritating it is that you must cross the room and get down on your stomach to confirm that it is actually recording. But I will just make one small passing observation. I recently bought a VCR, and one of the selling points — one of the things the manufacturer boasted about — was that it was capable of recording programs up to twelve months in advance. Now think about this for a moment and tell me any circumstance — and I mean any circumstance at all — in which you can envision wanting to set a video machine to record a program one year from now.

I don't want to sound like some old guy who is always moaning. I freely acknowledge that there are many excellent, well-engineered products that didn't exist when I was a boy — the pocket calculator and Post-it notes are two that fill me yet with gratitude and wonder — but it does seem to me that an awful lot of things out there have been designed by people who cannot possibly have stopped to think how they will be used.

Just think for a moment of all the everyday items you have to puzzle over — fax machines, scanners, photocopiers, hotel showers, hotel alarm clocks, airline tickets, television remote control units, microwave ovens, almost any electrical product owned by someone other than you — because they are ill thought out.

And why are they so ill thought out? Because all the best designers are making running shoes. Either that or they are just idiots. In either case, it really isn't fair.

Room Service

Something I have long wanted to do is visit the Motel Inn in San Luis Obispo, California.

On the face of it, this might seem an odd quest since the Motel Inn is not, by all accounts, a particularly prepossessing establishment. Built in 1925 in the Spanish colonial style much beloved by restaurant owners, Zorro, and almost no one else, it sits in the shadow of a busy elevated freeway amid a cluster of gas stations, fast-food outlets, and other, more modern motor inns.

Once, however, it was a famous stopping place on the coastal highway between Los Angeles and San Francisco. A Pasadena architect named Arthur Heineman gave it its exuberant style, but his most inspired legacy lies in the name he chose for it. Playing around with the words *motor* and *hotel,* he dubbed it a *mo-tel,* hyphenating the word to emphasize its novelty.

America already had lots of motels by

then (the very first apears to have been Askins' Cottage Camp built in 1901 in Douglas, Arizona), but they were all called something else — *auto court, cottage court, hotel court, tour-o-tel, auto hotel, bungalow court, cabin court, tourist camp, tourist court, trav-o-tel.* For a long time it looked like *tourist court* would become the standard designation for an overnight stopping place. It wasn't until about 1950 that motel achieved generic status.

I know all this because I have just been reading a book on the history of the motel in America called *The Motel in America*. Written by three academics, it is a ponderously heavy piece of work, full of sentences like "The needs of both consumers and purveyors of lodging strongly influenced the development of organized systems of distribution," but I bought it and devoured it anyway because I love everything about motels.

I can't help myself. I still get excited every time I slip a key into a motel room door and fling it open. It is just one of those things — airline food is another — that I get excited about and should know better.

The golden age of motels was also, as it happens, the golden age of me — the

1950s — and I suppose that's what accounts for my fascination. For anyone who didn't travel around America by car in the 1950s, it is almost impossible now to imagine how thrilling they were. For one thing, the national chains like Holiday Inn and Ramada barely existed then. As late as 1962, 98 percent of motels were individually owned, so each one had its own character.

Essentially they were of two types. The first type was the good ones. These nearly always had a welcoming, cottagey air. Typically, they were built around a generous lawn with shady trees and a flower bed decorated with a wagon wheel painted white. (The owners, for some reason, generally liked to paint all their rocks white, too, and array them along the edge of the drive.) Often they had a swimming pool or swings. Sometimes they had a gift shop or coffee shop, too.

Indoors they offered measures of comfort and elegance that would have the whole family cooing — thick carpet, purring air conditioner, a big TV, nightstand with a telephone and a built-in radio, gleaming bathroom, sometimes a dressing area, Vibro-matic beds, which gave you a massage for a quarter.

The second kind of motels consisted of the appalling ones. We always stayed at these. My father, who was one of history's great cheapskates, was of the view that there was no point in spending money on . . . well, on anything really, and certainly not on anything that you were mostly going to be asleep in.

In consequence, we generally camped in motel rooms where the beds sagged as if they had last been occupied by a horse and the cooling system was an open window and where you could generally count on being awakened in the night by a piercing shriek, the sound of splintering furniture, and a female voice pleading, "Put the gun down, Vinnie. I'll do anything you say." I don't wish to suggest that these experiences left me scarred and irrationally embittered, but I can clearly remember watching Janet Leigh being hacked up in the Bates Motel in *Psycho* and thinking, "At least she got a shower curtain."

All of this, even at its worst, gave highway travel a kind of exhilarating unpredictability. You never knew what quality of comfort you would find at the end of the day, what sort of small pleasures might be offered. It gave road trips a piquancy that the homogenized refinements of the modern age cannot match.

That changed very quickly with the rise of motel chains. Holiday Inn, for example, went from 79 outlets in 1958 to almost 1,500 in less than twenty years. Today just five chains account for one-third of all the motel rooms in America. Travelers these days evidently don't want uncertainty in their lives. They want to stay in the same place, eat the same food, watch the same TV wherever they go.

Recently, while driving from Washington, D.C., to New England with my own family, I tried explaining all this to my children and got the idea that we should stop for the night at an old-fashioned family-run establishment. Everyone thought this was an immensely stupid idea, but I insisted that it would be a great experience.

Well, we looked everywhere. We passed scores of motels, but they were all franchised to national chains. Eventually, after perhaps ninety minutes of futile hunting, I pulled off the interstate for the seventh or eighth time and — lo! — there shining out of the darkness was the Sleepy Hollow Motel, a perfect 1950s sort of place.

"There's a Comfort Inn across the street," one of my children pointed out.

"We don't want a Comfort Inn, Jimmy," I explained, temporarily forgetting in my excitement that I don't have a child named Jimmy. "We want a *real* motel."

My wife, being English, insisted on having a look at the room. It was awful, of course. The furnishings were battered and bare. The room was so cold you could see your breath. There was a shower curtain, but it hung by just three rings.

"It's got character," I insisted.

"It's got nits," said my wife. "We'll be across the road at the Comfort Inn."

In disbelief, I watched them troop out.

"You'll stay, won't you, Jimmy?" I said, but even he left without a backward glance.

I stood there for about fifteen seconds, then switched off the light, returned the key, and went across to the Comfort Inn. It was bland and characterless and just like every Comfort Inn I had ever stayed in. But it was clean, the TV worked, and, it must be said, the shower curtain was very nice.

Consuming Pleasures

I believe I have just secured definitive proof that America is the ultimate shopping paradise. It came in a video catalog that arrived unsolicited with the morning mail. There, among the usual diverse offerings — *Titanic*, *Tai Chi for Health and Fitness*, every movie ever made by John Wayne — was a self-help video called *Do the Macarena Totally Nude*, which promises to guide the naked home viewer through "the hot moves of this Latin-influenced dance that is sweeping the nation."

Among the catalog's other intriguing offerings were a documentary called *Antique Farm Tractors*, a boxed set representing the complete oeuvre of Don Knotts, and an interesting compilation entitled *Nude Housewives of America* (volumes 1 and 2), depicting ordinary housewives "doing their daily chores in the buff!" And to think I asked for a socket wrench for Christmas.

My point is that there is almost nothing you cannot buy in this remarkable country. Of course, shopping has been the national sport in America for decades, but three significant retailing developments have emerged in recent years to elevate the shopping experience to a higher, giddier plane. They are:

• *Telemarketing.* This is an all-new business in which platoons of salespeople phone up complete strangers, more or less at random, generally at suppertime, and doggedly read to them a prepared script promising a free set of steak knives or AM-FM radio if they buy a certain product or service. These people have become positively relentless.

The possibility that I would buy a timeshare in Florida over the telephone from a stranger is about as likely as the possibility that I would change religious affiliation on the basis of a doorstep visit from a brace of Mormons, but evidently this feeling is not universal. According to the *New York Times*, telemarketing in America is now worth $35 billion a year. That figure is so amazing that I cannot think about it without getting a headache, so let us move on to retail development number two.

• *Outlet malls.* These are malls in which companies like Ralph Lauren and Calvin Klein sell their own lines at discounts. In many cases, outlet malls are not malls at all but rather whole communities that have been taken over by outlet stores. Easily the most remarkable of these is Freeport, Maine, home of L. L. Bean.

We stopped there last summer on the way up the Maine coast, and I am still trembling from the experience. The procedure for a visit to Freeport is unvarying. You creep into town in a long line of traffic, spend forty minutes hunting for a parking space, then join a crowd of thousands shuffling along Main Street past a succession of shops selling every known brand name that ever was or will be.

At the center of it all is the L. L. Bean store, which is huge. It is open twenty-four hours a day, 365 days a year. You can buy a kayak there at 3 A.M. if you want. People apparently do. My brain is beginning to hurt again.

• *Catalogs.* Shopping by mail has been around for a long time, of course, but it has proliferated to a degree that is just beyond astounding. Almost from the moment we arrived in America catalogs

87

began plopping unbidden onto our mat with the daily mail. Now we get perhaps a dozen a week, sometimes more — catalogs for videos, gardening implements, lingerie, books, camping and fishing gear, things to make your bathroom a more stylish and convivial place, you name it.

For a long time I tossed these out with the rest of the unsolicited mail. What a fool I was. I now realize they not only provide hours of reading pleasure but open up a world of possibilities I scarcely knew existed.

Just today, along with the aforementioned nude macarena brochure, we received a catalog called "Tools for Serious Readers." It was full of the usual assortment of blotters and desk organizers, bed lights and lap trays, but what particularly caught my eye was something called the Briefcase Valet, a small wheeled trolley that sits about four inches off the floor.

Available in dark or natural cherry and attractively priced at $139, it is designed to alleviate one of the most intractable office storage problems of our age. As the catalog copy explains: "Most of us are faced with the same nagging problem of what to do with our briefcase when we put it down at home or in the office. That's why we designed our Briefcase Valet. It holds your briefcase up off the floor, making it easier to insert and retrieve things as the day progresses."

I especially like those last four words, "as the day progresses." How many times have I gotten to the end of a working day myself and thought: "Oh, what I'd give for a small wheeled device in a choice of wood tones to save me reaching those last four inches!"

The scary thing is that often these descriptions are written so artfully that you are almost taken in by them. I was just reading in another catalog about a fancy kitchen accessory from Italy called a *Porto Rotolo di Carta*, which boasts "a spring tension arm," "stainless steel guide," "crafted brass finial," and "rubber gasket for exceptional stability" — all for just $49.95 — when I realized that it was, in fact, a paper towel holder.

Obviously the catalog couldn't say, "No matter how you look at it, this is just a paper towel dispenser and you would be a sap to buy it," so they must try to dazzle you with its exotic pedigree and technical complexity.

In consequence, even the most mundane catalog items boast more design features than a 1954 Buick. I have before me a glossy book from another company announcing with undisguised pride that its flannel shirts feature, among much else, gauntlet buttons, extra-long sleeve plackets, two-ply 40S yarn construction ("for a superior nap"), boxed back pleat, double stitching at stress points, handy locker loop and non-fused collar, whatever all that may be. Even socks come with lengthy, scientific-sounding descriptions extolling their seamless closures, one-to-one fiber loops, and hand-linked yarns.

I confess I have sometimes been briefly tempted by these seductive blandishments to make a purchase, but in the end I realize that given a choice between paying $37.50 for a shirt with a superior nap and just having a nap, I will always go for the latter.

However, let me say right here that if anyone comes up with a Totally Nude Macarena Socket-Wrench Home Workout Video with handy locker loop in a choice of colors, I am ready to place my order now.

The Numbers Game

The U.S. Congress, which never ceases to be amazing, recently voted to give the Pentagon $11 billion more than it had asked for. Do you have any idea how much $11 billion is? Of course you don't. Nobody does. It is not possible to conceive of a sum that large.

No matter where you turn with regard to America and its economy you are going to bump into figures that are so large as to be beyond meaningful comprehension. Consider just a few figures culled at random from this week's papers. California has an economy worth $850 billion. The annual gross domestic product of the United States is $6.8 trillion. The federal budget is $1.6 trillion, the federal deficit nearly $200 billion.

It's easy to lose sight of just how enormous these figures really are. America's cumulative debt at last count, according to *Time* magazine, was "a hair" under $4.7 trillion. The actual figure was $4.692 trillion, so that statement is hard to argue with, yet it represents a difference of $8 billion — a pretty large hair in anybody's book.

I worked long enough on the business desk of a national newspaper in England to know that even the most experienced financial journalists often get confused when dealing with terms like *billion* and *trillion*, and for two very good reasons. First, they have usually had quite a lot to drink at lunch, and, second, such numbers really are confusing.

And that is the whole problem. Big numbers are simply beyond what we are capable of grasping. On Sixth Avenue in New York there is an electronic billboard, erected and paid for by some anonymous source, that announces itself as "The National Debt Clock." When I was last there, it listed the national debt at $4,533,603,804,000 — that's $4.5 trillion — and the figure was growing by $10,000 every second, or so fast that the last three digits on the electronic meter were a blur. But what does $4.5 trillion actually mean?

Well, let's just try to grasp the concept of $1 trillion. Imagine that you were in a vault filled with dollar bills and that you were told you could keep each one you initialed. Say, too, for the sake of argument that you could initial one dollar bill per second and that you worked straight through without ever stopping. How long do you think it would take to count a trillion dollars? Go on, humor me and take a guess. Twelve weeks? Two years? Five?

If you initialed one dollar per second, you would make $1,000 every seventeen minutes. After 12 days of nonstop effort you would acquire your first $1 million. Thus, it would take you 120 days to accumulate $10 million and 1,200 days — something over three years — to reach $100 million. After 31.7 years you would become a billionaire, and after almost a thousand years you would be as wealthy as Bill Gates. But not until after 31,709.8 years would you count your trillionth dollar (and even then you would be less than one-fourth of the way through the pile of money representing America's national debt).

That is what $1 trillion is.

What is interesting is that it is becoming increasingly evident that most of these inconceivably vast sums that get bandied about by economists and policy makers are almost certainly miles out anyway. Take gross domestic product, the bedrock of modern economic policy. GDP was a concept that was originated in the 1930s by the economist Simon Kuznets. It is very good at measuring physical things — tons of steel, board feet of lumber, potatoes, tires, and so on. That was all very well in a traditional industrial economy. But now the greater part of output for nearly all developed nations is in services and ideas — things like computer software, telecommunications, financial services — which produce wealth but don't necessarily, or even generally, result in a product that you can load on a pallet and ship out to the marketplace.

Because such activities are so difficult to measure and quantify, no one really knows what they amount to. Many economists now believe that America may have been underestimating its rate of GDP growth by as much as two to three percentage points a year for several years. That may not seem a great deal, but if it is correct then the American economy — which obviously is already staggeringly enormous — may be one-third larger than anyone had thought. In other words, there may be hundreds of billions of dollars floating around in the economy that no one suspected were there. Incredible.

Here's another even more arresting thought. None of this really matters because GDP is in any case a perfectly useless measurement. All that it is, literally, is a crude measure of national income — "the dollar value of finished goods and services," as the textbooks put it — over a given period.

Any kind of economic activity adds to the gross domestic product. It doesn't matter whether it's a good activity or a bad one. It has been estimated, for instance, that the O. J. Simpson trial added $200 million to America's GDP through lawyers' fees, court costs, hotel bills for the press, and so on, but I don't think many people would argue that the whole costly spectacle made America a noticeably greater, nobler place.

In fact, bad activities often generate more GDP than good activities. I was recently in Pennsylvania at the site of a zinc factory whose airborne wastes were formerly so laden with pollutants that they denuded an entire mountainside. From the factory fence to the top of the mountain there was not a single scrap of growing vegetation to be seen. From a GDP perspective, however, this was wonderful. First, there was the gain to the economy from all the zinc the factory had manufactured and sold over the years. Then there was the gain from the tens of millions of dollars the government must spend to clean up the site and restore the mountain. Finally, there will be a continuing gain from medical treatments for workers and townspeople made chronically ill by living amid all those contaminants.

In terms of conventional economic measurement, all of this is gain, not loss. So too is overfishing of lakes and seas. So too is deforestation. In short, the more recklessly we use up natural resources, the more the GDP grows.

As the economist Herman Daly once put it: "The current national accounting system treats the earth as a business in liquidation." Or as three other leading economists dryly observed in an article in the *Atlantic Monthly* last year: "By the curious standard of the GDP, the nation's economic hero is a terminal cancer patient who is going through a costly divorce."

So why do we persist with this preposterous gauge of economic performance? Because it's the best thing that economists have come up with yet. Now you know why they call it the dismal science.

Junk-Food Heaven

I decided to clean out the refrigerator the other day. We don't usually clean out our fridge — we just box it up every four or five years and send it off to the Centers for Disease Control in Atlanta with a note to help themselves to anything that looks scientifically promising — but we hadn't seen one of the cats for a few days and I had a vague recollection of having glimpsed something furry on the bottom shelf, toward the back. (Turned out to be a large piece of gorgonzola.)

So there I was down on my knees unwrapping pieces of foil and peering cautiously into Tupperware containers when I came across an interesting product called a breakfast pizza. I examined it with a kind of rueful fondness, as you might regard an old photograph of yourself dressed in clothes that you cannot believe you ever thought were stylish. The breakfast pizza, you see, represented the last surviving relic of a bout of very serious retail foolishness on my part.

Some weeks ago I announced to my wife that I was going to the supermarket with her next time she went because the stuff she kept bringing home was — how can I put this? — not fully in the spirit of American eating. I mean, here we were living in a paradise of junk food — the country that gave the world cheese in a spray can — and she kept bringing home healthy stuff like fresh broccoli and packets of Swedish crispbread.

It was because she was English, of course. She didn't really understand the rich, unrivaled possibilities for greasiness and goo that the American diet offers. I longed for artificial bacon bits, melted cheese in a shade of yellow unknown to nature, and creamy chocolate fillings, sometimes all in the same product. I wanted food that squirts when you bite into it or plops onto your shirt front in such gross quantities that you have to rise very, very carefully from the table and sort of limbo over to the sink to clean yourself up.

So I accompanied her to the supermarket and while she was off squeezing melons and pricing shiitake mushrooms, I made for the junk-food section — which was essentially all the rest of the store. Well, it was heaven.

The breakfast cereals alone could have occupied me for most of the afternoon. There must have been two hundred types. Every possible substance that could be dried, puffed, and coated with sugar was there. The most immediately arresting was a cereal called Cookie Crisp, which tried to pretend it was a nutritious breakfast but was really just chocolate chip cookies that you put in a bowl and ate with milk. Brilliant.

Also of note were cereals called Peanut Butter Crunch, Cinnamon Mini Buns, Count Chocula ("with Monster Marshmallows"), and a particularly hardcore offering called Cookie Blast Oat Meal, which contained *four* kinds of cookies. I grabbed one of each of the cereals and two of the oatmeal — how often I've said that you shouldn't start a day without a big, steaming bowl of cookies — and sprinted with them back to the shopping cart.

"What's that?" my wife asked in the special tone of voice with which she often addresses me in retail establishments.

I didn't have time to explain. "Breakfast for the next six months," I panted as I sprinted past, "and don't even think about putting any of it back and getting granola."

I had no idea how the market for junk food had proliferated. Everywhere I turned I was confronted with foods guaranteed to make you waddle — moon pies, pecan spinwheels, peach mellos, root beer buttons, chocolate fudge devil dogs, and a whipped marshmallow sandwich spread called Fluff, which came in a tub large enough to bathe a baby in. You really cannot believe the bounteous variety of nonnutritious foods available to the supermarket shopper these days or the quantities in which they are consumed. I recently read that the average American eats 17.8 pounds — 17.8 pounds! — of pretzels every year. And that, remember, is the average. Somebody somewhere is eating most of my share as well.

Aisle seven ("Food for the Seriously Obese") was especially productive. It had a whole section devoted exclusively to a product called Toaster Pastries, which included, among much else, eight different types of toaster strudel. And what exactly is toaster strudel? Who cares? It was coated in sugar and looked drippy. I grabbed an armload.

I admit I got a little carried away — but

there was so much and I had been away so long.

It was the breakfast pizza that finally made my wife snap. She looked at the box and said, "No."

"I beg your pardon, my sweet?"

"You are not bringing home something called breakfast pizza. I will let you have" — she reached into the cart for some specimen samples — "root beer buttons and toaster strudel and . . ." She lifted out a packet she hadn't noticed before. "What's this?"

I looked over her shoulder. "Microwave pancakes," I said.

"Microwave pancakes," she repeated, but with less enthusiasm.

"Isn't science wonderful?"

"You're going to eat it all," she said. "Every bit of everything that you don't put back on the shelves now. You do understand that?"

"Of course," I said in my sincerest voice.

And do you know she actually made me eat it. I spent weeks working my way through a symphony of junk food, and it was all awful. Every bit of it. I don't know whether junk food has gotten worse or whether my taste buds have matured, but even the treats I'd grown up with — even,

God help me, Hostess Cup Cakes — now seemed disappointingly pallid or sickly.

The most awful of all was the breakfast pizza. I tried it three or four times, baked it in the oven, zapped it with microwaves, and once in desperation served it with a side of marshmallow Fluff. But it never rose beyond a kind of limp, chewy listlessness. Eventually I gave up altogether and hid what was left in the Tupperware graveyard on the bottom shelf of the fridge.

Which is why, when I came across the box again the other day, I regarded it with mixed feelings. I started to toss it out, then hesitated and opened the lid. It didn't smell bad — I expect it was pumped so full of chemicals that there wasn't any room in it for bacteria — and I thought about keeping it a while longer as a reminder of my folly, but in the end I discarded it. And then, feeling hungry, I went off to the pantry to see if I couldn't find a nice plain piece of Swedish crispbread and maybe a stick of celery.

How to
Have Fun at Home

My wife thinks nearly everything about American life is wonderful. She loves having her groceries bagged for her. She adores free iced water and book matches. She thinks home-delivered pizza is a central hallmark of civilization. I haven't the heart to tell her that waiters and waitresses in the United States urge everyone to have a nice day.

Personally, while I am exceedingly fond of America and grateful for its many conveniences, I am not quite so slavishly accepting. Take the matter of having your groceries bagged for you. I appreciate the gesture and all, but when you come down to it what does it actually get you except the leisure to stand and watch your groceries being bagged? It's not as if it buys you some quality time.

However, there are certain things that are so wonderful in American life that I can hardly stand it myself. Chief among these, without any doubt, is the garbage disposal. A garbage disposal is everything a labor-saving device should be and so seldom is — noisy, fun, extremely hazardous, and so dazzlingly good at what it does that you cannot imagine how you ever managed without one. If you had asked me eighteen months ago what the prospects were that shortly my chief amusement in life would be placing assorted objects down a hole in the kitchen sink, I believe I would have laughed in your face, but in fact it is so.

I have never had a garbage disposal before, so I have been learning its tolerances through a process of trial and error. Chopsticks give perhaps the liveliest response (this is not recommended, of course, but there comes a time with every piece of machinery when you just *have* to see what it can do), but cantaloupe rinds make the richest, throatiest sound and result in less "down time." Coffee grounds in quantity are the most likely to provide a satisfying "Vesuvius effect," though for obvious reasons it is best not to attempt this difficult feat until your wife has gone out for the day and to have a mop and stepladder standing by.

The most exciting event with a garbage

disposal, of course, is when it jams and you have to reach in and unclog it, knowing that at any moment it might spring to life and abruptly convert your arm from a useful grasping tool into a dibber. Don't try to tell me about living life on the edge.

Equally satisfying in its way, and certainly no less ingenious, is the little-known fireplace ashpit. This is simply a metal plate — a kind of trapdoor — built into the floor of the living room fireplace above a deep, brick-lined pit. When you clean the fireplace, instead of sweeping the ash into a bucket and then trailing the dribblings through the house, you maneuver it into this hole and it disappears forever. Brilliant.

In theory the ashpit must eventually fill up, but ours seems to be bottomless. Down in the basement there's a small metal door in the wall that allows you to see how the pit is doing, and occasionally I go down to have a look. It isn't really necessary, but it gives me an excuse to go down in the basement, and I always welcome that because basements are, after the garbage disposal and the ashpit, the third great feature of American life. They are wonderful chiefly because they are so amazingly, so spaciously, unnecessary.

Now basements I know because I grew up with one. Every American basement is the same. They all have a clothesline that is rarely used, a trickle of water from an indeterminable source running diagonally across the floor, and a funny smell — a combination of old magazines, camping gear that should have been aired and wasn't, and something to do with a guinea pig named Mr. Fluffy that escaped down a central heating grate six months ago and has not been seen since (and presumably would now be better called Mr. Bones).

Basements are so monumentally surplus to normal requirements, in fact, that you seldom go down there, so it generally comes as something of a pleasant surprise to remember that you have one. Every dad who ever goes down in a basement pauses at some point to look around and think: "Gee, we really ought to do something with all this space. We could have a wet bar and a pool table and maybe a jukebox and a Jacuzzi and a couple of pinball machines . . ." But of course it's just one of those things that you intend to do one day, like learn Spanish or take up home barbering, and never do.

Oh, occasionally, especially in starter

homes, you will find that some young gung-ho mom and dad have converted the basement into a playroom for the children, but this is always a mistake as no child will play in a basement. This is because no matter how loving the parents, no matter how much the child would like, deep down, to trust them, there is always the thought that they will quietly lock the door at the top of the stairs and move to Florida. No, basements are deeply and inescapably scary — that's why they always feature in spooky movies, usually with a shadow of Joan Crawford carrying an axe thrown on the far wall. That may be why even dads don't go down there very often.

I could go on and on cataloging other small, unsung glories of American household life — refrigerators that dispense iced water and make their own ice cubes, walk-in closets, central heating that works — but I won't. I'm out of space, and, anyway, Mrs. B. has just gone out to do some shopping and it has occurred to me that I have not yet seen what the disposal can do with a juice carton. I'll get back to you on this one.

Tales of
the North Woods

Just over a year ago, in the depths of a snowy winter, a young college student left a party in a village near the small town in New Hampshire where I live to walk to his parents' house a couple of miles away. Foolishly — for it was dark and he had been drinking — he decided to take a shortcut through the woods. He never made it.

The next day, when his disappearance became known, hundreds of volunteers took to the woods to search for him. They hunted for days, but without success. It wasn't until spring that someone walking in the woods stumbled on his body.

Five weeks ago, something broadly similar happened. A small private jet with two people aboard had to abort its approach as it came in to land at our local airport in poor weather. As the pilot swung around to the northeast to make a new approach, he radioed his intentions to the control tower.

A moment later the little green blip that

was his plane disappeared from the airport radar screen. Somewhere out there, abruptly and for reasons unknown, the plane came down in the woods.

Over the next few days the biggest ground and air search in the state's history was undertaken, but the plane was not found. A big element of the mystery is that an exceptionally large number of people — 275 at last count — claim to have seen the jet just before it crashed. Some said they were close enough to see the two men peering out the windows. The trouble is that these witnesses were widely scattered across two states, in locations up to 175 miles apart. Clearly they can't all have seen the plane in the moments before it crashed, so what *did* they see?

A good deal of other news about that fateful flight has emerged in the weeks since the plane's disappearance. The most startling news to me was that a plane vanishing in the New Hampshire woods is not that exceptional an event. In 1959, according to our local paper, two professors from the university here went down in the woods in a light plane during a winter storm. Notes they left behind showed that they survived for at least four days. Unfortunately, their plane was not found for two and a half months. Two years later, another light plane disappeared in the woods and wasn't found for six months. A third plane crashed in 1966 and wasn't found until 1972, long after most people had forgotten about it. The woods, it seems, can swallow a lot of wreckage and not give much away.

Even so, the utter disappearance of a Lear jet seems inexplicable. To begin with, this was a big plane: an eighteen-seater, with a wingspan of forty feet. You wouldn't think that something that large could vanish without trace, but evidently it can. There is a great deal more technology available today than there was in previous years — heat sensors, infrared viewers, long-range metal detectors, and the like. The U.S. Air Force has even lent a reconnaissance satellite. All to no avail. For all the looking, there have been no signs of strewn wreckage, no crash paths through the trees. The plane has simply vanished.

I don't mean to imply that we live on the edge of some kind of Bermuda triangle of the deciduous world, merely that the woods of New Hampshire are a rather strange and sinister place.

To begin with, they are full of trees, and I don't mean that as a joke. I have spent a fair amount of time hiking the woods of New England, and I can tell you that the one thing you see in numbers beyond imagining is trees. At times it's actually unsettling because it is essentially just one endlessly repeated scene. Every bend in the path presents an outlook indistinguishable from every other, and it remains like that no matter how far you go. If you somehow lost the path, you could easily find yourself — very probably would find yourself — helplessly bereft of bearings.

Last fall, while out for a stroll not two miles from my home, I noticed just off the path a bluff I had not seen before and, below it, in a small, secret dell, the rooftop of a house. Since there must be a road or track to the house, it occurred to me that if there was a way down to the house, it would make a nice circular walk from my home. I ventured perhaps seventy-five yards from the path and explored the bluff top, but I couldn't see a way down and so made to return to the path. But could I find it? I could not.

I hunted around for perhaps five or six minutes in a state of mild perplexity and retraced my steps as carefully as I could, but the path seemed to have vanished. As I stood scratching my head, certain that this path I knew well should be right about where I was standing, two other hikers passed by through the trees. They were on the path but twenty yards from where I stood and moving at a completely different angle from what I expected. The woods are like that, you see: an incredible tangle without fixed reference points.

Knowing this, it's less surprising to learn that the woods sometimes keep forever people unfortunate enough to get lost in their featureless embrace, or even swallow aircraft whole. New Hampshire is as big as some European countries — Wales, for instance — and is 85 percent forest. There's a lot of forest out there to get lost in. Every year at least one or two people on foot go missing, sometimes never to be seen again.

Yet here's a remarkable thing. Until only about a century ago, and less than that in some areas, most of these woods didn't exist. Nearly the whole of rural New England — including all the area around our part of New Hampshire — was open, meadowy farmland.

I had this brought home to me with a certain potency the other week when the town council sent us, as a kind of New Year's present, a calendar containing old

112

photographs of the town from the local archives. One of the pictures, a hilltop panorama taken in 1874, showed a scene that looked vaguely familiar, though I couldn't tell why. It showed a corner of the Dartmouth College campus and a dirt road leading off into some distant hills. The rest was spacious farm fields.

It took me some minutes to work out that I was looking at the future site of my own neighborhood. It was odd because our street looks like a traditional New England street, with clapboard houses shaded by tall and shapely trees, but in fact nearly all of it dates from the early 1920s, half a century after the photograph was taken. The hill from which the picture was taken is now a twenty-acre woods and nearly all the landscape from the backs of our houses to the distant hills is swathed in dense, mature forest, but hardly a twig of it existed in 1874.

The farms disappeared because the farmers moved west, to richer lands in places like Illinois and Ohio, or migrated to the burgeoning industrial cities, where earnings were more reliable and generous. The farms they left behind — and sometimes the villages that supported them — sank into the ground and gradually returned to wilderness. All over New England if you go for a walk in the woods you will come across the remains of old stone walls and the foundations of abandoned barns and farmhouses hidden in the ferns and bracken of the forest floor.

The same path I got lost on follows, for part of its length, the route of an eighteenth-century post road. For eighteen miles the path winds through dark, tangled, seemingly ancient woodland, yet there are people alive who remember when all that land was farmland. Just off the old post road, four miles or so from here, there once stood a village called Quinntown. It was a reasonably thriving little place, with a mill and a school and a couple of streets of houses. It's still out there somewhere, or what remains of it.

I've looked for Quinntown several times as I've passed, but even with a good map the site is nearly impossible to find because the woods are so lacking in distinguishing landmarks. I know a man who has looked for Quinntown off and on for years and still not found it.

Last weekend I decided to try again. There was a fresh fall of snow, which always makes the woods agreeable. Naturally the thought flitted through my mind that I might stumble on some sign of the missing jet. I didn't *really* expect to find anything — I was seven or eight miles from the presumed crash site reported in the local paper — but on the other hand, the plane has to be out there somewhere and it was altogether possible that no one had looked in this area.

So I went out in the woods and had a good tramp around. I got a lot of healthful fresh air and exercise, and the woods were stunning in their snowy softness. It was strange to think that in all that vast stillness there were the remains of a once-robust little community, and stranger still that somewhere out there with me was a crumpled, unfound plane with two bodies aboard.

I would love to be able to tell you that I found Quinntown or the missing plane or both, but alas I did not. Sometimes life has inconclusive endings.

Columns, too, I'm afraid.

(*Author's note: On Christmas Eve 1998, as this book was being prepared for publication, the second anniversary of the plane's disappearance passed without any new news on what might have become of it. One theory is that the men, searching for an open space, tried to land on a lake but broke through the thin ice and sank to the bottom; in the night the ice reformed and was covered in fresh snow by morning. Working on that assumption, the lakes in the vicinity were checked by divers and airborne metal detectors in the summer of 1997. The search turned up nothing but some old cars and abandoned refrigerators.)*

The Cupholder Revolution

I am assured that this is a true story.

A man calls up his computer helpline complaining that the cupholder on his personal computer has snapped off, and he wants to know how to get it fixed.

"Cupholder?" says the computer helpline person, puzzled. "I'm sorry, sir, but I'm confused. Did you buy this cupholder at a computer show or receive it as a special promotion?"

"No, it came as part of the standard equipment on my computer."

"But our computers don't come with cupholders."

"Well, pardon *me*, friend, but they do," says the man a little hotly. "I'm looking at mine right now. You push a button on the base of the unit and it slides right out."

The man, it transpired, had been using the CD drawer on his computer to hold his coffee cup.

I bring this up here by way of introducing our topic this week: cupholders. Cupholders are taking over the world.

It would be almost impossible to exaggerate the importance of cupholders in automotive circles these days. The *New York Times* recently ran a long article in which it tested a dozen family cars. It rated each of them for ten important features, among them engine size, trunk space, handling, quality of suspension, and, yes, number of cupholders. A car dealer acquaintance of ours tells us that they are one of the first things people remark on, ask about, or play with when they come to look at a car. People buy cars on the basis of cupholders. Nearly all car advertisements note the number of cupholders prominently in the text.

Some cars, like the newest model of the Dodge Caravan, come with as many as seventeen cupholders. The largest Caravan holds seven passengers. Now you don't have to be a nuclear physicist, or even wide awake, to work out that that is 2.43 cupholders per passenger. Why, you may reasonably wonder, would each passenger in a vehicle need 2.43 cupholders? Good question.

Americans, it is true, consume positively staggering volumes of fluids. One of our local gas stations, I am reliably informed, sells a flavored confection called a Slurpee in containers up to 60 ounces in size. But even if every member of the family had a Slurpee *and* a personal bottle of Milk of Magnesia for dealing with the aftereffects, that would still leave three cupholders spare.

There is a long tradition of endowing the interiors of American cars with lots of gadgets and comforts, and I suppose a superfluity of cupholders is just an outgrowth of that tradition.

The reason Americans want a lot of comfort in their cars is because they live in them. Almost 94 percent of all American trips from home involve the use of a car. People in America don't just use their cars to get to the shops but also to get between shops. Most businesses in America have their own parking lots, so someone running six errands will generally move the car six times on a single outing, even to get between two places on opposite sides of the same street.

There are two hundred million cars in the United States — 40 percent of the world's total, for about 5 percent of its population — and an additional two million new ones hit the roads each month

119

(though obviously many are also retired). Even so, there are about twice as many cars in America as there were twenty years ago, driving on twice as many roads, racking up about twice as many miles.

So, because Americans have a lot of cars and spend a lot of time in them, they like a lot of comforts. However, there is a limit to how many different features you can fit into a car interior. What better, then, than to festoon it with a range of nifty cupholders, particularly when people seem to go for them in a big way? That's my theory.

What is certainly true is that not putting cupholders in a car is a serious mistake. I read a couple of years ago that Volvo had to redesign all its cars for the American market for this very reason. Volvo's engineers had foolishly thought that what buyers were looking for was a reliable engine, side-impact bars, and heated seats, when in fact what they craved was little trays into which they could insert their Slurpees. So a bunch of guys named Nils Nilsson and Lars Larsson were put to work designing cupholders into the system, and Volvo was thus saved from beverage ignominy, if not actual financial ruin.

Now from all the foregoing we can draw

one important conclusion — that no matter how hard you try, it is not quite possible to fill a column space with a discussion just of cupholders.

So let me tell you how I happen to know that those fellows at Volvo were called Nils Nilsson and Lars Larsson.

Some years ago when I was in Stockholm and had nothing better to do one evening (it was after 8 p.m., long after all the locals had turned in for the night), I passed the hours before bedtime thumbing through the local phone directory and tallying various names. I had heard that there were only a handful of surnames in Sweden, and this was essentially so. I counted over two thousand each for Eriksson, Svensson, Nilsson, and Larsson. Most of the rest of the book was taken up with Jonssons, Johanssens, and other similar variants. Indeed, there were so few names (or perhaps the Swedes were so cosmically dull) that many people used the same name twice. There were 212 people in Stockholm named Erik Eriksson, 117 named Sven Svensson, 126 named Nils Nilsson, and 259 named Lars Larsson. I wrote these figures down on a piece of paper and have been wondering all these years when I would ever find a use for it.

From this, I believe, we can draw two further conclusions. Save all scraps of paper bearing useless information, for one day you may be glad you did, and if you go to Stockholm, take drink. Now if you will excuse me, I am off for a Slurpee.

Number, Please

The other day I had an experience so startling and unexpected that it made me spill a soft drink down my shirt. (Though, having said that, I don't actually need an unexpected event to achieve this. All I need is a soft drink.) What caused this fizzy outburst was that I called a government office — specifically, the U.S. Social Security Administration — and someone answered the phone.

There I was all poised to have a recorded voice tell me: "All our agents are busy, so please hold while we play you some irritating music interrupted at fifteen-second intervals by a recorded voice telling you all our agents are busy so please hold while we play you some irritating music" and so on until suppertime.

So imagine my surprise when, after just 270 rings, a real person came on the line. He asked some of my personal details and then said, "Excuse me, Bill. I have to put you on hold a minute."

Did you catch that? He called me Bill. Not Mr. Bryson. Not Sir. Not O Mighty Taxpayer. But Bill. Two years ago, I would have regarded this as a small impertinence, but now I find I've grown to like it.

There are certain times when the informality and familiarity of American life strains my patience — when a waiter tells me his name is Bob and that he'll be my server this evening, I still have to resist an impulse to say, "I just want a cheeseburger, Bob. I'm not looking for a relationship" — but mostly I have come to like it. It's because it's symbolic of something more fundamental, I suppose.

There is no tugging of forelocks here, you see, but a genuine universal assumption that no person is better than any other. I think that's swell. My garbage collector calls me Bill. My doctor calls me Bill. My children's school principal calls me Bill. They don't tug for me. I don't tug for them. I think that's as it should be.

In England, I used the same accountant for over a decade, and our relations were always cordial but businesslike. She never called me anything but Mr. Bryson and I never called her anything but Mrs. Creswick. When I moved to America, I phoned an accountant for an appointment. When I came to his office, his first words to me were, "Ah, Bill, I'm glad you could make it." We were pals already. Now when I see him I ask him about his kids.

It shows itself in other ways, too. Hanover, where we live, is a college town. The local university, Dartmouth, is a private school and quite exclusive, but you would never guess it. None of its grounds are off limits to us, unlike, say, Oxford or Cambridge in England where virtually all the college property is closed to outsiders even though those venerable institutions are actually public and owned by the nation. Just you try to go into the Bodleian Library and have a look around, or take a stroll through one of the college quads outside an extremely limited number of hours and see what happens.

Dartmouth, by splendid contrast, could hardly be more accommodating to the community. One of my daughters skates on the college ice rink. My son's high school track team practices in the winter on the college's indoor track. The Hopkins Center, a performing arts center, shows movies and puts on live productions to which the general public is welcomed. Just last night I saw *North by Northwest* on a big screen with one of my teenagers, and afterward we had coffee and cheesecake in the student cafeteria. At none of these things do you ever have to show an ID or secure special permission, and never are you made to feel as if you are trespassing or unwelcome.

All this gives everyday encounters a sheen of openness and egalitarianism that I admire very much. It removes a lot of stuffiness from life. The one thing it won't do, however, is get you your wife's social security number when that number has been mislaid. We needed the number fairly urgently for some tax form. I explained this to the social security man when he came back on the line. He had, after all, just called me Bill, so I had reason to hope that we might get somewhere.

"I'm sorry," he said, "but we are only permitted to divulge that information to the designated individual."

"The person named on the card, you mean?"

"Correct."

"But she's my wife," I sputtered.

"We are only permitted to divulge that information to the designated individual."

"Let me get this straight," I said. "If I were my wife, you would give me the number over the phone?"

"Correct."

"But what if it was somebody just pretending to be her?"

A hesitant pause. "We would assume that the individual making the inquiry was the individual indicated as the designated individual."

"Just a minute please." I thought for a minute. My wife was out, so I couldn't call on her, but obviously I didn't want to have to go through all this again later. I came back on the phone and said in my normal voice: "Hello, it's Cynthia Bryson here. Please could I have my card number?"

There was a nervous chuckle. "I know it's you, Bill," the voice said.

"No, honestly. It's Cynthia Bryson. Please could I have my number?"

"I can't do that."

"Would it make a difference if I spoke in a female voice?"

"I'm afraid not."

"Let me ask you this — just out of curiosity. Is my wife's number on a computer screen in front of you right now?"

"Yes it is."

"But you won't tell me it?"

"I'm afraid I can't do that, Bill," he said, and sounded as if he meant it.

I have learned from years of experience that there is not the tiniest chance that a U.S. government employee will bend a rule, so I didn't press the matter. Instead I asked him if he knew how to get strawberry pop stains out of a white T-shirt.

"Baking soda," he replied without hesitation. "Leave it to soak overnight and it will come right out."

I thanked him and we parted.

I would have liked it, of course, if I had managed to get the information I needed, but at least I had made a friend and he was right about the baking soda. The T-shirt came out like new.

Friendly People

I was intending this week to write about some exasperation or other of modern American life when Mrs. Bryson (who is, may I say, a dear woman) brought me a cup of coffee, read the first few lines off the computer screen, muttered, "Bitch, bitch, bitch," and shuffled off.

"Pardon, my dewy English rose?" I called.

"You're always complaining in that column."

"But the world needs righting, my luscious, cherry-cheeked daughter of Boadicea," I rejoined tranquilly. "Besides, complaining is what I do."

"Complaining is all you do."

Well, excuse me, but not quite. I believe on these very pages I once said a few words of praise for the American garbage disposal, and I clearly recall commending our local post office for providing me with a free doughnut on Customer Appreciation Day. But perhaps she had a point.

There are many wonderful things about the United States of America that deserve praise — the Bill of Rights, the Freedom of Information Act, and free refills are three that leap to mind — but none is more outstanding than the friendliness of the people.

When we moved to this little town in New Hampshire, people received us as if the one thing that had kept them from total happiness to this point was the absence of us in their lives. They brought us cakes and pies and bottles of wine. Not one of them said, "So you're the people who paid a fortune for the Smith place," which I believe is the traditional greeting in England. Our next-door neighbors, upon learning that we were intending to go out to eat, protested that it was too, too dreary to dine in a restaurant on one's first night in a new town and insisted we come to them for dinner there and then, as if feeding six extra mouths was the most trifling of burdens.

When word got around that our furniture was on a containership making its way from Liverpool to Boston, evidently by way of Port Said, Mombasa, and the Galápagos Islands, and that we were temporarily without anything to sleep on, sit on, or eat from, a stream of friendly strangers (some of whom I have not seen since) began traipsing up the walk with chairs, lamps, tables, even a microwave oven.

It was dazzling, and it has remained so. At Christmas this year we went to England for ten days and returned home late at night and hungry to find that a neighbor had stocked the fridge with both essentials and goodies and filled vases with fresh flowers. This sort of thing happens all the time.

Recently I went with one of my children to a Dartmouth College basketball game. We arrived just before game time and joined a long line at one of the ticket windows. After a minute a man came up to me and said, "Are you waiting to buy tickets?"

"No, I'm standing here to make the line more impressive," was the reply that leapt to mind, but of course all I said was, "Yes, I am."

"Because you can have these," he said, and thrust two tickets at me.

My immediate thought, born of years of stupidly misreading situations, was that there must be some catch. "How much?" I said warily.

"No, no, you can have them. For free.

We can't go to the game, you see." He indicated a car outside with the engine running and a woman in the passenger seat.

"Really?" I said. "Well, thank you very much." And then I was struck by a thought. "Did you make a special trip here to give away two tickets?"

"They were going to go to waste otherwise," he said apologetically. "Enjoy the game."

Perhaps the most singular thing is that there is no crime here. I mean none. People will casually leave a $500 bicycle propped against a tree and go off to do their shopping. If someone did steal it, I am almost certain the victim would run after the thief shouting, "Could you please return it to 32 Wilson Avenue when you've finished with it? And watch out for the third gear — it sticks."

No one locks anything. I remember being astounded by this on my first visit when a realtor took me out to look at houses and she kept leaving her car unlocked, even when we went into a restaurant for lunch and even though there was a mobile phone on the front seat and some shopping in the back.

At one of the houses, she discovered she

had brought the wrong key. "Back door'll be unlocked," she announced confidently, and it was. I subsequently realized that there was nothing unusual in this. We know people who go away on vacation without locking their doors, don't know where their house key is, aren't even sure if they still have one.

Now you might reasonably wonder why, then, this is not a thief's paradise. There are two reasons, I believe. First, there is no market for stolen goods here. If you sidled up to anyone in New Hampshire and said, "Want to buy a car stereo?" the person would look at you as if you were out of your mind and say, "No, I already have a car stereo." Then they would report you to the police and — here is the second thing — the police would come and shoot you.

But of course the police don't shoot people here because they don't need to because there is no crime. It is a rare and heartwarming example of a virtuous circle. We have grown used to this now, but when we were still new in town and I expressed wonder about it all to a woman who grew up in New York City but has lived here for twenty years, she laid a hand on my arm and said, as if imparting a great secret, "Honey, you're not in the real world any longer. You're in New Hampshire."

Why Everyone Is Worried

Here's a fact for you: In 1995, according to the *Washington Post*, computer hackers successfully breached the Pentagon's security systems 161,000 times. That works out to eighteen illicit entries every hour around the clock, one every 3.2 minutes.

Oh, I know what you're going to say. This sort of thing could happen to any monolithic defense establishment with the fate of the earth in its hands. After all, if you stockpile a massive nuclear arsenal, it's only natural that people are going to want to go in and have a look around, maybe see what all those buttons marked "Detonate" and "Code Red" mean. It's only human nature.

Besides, the Pentagon has got quite enough on its hands, thank you, with trying to find its missing logs from the Gulf War. I don't know if you have read about this, but the Pentagon has mislaid — irretrievably lost, actually — all but thirty-six of the two hundred pages of official records of its brief but exciting desert adventure. Half of the missing files, it appears, were wiped out when an officer at Gulf War headquarters — I wish I was making this up, but I'm not — incorrectly downloaded some games into a military computer.

The other missing files are, well, missing. All that is known is that two sets were dispatched to Central Command in Florida, but now nobody can find them (probably those cleaning ladies again), and a third set was somehow "lost from a safe" at a base in Maryland, which sounds eminently plausible in the circumstances.

Now to be fair to the Pentagon, its mind has no doubt been distracted by the unsettling news that it has not been getting very reliable dispatches from the CIA. I refer to the recent news that, despite spending $2 billion a year monitoring developments in the Soviet Union, the CIA failed completely to foresee the breakup of the U.S.S.R., and this has naturally unnerved the top brass at the Pentagon. I mean to say, you can't expect people to keep track of their wars if they're not getting reliable reports from the field, now can you?

The CIA, in its turn, was almost certainly distracted from its missions by the news — and again let me stress that I am not making any of this up — that the FBI had spent years filming one of the CIA's agents, Aldrich Ames, going into the Soviet embassy in Washington with bulging files and coming out empty-handed but had not yet quite figured out what he was up to. The FBI knew that Ames was a CIA employee, knew he made regular visits to the Soviet embassy, and knew the CIA was looking for a mole in its midst but had never managed to make the leap of imagination necessary to pull these tantalizing strands together.

Ames was eventually caught and sentenced to a zillion years in prison for passing information, but no thanks to the FBI. But then, to be fair, the FBI has been absolutely snowed under with screwing up everything it comes in contact with. First, there was its wrongful arrest of Richard Jewell, the security guard it suspected of last year's bombing in Atlanta's Olympic Park. Jewell, according to the FBI, planted the bomb and made a phone call alerting authorities, then raced a couple of miles in a minute or so in order to be back at the scene in time to be a hero. Even though there was not a shred of evidence to connect him with the bomb and even though it was conclusively demonstrated that he could not have made the call and returned to the park in the time alleged, it took the FBI months to realize it had the wrong man.

Then in April came news that FBI forensic labs had for years been botching, losing, spilling, contaminating, stepping in and tracking out to the parking lot most of the vital evidence that came its way. Occasionally its agents just made things up. In one incident, a lab scientist wrote an incriminating report based on microscopic findings without actually bothering to look through a microscope. Thanks to the lab's dogged and inventive work, at least one thousand convictions, and perhaps many thousands more, will now be subject to costly reviews and appeals. Among its other ongoing achievements, the FBI has still not found the perpetrator of the Atlanta bombing nor of a series of church bombings across the South, hasn't arrested anyone in a mysterious fatal derailment of a passenger train in Arizona in 1995, failed to catch the Unabomber (he was turned in by his brother), and still isn't able to say whether the crash of TWA flight 800 last year was a crime or an accident or what.

(It later emerged that an FBI official had allowed a psychic to examine the crash site and the wreckage. Never let it be said that our tax dollars aren't spent wisely.)

A lot of people conclude from this that the FBI and its agents are dangerously inept. They are correct, of course, but there are extenuating circumstances for the bureau's low morale and poor performance — namely, the discovery last year that there is a group of people even more astoundingly incompetent. I refer to America's sheriffs' departments.

Space does not permit a comprehensive survey of the singular accomplishments of America's sheriffs' departments, so I will cite just two. First, there was the news that the Los Angeles County Sheriff's Department set a departmental, and possibly national, record last year by incorrectly releasing no fewer than twenty-three prisoners, some of them quite dangerous and cranky. After the release of prisoner number twenty-three, a supervisor explained to reporters that a clerk had received papers ordering that the prisoner be sent to Oregon to serve out a long sentence for burglary and rape but, as could happen to anyone, had taken this to mean giving him back all his possessions, escorting him to the door, and recommending a good pizza place around the corner.

Even better were the sheriff's deputies in Milwaukee who were sent to the local airport with a team of sniffer dogs to practice hunting out explosives. The deputies hid a five-pound package of live explosives somewhere in the airport and then — I just love this — forgot where. Needless to say, the dogs couldn't find it. That was in February, and they're still looking. It was the second time that the Milwaukee sheriff's department has managed to mislay explosives at the airport.

I could go on and on, but I'm going to break off here because I want to see if I can get into the Pentagon's computer. Call me a devil, but I've always had a hankering to blow up a minor country. It will be the perfect crime. The CIA won't notice it, the Pentagon will notice it but will lose the records, the FBI will spend eighteen months investigating and then arrest Mr. Ed the Talking Horse, and the Los Angeles County Sheriff's Department will let him go. If nothing else, it will take people's minds off all these other things they have to worry about.

The Risk Factor

Now here is something that seems awfully unfair to me. Because I am an American it appears that I am twice as likely as an English person to suffer an untimely and accidental death. I know this because I have just been reading something called *The Book of Risks: Fascinating Facts About the Chances We Take Every Day* by a statistical wonk named Larry Laudan.

It is full of interesting and useful charts, graphs, and factual analyses, mostly to do with coming irremediably a cropper in the United States. Thus, I know that if I happen to take up farm work this year I am three times more likely to lose a limb, and twice as likely to be fatally poisoned, than if I just sit here quietly. I now know my chances of being murdered sometime in the next twelve months are 1 in 11,000; of choking to death 1 in 150,000; of being killed by a dam failure 1 in 10 million; and of being fatally conked on the head by something falling from the sky about 1 in

250 million. Even if I stay indoors, away from the windows, it appears that there is a 1 in 450,000 chance that something will kill me before the day is out. I find that rather alarming.

However, nothing is more galling than the discovery that just by being an American, by standing to attention for "The Star-Spangled Banner" and having a baseball cap as a central component of my wardrobe, I am twice as likely to die in a mangled heap as, say, Prince Philip or Posh Spice. This is not a just way to decide mortality, if you ask me.

Mr. Laudan does not explain why Americans are twice as dangerous to themselves as Britons (too upset, I daresay), but I have been thinking about it a good deal, as you can imagine, and the answer — very obvious when you reflect for even a moment — is that America is an outstandingly dangerous place.

Consider this: Every year in New Hampshire a dozen or more people are killed crashing their cars into moose. Now correct me if I am wrong, but this is a fate unlikely to await anyone in the United Kingdom. Nor, we may safely assume, is anyone there likely to be eaten by a grizzly bear or mountain lion, butted senseless by bison, seized about the ankle by a seriously perturbed rattlesnake, or subjected to an abrupt and startling termination from tornadoes, earthquakes, hurricanes, rock slides, avalanches, flash floods, or paralyzing blizzards — all occurrences that knock off scores, if not hundreds, of my fellow citizens each year.

Finally, and above all, there is the matter of guns. There are 200 million guns in the United States and we do rather like to pop them off. Each year, 40,000 Americans die from gunshot wounds, the great majority of them by accident. Just to put that in perspective for you, that's a rate of 6.8 gunshot deaths per 100,000 people in America, compared with a decidedly unambitious 0.4 per 100,000 in the United Kingdom.

America is, in short, a pretty risky place. And yet, oddly, we get alarmed by all the wrong things. Eavesdrop on almost any conversation at Lou's Cafe here in Hanover and the talk will all be of cholesterol and sodium levels, mammograms and resting heart rates. Show most Americans an egg yolk and they will recoil in terror, but the most palpable and avoidable risks scarcely faze them.

Forty percent of the people in this

country still don't use a seat belt, which I find simply amazing because it costs nothing to buckle up and clearly has the potential to save you from exiting through the windshield like Superman. (Vermont, which is one of the few states to keep careful track of these things, reported that in the first ten months of 1998, eighty-one people were killed on the state's roads — and 76 percent of those people were not wearing seat belts.) Even more remarkably, since a spate of recent newspaper reports about young children being killed by airbags in minor crashes, people have been rushing to get their airbags disconnected. Never mind that in every instance the children were killed because they were sitting in the front seat, where they should not have been in the first place, and in nearly all cases weren't wearing seat belts. Airbags save thousands of lives, yet many people are having them disabled on the bizarre assumption that they present a danger.

Much the same sort of statistical illogic applies to guns. Forty percent of Americans keep guns in their homes, typically in a drawer beside the bed. The odds that one of those guns will ever be used to shoot a criminal are comfortably under one in a million. The odds that it will be used to shoot a member of the household — generally a child fooling around — are at least twenty times that figure. Yet over 100 million people resolutely ignore this fact, even sometimes threaten to pop you one themselves if you make too much noise about it.

Nothing, however, better captures the manifest irrationality of people toward risks as one of the liveliest issues of recent years: passive smoking. Four years ago, the Environmental Protection Agency released a report concluding that people who are over thirty-five and don't smoke but are regularly exposed to the smoke of others stand a 1 in 30,000 risk of contracting lung cancer in a given year. The response was immediate and electrifying. All over the country smoking was banned at work and in restaurants, shopping malls, and other public places.

What was overlooked in all this was how microscopically small the risk from passive smoking actually is. A rate of 1 in 30,000 sounds reasonably severe, but it doesn't actually amount to much. Eating one pork chop a week is statistically more likely to give you cancer than sitting routinely in a roomful of smokers. So, too, is consuming a carrot every seven days, a glass of orange juice twice a month, or a head of lettuce every two years. You are five times more likely to contract lung cancer from your pet parakeet than you are from secondary smoke.

Now I am all for banning smoking on the grounds that it is dirty and offensive, unhealthy for the user, and leaves unsightly burns in the carpet. All I am saying is that it seems a trifle odd to ban it on grounds of public safety when you are happy to let any old fool own a gun or drive around unbuckled.

But then logic seldom comes into these things. I remember some years ago watching my brother buy a lottery ticket (odds of winning: about 1 in 12 million), then get in his car and fail to buckle up (odds of having a serious accident in any year: 1 in 40). When I pointed out the inconsistency of this, he looked at me for a moment and said: "And what are the odds, do you suppose, that I will drop you four miles short of home?"

Since then, I have kept these thoughts pretty much to myself. Much less risky, you see.

The War on Drugs

I recently learned from an old friend in Iowa that if you are caught in possession of a single dose of LSD in my native state you face a mandatory sentence of seven years in prison without possibility of parole.

Never mind that you are, say, eighteen years old and of previous good character, that this will ruin your life, that it will cost the state $25,000 a year to keep you incarcerated. Never mind that perhaps you didn't even know you had the LSD — that a friend put it in the glovebox of your car without your knowledge or maybe saw police coming through the door at a party and shoved it into your hand before you could react. Never mind any extenuating circumstances whatever. This is America in the 1990s and there are no exceptions where drugs are concerned. Sorry, but that's the way it is. Next.

It would be nearly impossible to exaggerate the ferocity with which the United States now prosecutes drug offenders. In fifteen states you can be sentenced to life in prison for owning a single marijuana plant. Newt Gingrich, the House Speaker, recently proposed that anyone caught bringing as little as two ounces of marijuana into the United States should be imprisoned for life without possibility of parole. Anyone caught bringing more than two ounces would be executed.

According to a 1990 study, 90 percent of all first-time drug offenders in federal courts were sentenced to an average of five years in prison. Violent first-time offenders, by contrast, were imprisoned less often and received on average just four years in prison. You are, in short, less likely to go to prison for kicking an old lady down the stairs than you are for being caught in possession of a single dose of any illicit drug. Call me soft, but that seems to me a trifle disproportionate.

Please understand it is not remotely my intention here to speak in favor of drugs. I appreciate that drugs can mess you up in a big way. I have an old school friend who made one LSD voyage too many in about 1977 and since that time has sat on a rocker on his parents' front porch examining the backs of his hands and smiling to himself. So I know what drugs can do. I just haven't reached the point where it seems to me appropriate to put someone to death for being an idiot.

Not many of my fellow countrymen would agree with me. It is the clear and fervent wish of most Americans to put drug users behind bars, and they are prepared to pay almost any price to achieve this. The people of Texas recently voted down a $750 million bond proposal to build new schools but overwhelmingly endorsed a $1 billion bond for new prisons, mostly to house people convicted of drug offenses.

America's prison population has more than doubled since 1982. There are now 1,630,000 people in prison in the United States. That is more than the populations of all but the three largest cities in the country. Sixty percent of federal prisoners are serving time for nonviolent offenses, mostly to do with drugs. America's prisons are crammed with nonviolent petty criminals whose problem is a weakness for illegal substances.

Because most drug offenses carry mandatory sentences and exclude the possibility of parole, other prisoners are having to be released early to make room for all the new drug offenders pouring into the system. In consequence, the average convicted murderer in the United States now serves less than six years, the average rapist just five. Moreover, once he is out, the murderer or rapist is immediately eligible for welfare, food stamps, and other federal assistance. A convicted drug user, no matter how desperate his circumstances may become, is denied these benefits for the rest of his life.

The persecution doesn't end there. My friend in Iowa once spent four months in a state prison for a drug offense. That was almost twenty years ago. He did his time and since then has been completely clean. Recently, he applied for a temporary job with the U.S. Postal Service as a holiday relief mail sorter. Not only did he not get the job, but a week or so later he received by recorded delivery an affidavit threatening him with prosecution for failing to declare on his application that he had a felony conviction involving drugs.

The Postal Service had taken the trouble, you understand, to run a background check for drug convictions on someone applying for a temporary job sorting mail. Apparently it does this as a matter of routine — but only with respect to drugs. Had he killed his grandmother and raped his sister twenty-five years ago, he would in all likelihood have gotten the job.

It gets more amazing. The government can seize your property if it was used in connection with a drug offense, even if you did not know it. In Connecticut, according to a recent article in the *Atlantic Monthly* magazine, a federal prosecutor named Leslie C. Ohta made a name for herself by seizing the property of almost anyone even tangentially connected with a drug offense — including a couple in their eighties whose grandson was found to be selling marijuana out of his bedroom. The couple had no idea that their grandson had marijuana in the house (let me repeat: they were in their eighties) and of course had nothing to do with it themselves. They lost the house anyway.

The saddest part of this zealous vindictiveness is that it simply does not work. America spends $50 billion a year fighting drugs, and yet drug use goes on and on. Confounded and frustrated, the government enacts increasingly draconian laws until we find ourselves at the ludicrous point where the Speaker of the House can seriously propose to execute people — strap them to a gurney and snuff out their lives — for possessing the botanical equivalent of two bottles of vodka, and no one anywhere seems to question it.

My solution to the problem would be twofold. First, I would make it a criminal offense to be Newt Gingrich. This wouldn't do anything to reduce the drug problem, but it would make me feel much better. Then I would take most of that $50 billion and spend it on rehabilitation and prevention. Some of it could be used to take busloads of youngsters to look at that school friend of mine on his Iowa porch. I am sure it would persuade most of them not to try drugs in the first place. It would certainly be less brutal and pointless than trying to lock them all up for the rest of their lives.

Dying Accents

We have a man named Walt who does a little carpentry around the house from time to time. He looks to be about 112 years old, but goodness me the man can saw and hammer. He has been doing handiwork around town for at least fifty years.

Walt lives in Vermont, just across the Connecticut River from our little town, and is a proper New Englander — honest, hardworking, congenitally disinclined to waste time, money, or words. (He converses as if he has heard that someday he will be billed for it.) Above all, like all New Englanders, he is an early riser. Boy, do New Englanders like to get up early. We have some English friends who moved here a few years ago. Soon after arriving the woman called the dentist for an appointment and was told to come at 6:30 the following day. She showed up the next evening to find the dentist's office in darkness. They had meant 6:30 A.M., of course. If Walt were told to come for a dental appointment at that hour I am positive he would ask if they had anything a little earlier.

Anyway, the other day he arrived at our house a few minutes before seven and apologized for being late because the traffic through Norwich had been "fierce." What was interesting about this was not the notion that traffic in Norwich could ever be fierce but that he pronounced it "Norritch," like the English city. This surprised me because everyone in Norwich and for miles around pronounces it "Nor-wich" (i.e., with the "w" sounded, as in "sandwich").

I asked him about that.

"Ayuh," he said, which is an all-purpose New England term, spoken in a slow drawl and usually accompanied by the removal of a cap and a thoughtful scratching of the head. It means, "I may be about to say something . . . but then again I may not." He explained to me that the village was pronounced "Norritch" until the 1950s, when outsiders from places like New York and Boston began to move in and, for whatever reason, started to modify the pronunciation. Now virtually everyone who is younger than Walt, which is virtually everyone, pronounces it "Nor-wich." That seemed to me quite sad, the idea that a traditional local pronunciation could be lost simply because outsiders were too inattentive to preserve it, but it's only symptomatic of a much wider trend.

Thirty years ago, three-quarters of the people in Vermont were born there. Today the proportion has fallen to barely half, and in some places it is much lower. In consequence, these days you are far less likely than you once were to hear locals pronouncing cow as "kyow," saying "so don't I" for "so do I," or employing the colorful, if somewhat cryptic, expressions for which the state was once widely noted. "Heavier than a dead minister" and "jeezum-jee-hassafrats" are two that spring to mind if not, alas, to many Vermont tongues any longer.

If you go to the remoter corners of the state and hang out at a general store you might just overhear a couple of old farmers (pronounced "fahmuhs") asking for "a frog skin more" of coffee or saying "Well, wouldn't that just jar your mother's preserves," but more probably it will be urban refugees in L. L. Bean attire asking the storekeeper if he has any guavas.

The same thing has been happening all over the country. I have just been reading

155

an academic study on the dialect of Ocracoke Island off the coast of North Carolina. Ocracoke is part of the Outer Banks, a chain of barrier islands where the inhabitants once spoke a hearty patois so rich and mysterious that visitors sometimes supposed they had stumbled on some half-lost outpost of Elizabethan England.

The locals — sometimes called "Hoi-Toiders" for the way they pronounced "high tide" — had an odd, lilting accent that incorporated many archaic terms, like "quammish" (meaning to feel sick or uneasy), "fladget" (for a piece of something), and "mommuck" (meaning to bother) that hadn't been heard since Shakespeare put away his quill. Being a maritime people they also used nautical terms in distinctive ways. For instance, "scud," meaning to run before a gale with a small amount of sail, was employed for land-based movements, so that an Ocracoker might invite you to go for a scud in his car. Finally, just to make the bewilderment of outsiders complete, they absorbed a number of non-English words, like "pizer" (apparently from the Italian "piazza") for a porch, and pronounced the lot in a way that brought to mind Ringo

Starr doing a Dorset accent. It was, in short, an interesting dialect.

All this scudded along, as you might say, in a dependable fashion until 1957 when the federal government built Ocracoke a bridge to the mainland. Almost at once tourists came in and the Ocracoke dialect began to go out.

All of this was scientifically monitored and recorded by linguists from North Carolina State University, who made periodic field trips to the island over half a century, on each visit noting a steady and seemingly terminal decline in the fragile idiolect. Then, to everyone's surprise, the Ocracoke dialect began to undergo a revival. The researchers found that middle-aged people — those who had grown up in the 1950s and 1960s when tourism first became a dominant feature of island life — not only were returning to the old speechways but actually had more pronounced accents than their elders. The explanation, the researchers surmise, is that the islanders "exaggerate their island dialect features, whether consciously or not, because they want there to be no mistake that they are 'real' Ocracokers and not tourists or new residents recently relocated from the mainland."

Much the same sort of phenomenon has been found elsewhere. A study of the dialect on Martha's Vineyard revealed that certain traditional pronunciations there, such as flattening of the "ou" sound in words like "house" and "mouse," making them something more like "hawse" and "mawse," staged an unexpected rally after nearly going extinct. The driving force, it turned out, was natives who returned to the island after living away and embraced the old speech forms as a way of distinguishing themselves from the mass of nonnatives.

So does this mean that the rich and chewy Vermont accent will likewise recover and that once again we can expect to hear people say that something "would give you a pain where you never had an ache" or that they "felt rougher than a boar's rear end"? Sadly, it seems not. From the evidence, it appears that these dialectal revivals happen only on islands or in communities that are in some way still comparatively isolated.

So it seems likely that when old Walt finally hangs up his saw and hammer whoever takes his place won't sound like an old-time Vermonter even if he was born and reared there. I only hope he's not such an early riser.

Inefficiency
Report

The other day something in our local newspaper caught my eye. It was an article reporting that the control tower and related
facilities at our local airport are to be privat-
ized. The airport loses money, so the Federal Aviation Administration is trying to cut
costs by contracting out landing services to
someone who can do it more cheaply. What
especially caught my attention was a sentence deep in the article that said, "A
spokeswoman with the Federal Aviation Administration's regional office in New York
City, Arlene Sarlac, could not provide the
name of the company that will be taking
over the tower."

Well, that's really reassuring to hear.
Now maybe I am hypertouchy because I
use the airport from time to time and have
a particular interest in its ability to bring
planes down in an approximately normal
fashion, so I would rather like to know that
the tower hasn't been bought by, say, the

New England Roller Towel Company or Crash Services (Panama) Ltd., and that the next time I come in to land, the plane won't be guided in by some guy on a stepladder waving a broom. I would hope, at the very least, that the Federal Aviation Administration would have some idea of whom they were selling the tower to. Call me particular, but it seems to me that that's the sort of thing you ought to have on file somewhere.

The FAA, it must be said, is not the most efficient of enterprises. A recent report noted that the agency had been plagued for years by power failures, malfunctioning and antiquated equipment, overworked and overstressed staff, inadequate training programs, and mismanagement owing to a fragmented chain of command. With regard to equipment standards, the report found that "21 separate offices issued 71 orders, 7 standards, and 29 specifications." The upshot was that the FAA didn't have any idea what equipment it owned, how it was being maintained, or even whose turn it was to make the coffee.

Even more ominously, according to the *Los Angeles Times*, "at least three airliner accidents may have been prevented had the FAA not fallen behind schedule in planned modernization of air traffic control equipment."

I mention this because our subject today is large-scale incompetence in my native land. I wouldn't say that America is a particularly outstanding place to find incompetence. But when you do find incompetence here it does tend to be particularly outstanding. Partly this is because it is a big country. Big countries spawn big bureaucracies. Those bureaucracies spawn lots of departments, and each of those departments issues lots of rules and regulations. An inevitable consequence is that with so many departments the left hand not only doesn't know what the right hand is doing but doesn't seem to know that there is a right hand. This is interestingly illustrated by frozen pizza.

In the United States, frozen cheese pizza is regulated by the Food and Drug Administration. Frozen pepperoni pizza, on the other hand, is regulated by the Department of Agriculture. Each sets its own standards with regard to content, labeling, and so on and has its own team of inspectors and set of regulations that require licenses, compliance certificates, and all kinds of other costly paperwork. And that's just for frozen pizza. Altogether, it has been estimated, the cost to the nation of complying with the full whack of federal regulations is $668 billion a year, an average of $7,000 per household. That's a lot of compliance.

What gives American inefficiency its particular tang, however, is a peculiar affection for parsimony. There is a short-termism here, particularly in official circles, that is often simply arresting. Consider an experience of the Internal Revenue Service.

Every year an estimated $100 billion in taxes — a sum larger than the gross national product of many countries — goes unreported and uncollected. In 1995, as an experiment, Congress gave the IRS $100 million of extra funding to go looking for some of this extra money. At the end of the year it had found and collected $800 million — only a fraction of the missing money but still $8 of extra government revenue for every $1 of additional collection costs.

The IRS confidently predicted that if the program were extended it would net the government at least $12 billion of missing tax revenues the following year, with more to come in succeeding years. Instead of expanding the program, Congress chopped it as — wait for it — part of its federal deficit reduction program. Do you begin to see what I mean?

Or take food inspection. All kinds of high-tech gizmos exist to test meat for microbial infestations like salmonella and *E. coli*. But the government is too cheap to invest in these, so federal food inspectors continue to inspect meat visually, as it rolls past on assembly lines. Now you can imagine how attentively a low-paid federal food inspector is going to be looking at each of 18,000 identical plucked chickens sliding past him on a conveyor belt every day of his working life. Call me a cynic, but I very much doubt that after a dozen years or so of this an inspector is likely to be thinking: "Hey, here come some more chickens. These might be interesting." In any case — and here's a point that you would think might have occurred to somebody by now — microorganisms are invisible.

As a result, by the government's own admission, as much as 20 percent of all chicken and 49 percent of turkey is contaminated. What all this costs in illness is anybody's guess, but it is thought that as many as 80 million people may get sick each year from factory-contaminated food, costing the economy somewhere between $5 billion and $10 billion in additional health care costs, lost productivity, and so on. Every year nine thousand people die of food poisoning in the United States.

All of which brings us back to the good old Federal Aviation Administration. (Actually it doesn't, but I had to get here somehow.) The FAA may or may not be the most inefficient bureaucracy in the United States, but it is indubitably the only one that has my life in its hands when I am 32,000 feet above the earth, so you may imagine my disquiet at learning that it is handing over our control tower to some people whose names it can't remember.

According to our newspaper, the hand-over will be complete by the end of the month. Three days after that, I am irrevocably committed to flying to Washington from that airport. I mention this merely in case you find a blank space here in a couple of weeks.

But it probably won't come to that. I just asked my wife what we are having for dinner.

Turkey burgers, she said.

Why No One Walks

A researcher at the University of California at Berkeley recently made a study of the nation's walking habits and found that the average person in the United States walks less than 75 miles a year — about 1.4 miles a week, barely 350 yards a day. I'm no stranger to sloth myself, but that's appallingly little. I rack up more mileage than that just looking for the channel changer.

Eighty-five percent of us, according to the Berkeley study, are "essentially" sedentary and 35 percent are "totally" sedentary. We have become a nation of sitters and riders.

One of the things my wife and I wanted when we decided to move back to America was to live in a manageably sized town within walking distance of a central business district. Hanover, where we settled, is a small, typical New England town, pleasant, sedate, and compact. It has a broad central green surrounded by the venerable buildings of Dartmouth College,

165

a trim Main Street, and leafy residential streets. It is, in short, an agreeable, easy place to go about one's business on foot, and yet as far as I can tell almost no one does.

I walk to town nearly every day when I am at home. I go to the post office or library or bookstore, and sometimes, if I am feeling particularly debonair, I stop at Rosey Jekes Cafe for a cappuccino. Occasionally in the evenings my wife and I stroll up to the Nugget Theater for a movie or to Murphy's for a beer. All this is a big part of my life and I wouldn't dream of doing it other than on foot. People have gotten used to this curious and eccentric behavior now, but several times in the early days passing acquaintances would slow by the curb and ask if I wanted a ride.

"But I'm going your way," they would insist when I politely declined. "Really, it's no bother."

"Honestly, I enjoy walking."

"Well, if you're absolutely *sure*," they would say and depart reluctantly, even guiltily, as if leaving the scene of an accident without giving their name.

People have become so habituated to using the car for everything that it would never occur to them to unfurl their legs and see what those lower limbs can do. It is worth noting that 93 percent of all trips outside the property in the United States now involve the use of a car.

As with most old New England towns designed for another age of transportation, Hanover isn't a particularly obliging place for cars. Nearly any visit to town by automobile will be characterized by a long and exasperating hunt for a parking space. To alleviate this, the local authorities are forever widening roads to speed traffic flow and building new parking lots — Dartmouth recently tore down an unexceptionable old hospital building in order to insert into the heart of the campus a couple of more acres of numbingly soulless parking lot — failing to understand that it is the absence of these features that makes the town desirable in the first place.

But it isn't really the authorities who are to blame. It is the people who wish to take two tons of metal with them wherever they go. We have reached an age where college students expect to drive between classes, where parents will get in a car and drive three blocks to pick up their children from a friend's house, where the mailman takes his van up and down every driveway on a street. We will go through the most

167

extraordinary contortions to save ourselves twenty feet of walking.

Sometimes it's almost ludicrous. The other day I was in the little nearby town of Etna waiting to bring home one of my children from a piano lesson when a car stopped outside the local post office and a man about my age popped out and dashed inside (and left the engine running — something else that exercises me inordinately). He was inside for about three or four minutes, then came out, got in the car, and drove exactly sixteen feet (I had nothing better to do so I paced it off) to the general store next door, and popped in again, engine still running.

And the thing is, this man looked really fit. I'm sure he jogs extravagant distances and plays squash and does all kinds of exuberantly healthful things, but I am just as sure that he drives to each of these undertakings. It's crazy. An acquaintance of ours was complaining the other day about the difficulty of finding a place to park outside the local gymnasium. She goes there several times a week to walk on a treadmill. The gymnasium is, at most, a six-minute walk from her front door. I asked her why she didn't walk to the gym and do six minutes less on the treadmill.

She looked at me as if I were tragically simple-minded and said, "But I have a program for the treadmill. It records my distance and speed and calorie-burn rate, and I can adjust it for degree of difficulty." It had not occurred to me how thoughtlessly deficient nature is in this regard.

According to a concerned and faintly horrified recent editorial in the *Boston Globe*, the United States spends less than 1 percent of its $25 billion-a-year highway budget on facilities for pedestrians. Actually, I'm surprised it's that much. Go to almost any suburb developed in the last thirty years and you will not find a sidewalk anywhere. Often you won't find a single pedestrian crossing.

I had this brought home to me last summer when we were driving across Maine and stopped for coffee on Route 1 in one of those endless zones of shopping malls, motels, gas stations, and fast food places that sprout everywhere these days. I noticed there was a bookstore across the street, so I decided to skip coffee and pop over. I needed a particular book for some work I was doing and anyway I figured this would give my wife a chance to spend some important quality time with four restive, overheated children.

Although the bookshop was no more than seventy or eighty feet away, I discovered that there was no way to get there on foot. There was a traffic outlet for cars, but no provision for pedestrians, and no way to cross on foot without dodging over six lanes of swiftly moving traffic. In the end, I had to get in our car and drive across. There was simply no other way. At the time it seemed ridiculous and exasperating, but afterward I realized that I was possibly the only person ever even to have entertained the notion of negotiating that intersection on foot.

The fact is, we not only don't walk anywhere anymore in this country, we *won't* walk anywhere, and woe to anyone who tries to make us, as a town here in New Hampshire called Laconia discovered to its cost. A few years ago, Laconia spent $5 million pedestrianizing its downtown, to make it a pleasant shopping environment. Esthetically it was a triumph — urban planners came from all over to coo and take photos — but commercially it was a disaster. Forced to walk one whole block from a parking lot, shoppers abandoned downtown Laconia for suburban malls.

In 1994, Laconia dug up its pretty brick paving, took away the benches, tubs of geraniums, and decorative trees, and put the street back to the way it had been in the first place. Now people can park right in front of the stores again, and downtown Laconia thrives anew.

And if that isn't sad, I don't know what is.

Wide-Open Spaces

Here are a couple of things to bear in mind as you go through life: Daniel Boone was an idiot, and it's not worth trying to go to Maine for the day from Hanover, New Hampshire. Allow me to explain.

I was fooling around with a globe the other evening and was mildly astounded to discover that here in Hanover I am much closer to our old house in Yorkshire than I am to many other parts of the United States. Indeed, from where I sit to Attu, the westernmost of Alaska's Aleutian Islands, is almost four thousand miles. Put another way, a person in London is closer to Johannesburg than I am to the outermost tip of my own country.

Of course, you could argue that Alaska is not a fair comparison because there is so much non-U.S. territory between here and there. But even if you confine yourself to the mainland United States, the distances are imposing, to say the least. From my house to Los Angeles is about the same as from London to Lagos. We are, in a word, talking big scale here.

Here is another arresting fact to do with scale. In the past twenty years (a period in which, let the record show, I was doing my breeding elsewhere), the population of the United States increased by almost exactly the equivalent of Great Britain's. I find that quite amazing, not least because I don't know where all these new people are.

A remarkable thing about America, if you have been living for a long time in a crowded little place like the United Kingdom, is how very big and very empty so much of it is. Consider this: Montana, Wyoming, and North and South Dakota have an area twice the size of France but a population less than that of south London. Alaska is bigger still and has even fewer people. Even my own adopted state of New Hampshire, in the relatively crowded Northeast, is 85 percent forest, and most of the rest is lakes. You can drive for very long periods in New Hampshire and never see anything but trees and mountains — not a house or a hamlet or even, quite often, another car.

I am constantly caught by this. Not long ago, I had a couple of friends over from England and we decided to take a drive over to the lakes of western Maine. It had the makings of a nice day out. All we had to do was cross New Hampshire — which is, after all, the fourth tiniest state in America — and go a little way over the state line into our lovely, moose-strewn neighbor to the east. I figured it would take about two hours — two and a half tops.

Well, of course you have anticipated the punchline. Six hours later we pulled up exhausted at the shore of Rangeley Lake, took two pictures, looked at each other, and wordlessly got back in the car and drove home. This sort of thing happens all the time.

The curious thing is that a very great many Americans don't seem to see it this way. They think the country is way too crowded. Moves are constantly afoot to restrict access to national parks and wilderness areas on the grounds that they are dangerously overrun. Parts of them *are* unquestionably crowded, but that is only because 98 percent of visitors arrive by car, and 98 percent of those venture no more than a couple of hundred feet from their metallic wombs. Elsewhere, however, you can have whole mountains to yourself, even in the most popular parks on the busiest days. Yet I may soon find myself barred from hiking in many wilderness areas unless I had the foresight to book a visit weeks beforehand, because of perceived overcrowding.

Even more ominously, there is a growing belief that the best way of dealing with this supposed crisis is by expelling most of those not born here. There is an organization whose name escapes me (it may be "Dangerously Small-Minded Reactionaries for a Better America") that periodically runs earnest, carefully reasoned ads in the *New York Times*, *Atlantic Monthly*, and other important and influential publications calling for an end to immigration because, as one of its ads explains, it "is devastating our environment and the quality of our lives." Elsewhere it adds, "Primarily because of immigration we are rushing at breakneck speed toward an environmental and economic disaster." Oh, give me a break, please.

You could, I suppose, make an economic or even cultural case for cutting back on immigration, but not on the grounds that the country is running out of room. Anti-immigration arguments conveniently overlook the fact that America already expels a million immigrants a year and that those who are here mostly do jobs that are too dirty, low-paying, or unsatisfying for the rest of us to do. Getting rid of immigrants is not suddenly going to open employment opportunities for those born here; all it's going to do is leave a lot of dishes unwashed, a lot of beds unmade, and a lot of fruit unpicked. Still less is it going to miraculously create a lot more breathing space for the rest of us.

America already has one of the lowest proportions of immigrants in the developed world. Just 6 percent of people in the United States are foreign born, compared with, for instance, 8 percent in Britain and 11 percent in France. America may or may not be heading for an environmental and economic disaster, but if so it certainly isn't because six people in every hundred were born somewhere else.

There aren't many human acts more foolishly simplistic or misguided, or more likely to lead to careless evil, than blaming general problems on small minorities, yet that seems to be quite a respectable impulse where immigration is concerned these days. Two years ago, Californians voted overwhelmingly for Proposition 187, which would deny health and education services to illegal immigrants. Almost immediately upon passage of the proposition, Governor Pete Wilson ordered the state health authorities to stop providing prenatal care to any woman who could not prove that she was here legally. Now please correct me by all means, but does it not seem just a trifle harsh — a trifle barbaric even — to imperil the well-being of an unborn child because of the actions of its parents?

No less astounding in its way, the federal government recently began removing basic rights and entitlements even from legal immigrants. We are in effect saying to them: "Thank you for your years of faithful service to our economy, but things are a little tough at the moment, so we aren't prepared to help you. Besides, you have a funny accent."

I'm not arguing for unlimited immigration, you understand, just a sense of proportion in how we treat those who are here already. The fact is, America is one of the least crowded countries on earth, with an average of just 68 people per square mile, compared with 256 in France and over 600 in Britain. Altogether, only 2 percent of the United States is classified as "built up."

Of course, Americans have always tended to see these things in a different way. Daniel Boone famously is supposed to have looked out his cabin window one day, seen a wisp of smoke rising from a homesteader's dwelling on a distant mountain, and announced his intention to move on, complaining bitterly that the neighborhood was getting too crowded.

Which is why I say Daniel Boone was an idiot. I just hate to see the rest of my country going the same way.

Snoopers at Work

Now here is something to bear in mind should you ever find yourself using a changing room in a department store or other retail establishment. It is perfectly legal — indeed, it is evidently routine — for the store to spy on you while you are trying on their clothes.

I know this because I have just been reading a book by Ellen Alderman and Caroline Kennedy called *The Right to Privacy*, which is full of alarming tales of ways that businesses and employers can — and enthusiastically do — intrude into what would normally be considered private affairs.

The business of changing-cubicle spying came to light in 1983 when a customer trying on clothes in a department store in Michigan discovered that a store employee had climbed a stepladder and was watching him through a metal vent. (Is this tacky or what?) The customer was sufficiently outraged that he sued the store for invasion of privacy. He lost. A state court held that it was reasonable for retailers to defend against shoplifting by engaging in such surveillance.

He shouldn't have been surprised. Nearly everyone is being spied on in some way in America these days. A combination of technological advances, employer paranoia, and commercial avarice means that many millions of Americans are having their lives delved into in ways that would have been impossible, not to say unthinkable, a dozen years ago.

Worse still, there are now scores of information brokers — electronic private investigators — who make a living going through the Internet digging out personal information on people for a fee. If you have ever registered to vote they can get your address and date of birth, since voter registration forms are a matter of public record in most states. With these two pieces of information, they can (and for as little as $8 or $10 will) provide almost any personal information about any person you might wish to know: court records, medical records, driving records, credit history, hobbies, buying habits, annual income, phone numbers (including unlisted numbers), you name it.

Most of this was possible before, but it would take days of inquiries and visits to various government offices. Now it can be done in minutes, in complete anonymity, through the Internet.

Many companies are taking advantage of these technological possibilities to make their businesses more ruthlessly productive. In Maryland, according to *Time* magazine, a bank searched through the medical records of its borrowers — apparently quite legally — to find out which of them had life-threatening illnesses and used this information to cancel their loans. Other companies have focused not on customers but on their own employees — for instance, to check what prescription drugs the employees are taking. One large, well-known company teamed up with a pharmaceutical firm to comb through the health records of employees to see who might benefit from a dose of antidepressants. The idea was that the company would get more serene workers; the drug company would get more customers.

According to the American Management Association two-thirds of companies in the United States spy on their employees in some way. Thirty-five percent track phone calls, and 10 percent actually tape phone

181

conversations to review at leisure later. About a quarter of companies surveyed admitted to going through their employees' computer files and reading their e-mail.

Still other companies are secretly watching their employees at work. A secretary at a college in Massachusetts discovered that a hidden video camera was filming her office twenty-four hours a day. Goodness knows what the school authorities were hoping to find. What they got were images of the woman changing out of her work clothes and into a track suit each night in order to jog home from work. She is suing and will probably get a pot of money. But elsewhere courts have upheld companies' rights to spy on their workers.

In 1989, when an employee of a large Japanese-owned computer products company discovered that the company was routinely reading employees' e-mail, even though it had assured the employees that it was not, she blew the whistle, and was promptly fired. She sued for unfair dismissal and lost the case. A court upheld the right of companies not only to review employees' private communications but to lie to them about doing it. Whoa.

There is a particular paranoia about

drugs. I have a friend who got a job with a large manufacturing company in Iowa a year or so ago. Across the street from the company was a tavern that was the company after-hours hangout. One night my friend was having a beer after work with his colleagues when he was approached by a fellow employee who asked if he knew where she could get some marijuana. He said he didn't use the stuff himself, but to get rid of her — for she was very persistent — he gave her the phone number of an acquaintance who sometimes sold it.

The next day he was fired. The woman, it turned out, was a company spy employed solely to weed out drug use in the company. He hadn't supplied her with marijuana, you understand, hadn't encouraged her to use marijuana, and had stressed that he didn't use marijuana himself. Nonetheless he was fired for encouraging and abetting the use of an illegal substance.

Already, 91 percent of large companies — I find this almost unbelievable — now test some of their workers for drugs. Scores of companies have introduced what are called TAD rules — TAD being short for "tobacco, alcohol, and drugs" — which prohibit employees from using any of these substances at any time, including at home. There are companies, if you can believe it, that forbid their employees to drink or smoke at any time — even one beer, even on a Saturday night — and enforce the rules by making their workers give urine samples.

But it gets even more sinister than that. Two leading electronics companies working together have invented something called an "active badge," which tracks the movements of any worker compelled to wear one. The badge sends out an infrared signal every fifteen seconds. This signal is received by a central computer, which is thus able to keep a record of where every employee is and has been, whom they have associated with, how many times they have been to the toilet or water cooler — in short, to log every single action of their working day. If that isn't ominous, I don't know what is.

However, there is one development, I am pleased to report, that makes all of this worthwhile. A company in New Jersey has patented a device for determining whether restaurant employees have washed their hands after using the lavatory. Now *that* I can go for.

Lost at the Movies

Every year about this time I do a mildly foolish thing. I gather up some of the smaller children and take them to one of the summer movies.

Summer movies are big business in America. This year between Memorial Day and Labor Day Americans will spend $2 billion on movie tickets, plus half as much again on chewy things to stuff into their mouths while staring saucer-eyed at images of extremely costly mayhem.

Summer movies are nearly always bad, of course, but I believe this may be the worst summer ever. I base this entirely, but confidently, on a quotation I saw in the *New York Times* from Jan de Bont, director of *Speed 2: Cruise Control*, who boasted that the movie's biggest dramatic event — in which an out-of-control cruise ship carrying Sandra Bullock plows into a Caribbean village — came to him in a dream. "The entire screenplay was written backward from that image," he revealed proudly. There, I think, you have all you need to know about the intellectual quality of the average summer movie.

I always tell myself not to set my expectations too high, that summer movies are the cinematic equivalent of amusement park rides, and no one ever expected a roller coaster to provide a satisfying plot line. But the thing is, summer movies have become so dumb — so very, very dumb — that it is hard to abide them. No matter how much money has been spent on them — and it is worth noting that at least eight of this year's crop have budgets over $100 million — there is always such a large measure of implausibility as to make you wonder whether the script was concocted over canapés the night before filming began.

This year we went to the new Jurassic Park movie, *Lost World*. Now never mind that it is largely identical to the last Jurassic Park movie — same booming footfalls and trembling puddles whenever T-rex comes into the vicinity, same mortified people backing away from a door against which velociraptors are hurling themselves (only to find another toothy creature looming over their shoulder), same scenes of vehicles dangling precariously from a jungly bluff while the heroes hold on for dear life. No matter. The dinosaurs are terrific and a dozen or so people get squashed or eaten in the first hour. This is what we've come for!

And then it all falls apart. In a culminating scene, a Tyrannosaurus escapes, in an improbable manner, from a ship, runs rampant through downtown San Diego, crushing buses and destroying gas stations, and then — suddenly, inexplicably — is in the middle of a heavily slumbering suburban neighborhood, alone and unobserved. Now does it strike you as remotely likely that a prehistoric, twenty-foot-high creature not seen on earth for sixty-five million years could cause mayhem in a business district and then slip off into a residential zone without anyone's noticing? Does it not seem a trifle nagging and unsatisfactory that while downtown San Diego is full of people doing lively, mid-evening sorts of things — lining up at movie theaters, strolling around hand in hand — out in the residential area the streets are silent and every last soul is fast asleep?

And so it goes on from there. While police cars are dashing around bumping helplessly into each other, the hero and heroine manage to find the T-rex unaided and — undetected by anyone in this curiously unobservant city — lure her some miles back to the boat, so that she can be returned to her tropical island home, thus setting up the happy, inevitable, and commercially gratifying possibility of a Jurassic Park 3.

Lost World is slack and obvious and, for all its $100 million-plus budget, contains about $2.35 worth of actual thought, and so of course it is on its way to setting all kinds of records at the box office. In its first weekend alone, it took in $92.7 million.

However, my problem is not really with *Lost World* or any of the other summer fare. I'm way past expecting Hollywood to provide me with a cerebral experience during the warmer months. My problem is with the Sony 6 Theaters of West Lebanon, New Hampshire, and the thousands of other suburban cinema complexes like it, which are doing to the American movie-going experience essentially what Steven Spielberg's Tyrannosaurus rex did to San Diego.

Anyone who grew up in America in the 1960s or before will remember the days when going to the pictures meant visiting a single-screen institution, usually vast, usually downtown. In my hometown, Des Moines, the main movie theater (imaginatively called "The Des Moines") was a palatial extravaganza with spooky lighting and a decor that brought to mind an Egyptian crypt. By my era, it was something of a dump — I am sure there was a dead horse in there somewhere, and certainly it hadn't been cleaned since Theda Bara was in her prime — but just being there, facing a vast screen in a cubic acre of darkness, was an entrancing experience.

Except in a few major cities, nearly all those great downtown cinemas are gone now. (The Des Moines went in about 1965.) Instead what you get nowadays are suburban multiplexes with an abundance of tiny screening rooms. Although *Lost World* was the hottest movie around, we saw it in a chamber of almost laughable minuteness, barely large enough to accommodate nine rows of seats, which were grudgingly padded and crammed so close together that my knees ended up more or less hooked around my ears. The screen had the dimensions of a large beach towel and was so ill-placed that everyone in the first three rows had to look almost straight up, as if in a planetarium. The sound was bad and the picture frequently jerky. Before it started, we had to sit through thirty minutes of commercials. The popcorn, candy, and soft drinks were outrageously expensive, and the salespeople had been programmed to try to sell you things you didn't want and had not asked for. In short, every feature of this movie complex seemed carefully designed to make a visit a deeply regretted experience.

I'm not cataloging all this to make you feel sorry for me, though sympathy is always welcome, but to point out that this is increasingly the standard experience for moviegoers in America. I can handle a little audiovisual imbecility, but I can't bear to see the magic taken away.

I was talking about this to one of my older children the other day. She listened attentively, even sympathetically, then said a sad thing. "Dad," she told me, "you need to understand that people don't want the smell of a dead horse when they go to the movies."

She's right, of course. But if you ask me, they don't know what they are missing.

Gardening
with My Wife

I'm going to have to be quick because it's a Sunday and the weather is glorious and Mrs. Bryson has outlined a big, ambitious program of gardening. Worse, she's wearing what I nervously call her Nike expression — the one that says, "Just do it."

Now don't get me wrong. Mrs. Bryson is a rare and delightful creature and goodness knows my life needs structure and supervision, but when she gets out a pad and pen and writes the words "Things To Do" (vigorously underscored several times) you know it's going to be a long time till Monday.

I love to garden — there is something about the combination of mindless activity and the constant unearthing of worms that just suits me somehow — but frankly I am not crazy about gardening with my wife. The trouble, you see, is that she is English and thus can intimidate me. She can say things like, "Have you heeled in the nodes on the *Dianthus chinensis?*" and "Did you remember to check the sequestrene levels on the *Phlox subulata?*"

All British people can do this, I find, and it's awful — terrifying even. Even now I remember the astonishment of listening to the ever-popular BBC radio program "Gardeners' Question Time" for the first time many years ago and realizing with quiet horror that I was in a nation of people who not only knew and understood things like powdery mildew, peach leaf curl, optimum pH levels, and the difference between *Coreopsis verticillata* and *Coreopsis grandiflora* but cared about them — indeed, found it gratifying to engage in long and lively discussions on such matters.

I come from a background where you are considered to have a green thumb if you can grow a cactus on a windowsill, so my own approach to gardening has always been rather less scientific. My method, which actually works pretty well, is to treat as a weed anything that hasn't flowered by August and to sprinkle everything else with bone meal, slug pellets, and whatever else I find lying around the potting shed. Once or twice a summer I tip everything with a skull and crossbones on the label into a spray canister and give everything a jolly good dousing. It's an unorthodox approach and occasionally, I admit, I have to leap out of the way of an abruptly falling tree that has failed to respond to ministrations, but generally it has been a success and I have achieved some interesting and novel mutational effects. I once got a fence post to fruit, for instance.

For years, especially when the children were small and capable of almost any kind of mischief, my wife left me to the garden. Occasionally she would step out to ask what I was doing, and I would have to confess that I was dusting some weedy-looking things with an unknown powdery substance that I had found in the garage and that I was pretty confident was either nitrogen or possibly cement mix. Usually at that moment one of the children would come out to announce that little Jimmy's hair was on fire, or something else similarly but usefully distracting, and she would fly off, leaving me to get on with my experiments in peace. It was a good arrangement and our marriage prospered.

Then the children grew large enough to attend to their own cranial blazes and we moved to America, and now I find Mrs. B. out there with me. Or rather I am there with her, for I seem to have acquired a subsidiary role that principally involves bringing or taking away the wheelbarrow at a trot. I used to be a keen gardener; now I'm a kind of rickshaw boy.

Anyway, gardening isn't the same here. People don't even have gardens in America. They have yards. And they don't garden in those yards. They do "yard-work." Takes all the fun out of it some-how.

In Britain, nature is fecund and kindly. The whole country is a kind of garden, really. In America, the instinct of nature is to be a wilderness — glorious in its way, of course, but much harder to subdue. What you get here are triffid-like weeds that come creeping in from every margin and must be continually hacked back with sabers and machetes. I am quite sure that if we left the property for a month we would come back to find that the weeds had captured the house and dragged it off to the woods to be slowly devoured.

American gardens are mostly lawn, and American lawns are mostly big. This means that you spend your life raking. In the autumn the leaves fall together with a single great *whoomp* — a sort of vegetative mass suicide — and you spend about two months dragging them into piles, while the wind does its best to put them all back where you found them. You rake and rake, and cart the leaves off to the woods, then hang up your rake and go inside for the next seven months.

But as soon as you turn your back, the leaves begin creeping back. I don't know how they do it, but when you come out in spring, there they all are again, spread ankle deep across your lawn, choking thorny shrubs, clogging drains. So you spend weeks and weeks raking them up and carting them back to the woods. Finally, just when you get the lawn pristine, there is a great *whoomp* sound and you realize it's autumn again. It's really quite dispiriting.

And now on top of all that my dear spouse has suddenly taken a commanding interest in the whole business of domestic horticulture. It's my own fault, I have to admit. Last year, I filled the lawn spreader with a mixture of my own devising — essentially fertilizer, moss killer, rabbit food (initially by mistake, but then I thought, "What the heck?" and tossed in the rest) and a dash of something lively called buprimate and triforine. Two days later the front lawn erupted in vivid orange stripes of a sufficiently arresting and persistent nature to attract sightseers from as far away as west-central Massachusetts. So now I find myself on a kind of permanent probation.

Speaking of which, I've got to go. I've just heard the hard, clinical snap of gardening gloves going on and the ominous sound of metal tools being taken down from their perches. It's only a matter of time before I hear the cry of "Boy! Bring the barrow — and look sharp!" But you know the part I really hate? It's having to wear this stupid coolie hat.

Ah, Summer!

In New England, a friend here recently explained to me, the year divides into three parts. Either winter has just been, or winter is coming, or it's winter.

I know what he meant. Summers here are short — they start on the first of June and end on the last day of August, and the rest of the time you had better know where your mittens are — but for the whole of those three months the weather is agreeably warm and nearly always sunny. Best of all, the weather stays at a generally congenial level, unlike Iowa, where I grew up and where the temperature and humidity climb steadily with every passing day of summer until by mid-August it is so hot and airless that even the flies lie down on their backs and just quietly gasp.

It's the mugginess that gets you. Step outside in Iowa in August and within twenty seconds you will experience a condition that might be called perspiration incontinence. It gets so hot that you see department store mannequins with sweat circles under their arms. I have particularly vivid memories of Iowa summers because my father was the last person in the Midwest to buy an air conditioner. He thought they were unnatural. (He thought anything that cost more than $30 was unnatural.)

The one place you could get a little relief was the screened porch. Up until the 1950s nearly every American home had one of these, though they seem to be getting harder and harder to find now. They give you all the advantages of being outdoors and indoors at the same time. They are wonderful and will always be associated in my mind with summer things — corn on the cob, watermelon, the nighttime chirr of crickets, the sound of my parents' neighbor Mr. Piper arriving home late from one of his lodge meetings, parking his car with the aid of his garbage cans, then serenading Mrs. Piper with two choruses of "Rose of Seville" before settling down for a nap on the lawn.

So when we came to the States, the one thing I asked for in a house was a screened porch, and we found one. I live out there in the summer. I am writing this on the screened porch now, staring out on a sunny garden, listening to twittering birds and the hum of a neighbor's lawnmower, caressed by a light breeze, and feeling pretty darned chipper. We will have our dinner out here tonight (if Mrs B. doesn't trip over a rucked carpet with the tray again, bless her) and then I will lounge around reading until bedtime, listening to the crickets and watching the cheery blink of fireflies. Summer wouldn't be summer without all this.

Soon after we moved into our house, I noticed that a corner of screen had come loose near the floor and that our cat was using it as a kind of cat flap to come in and sleep on an old sofa we kept out there, so I just left it. One night after we had been here about a month, I was reading unusually late when out of the corner of my eye I noticed the cat come in. Only here's the thing: The cat was with me already.

I looked again. It was a skunk. Moreover, it was between me and the only means of exit. It headed straight for the table and I realized it probably came in every night about this time to hoover up any dinner bits that had fallen on the floor. (And there very often are, on account of a little game the children and I play called Vegetable Olympics when Mrs. Bryson goes off to answer the phone or get more gravy.)

199

Being sprayed by a skunk is absolutely the worst thing that can happen to you that doesn't make you bleed or put you in the hospital. If you smell skunk odor from a distance, it doesn't smell too bad at all. It's rather strangely sweet and arresting — not attractive exactly, but not revolting. Everybody who has ever smelled a skunk from a distance for the first time thinks, "Well, that's not so bad. I don't know what all the fuss is about."

But get close — or, worse still, get sprayed — and believe me it will be a long, long time before anyone asks you to dance slow and close. The odor is not just strong and disagreeable but virtually ineradicable. The most effective treatment, apparently, is to scrub yourself thoroughly with tomato juice. But even with gallons of the stuff the best you can hope for is to subdue the smell fractionally.

A classmate of my son's had a skunk get into her family's basement one night. It sprayed and the family lost virtually everything in their home. All their curtains, bedding, clothes, soft furnishings — everything, in short, that could absorb an odor — had to be thrown on a bonfire, and the rest of the house scrubbed from top to bottom. The classmate of my son's never got near the skunk, left the house immediately, and spent a weekend scouring herself with tomato juice and a stiff brush, but it was weeks before anyone would walk down the same side of a street as her. So when I say you don't want to be sprayed by a skunk, believe me, you don't want to be sprayed by a skunk.

All of this went through my mind as I sat agog watching a skunk perhaps eight feet away. The skunk spent about thirty seconds snuffling around under the table, then calmly padded out the way it had come. As it left, it turned and gave me a look that said: "I knew you were there the whole time." But it didn't spray me, for which I am grateful even now.

The next day I tacked the loose corner of screen back into place, but to show my appreciation I put a handful of dried cat food on the step, and about midnight the skunk came and ate it. After that, for two summers, I put a little food out regularly and the skunk always came to collect it. This year it hasn't been back. There has been a rabies epidemic among small mammals that has seriously reduced the populations of skunks, raccoons, and even squirrels. Apparently this happens every fifteen years or so as part of a natural cycle.

So I seem to have lost my skunk. In a year or so, the populations will recover and I may be able to adopt another. I hope so because the one thing about being a skunk is that you don't have a lot of friends.

In the meantime, partly as a mark of respect and partly because Mrs. B. caught one in the eye at an inopportune moment, we have stopped playing food games even though, if I say it myself, I was comfortably in line for a gold.

A Day
at the Seaside

Every year about this time, my wife wakes me up with a playful slap and says: "I've got an idea. Let's drive for three hours to the ocean, take off most of our clothes, and sit on some sand for a whole day."

"What for?" I will say warily.

"It will be fun," she will insist.

"I don't think so," I will reply. "People find it disturbing when I take my shirt off in public. I find it disturbing."

"No, it will be great. We'll get sand in our hair. We'll get sand in our shoes. We'll get sand in our sandwiches and then in our mouths. We'll get sunburned and windburned. And when we get tired of sitting, we can have a dip in water so cold it actually hurts. At the end of the day, we'll set off at the same time as thirty-seven thousand other people and get in such a traffic jam that we won't get home till midnight. I can make trenchant observations about your driving skills, and the children can pass the time in back sticking each other with sharp objects. It will be such fun."

The tragic thing is that because my wife is English, and therefore beyond the reach of reason where saltwater is concerned, she really will think it's fun. Frankly I have never understood the British attachment to the seaside.

I grew up in Iowa, a thousand miles from the nearest ocean, so to me (and I believe to most other Iowans, though I haven't had a chance to check with all of them yet) the word *ocean* suggests alarming things like riptides and under-tows. (I expect people in New York suffer similar terrors when you mention words like *cornfields* and *county fair*.) Lake Ahquabi, where I did all my formative swimming and sunburning, may not have the romance of Cape Cod or the grandeur of the rockribbed coast of Maine, but then neither did it grab you by the legs and carry you off helplessly to Newfound-land. No, you may keep the sea, as far as I am concerned, and every drop of water in it.

So when last weekend my wife suggested that we take a drive to the ocean, I put my foot down and said, "Never — absolutely not," which is of course why we ended up, three hours later, at Kennebunk Beach in Maine.

Now you may find this hard to believe, given the whirlwind of adventure that has been my life, but in all my years I had been to American ocean beaches just twice — once in California when I was twelve and managed to scrape all the skin from my nose and chest (this is a true story) by mistiming a retreating wave as only someone from Iowa can and diving headlong into bare, gritty sand, and once in Florida when I was a college student on spring break and far too intoxicated to notice a landscape feature as subtle as an ocean.

So I can't pretend to speak with authority here. All I can tell you is that if Kennebunk Beach in Maine is anything to go by, then American beaches are entirely unlike British ones. To begin with, there was no pier, promenade, or arcades; no shops where everything is miraculously priced at £1; no places to buy saucy postcards or jaunty hats; no tearooms and fish and chip shops; no fortune tellers; no disembodied voice from a bingo parlor breathing out those strange, coded calls: *"Number 37 — the vicar's in the shrubs again,"* or whatever it is they say.

Indeed, there was nothing commercial at

all — just a street lined with big summer homes, a vast, sunny beach, and an infinite and hostile sea beyond.

That isn't to say the people on the beach — of whom there were many hundreds — were going to go without, for they had brought everything they would ever need again in the way of food, beverages, beach umbrellas, windbreaks, folding chairs, and sleek inflatables. Amundsen went to the South Pole with fewer provisions than most of these people had.

We were a pretty pathetic sight in contrast. Apart from being whiter than an old man's flanks, we had in the way of equipment just three beach towels and a raffia bag filled, in the English style, with a bottle of sunscreen, an inexhaustible supply of Wet Wipes, spare underpants for everyone (in case of vehicular accidents involving visits to an emergency room), and a modest packet of sandwiches.

Our youngest — whom I've taken to calling Jimmy in case he should one day become a libel lawyer — surveyed the scene and said: "OK, Dad, here's the situation. I need an ice cream cone, an inflatable lounger, a deluxe bucket and spade set, a hot dog, scuba equipment, some cotton candy, a zodiac with an outboard, my own water slide, a cheese pizza with extra cheese, and a bathroom."

"They don't have those things here, Jimmy," I chuckled.

"I really need the bathroom."

I reported this to my wife. "Then you'll have to take him to Kennebunkport," she said serenely from beneath a preposterous sun hat.

Kennebunkport is an old town, at a crossroads, laid out long before anyone thought of the automobile, and some miles from the beach. It was jammed with traffic from all directions. We parked an appallingly vast distance from the center and searched all over for rest rooms. By the time we found a rest room (actually it was the back wall of the Rite-Aid Pharmacy — but please don't tell my wife), little Jimmy didn't need to go any longer.

So we returned to the beach. By the time we got there, some hours later, I discovered that everyone had gone off for a swim and there was only one half-eaten sandwich left. I sat on a towel and nibbled at the sandwich.

"Oh, look, Mummy," said number two daughter gaily when they emerged from the surf a few minutes later, "Daddy's eating the sandwich the dog had."

"Tell me this isn't happening," I whispered.

"Don't worry, dear," my wife said soothingly. "It was an Irish setter. They're very clean."

I don't remember much after that. I had a little nap and woke to find that Jimmy was burying me up to my chest in sand, which was fine except that he had started at my head, and I managed to get so sunburned that a dermatologist invited me to a convention in Cleveland the following week as an exhibit.

We lost the car keys for two hours, the Irish setter came back and stole one of the beach towels, then nipped me on the hand for eating his sandwich, and number two daughter got tar in her hair. It was a typical day at the seaside, in other words. We got home about midnight after an inadvertent detour to the Canadian border — though this at least gave us something to talk about on the long drive across Pennsylvania.

"Lovely," said my wife. "We must do that again soon."

And the heartbreaking thing is she really meant it.

On Losing a Son

This may get a little sentimental, and I'm sorry, but yesterday evening I was working at my desk when my youngest child came up to me, a baseball bat perched on his shoulder and a cap on his head, and asked me if I felt like playing a little ball with him. I was trying to get some important work done before going away on a long trip, and I very nearly declined with regrets, but then it occurred to me that never again would he be seven years, one month, and six days old, so we had better catch these moments while we can.

So we went out onto the front lawn and here is where it gets sentimental. There was a kind of beauty about the experience so elemental and wonderful I cannot tell you — the way the evening sun fell across the lawn, the earnest eagerness of his young stance, the fact that we were doing this most quintessentially dad-and-son thing, the supreme contentment of just being together — and I couldn't believe that it would ever have occurred to me that finishing an article or writing a book or doing anything at all could be more important and rewarding than this.

Now what has brought on all this sudden sensitivity is that a week or so ago we took our eldest son off to a small university in Ohio. He was the first of our four to fly the coop, and now he is gone — grown up, independent, far away — and I am suddenly realizing how quickly they go.

"Once they leave for college they never really come back," a neighbor who has lost two of her own in this way told us wistfully the other day.

This isn't what I wanted to hear. I wanted to hear that they come back a lot, only this time they hang up their clothes, admire you for your intelligence and wit, and no longer have a hankering to sink diamond studs into various odd holes in their heads. But the neighbor was right. He is gone. There is an emptiness in the house that proves it.

I hadn't expected it to be like this because for the past couple of years even when he was here he wasn't really here, if you see what I mean. Like most teenagers, he didn't live in our house in any meaningful sense — more just dropped by a couple of times a day to see what was in the refrigerator or to wander between rooms, a towel round his waist, calling out "Mom, where's my . . . ?" as in "Mom, where's my yellow shirt?" and "Mom, where's my deodorant?" Occasionally I would see the top of his head in an easy chair in front of a television on which Asian people were kicking each other in the heads, but mostly he resided in a place called "Out."

My role in getting him off to college was simply to write checks — lots and lots of them — and to look suitably pale and aghast as the sums mounted. I was staggered at the cost of sending a child to college these days. Perhaps it is because we live in a community where these matters are treated earnestly, but nearly every college-bound youth in our town goes off and looks at half a dozen or more prospective universities at enormous cost. Then there are fees for college entrance examinations and a separate fee for each university applied to.

But all this pales beside the cost of college itself. My son's tuition is $19,000 a year, which I am told is actually quite reasonable these days. Some schools charge as much as $28,000 for tuition. Then there is a fee of $3,000 a year for his room, $2,400 for food, $700 or so for books, $650 for health center fees and insurance, and $710 for "activities." Don't ask me what that is. I just sign the checks.

Still to come are the costs of flying him to and from Ohio at Thanksgiving, Christmas, and Easter, plus all the other incidental expenses like spending money and long-distance phone bills. Already my wife is calling him every other day to ask if he has enough money, when in fact, as I point out, it should be the other way around. And here's one more thing. Next year, I have a daughter who goes off to college, so I get to do this twice.

So you will excuse me, I hope, when I tell you that the emotional side of this event was rather overshadowed by the ongoing financial shock. It wasn't until we dropped him at his university dormitory and left him there looking touchingly lost and bewildered amid an assortment of cardboard boxes and suitcases in a spartan room not unlike a prison cell that it really hit home that he was vanishing out of our lives and into his own.

Now that we are home it is even worse. There is no kickboxing on the TV, no astounding clutter of sneakers in the back hallway, no calls of "Mom, where's my . . . ?" from the top of the stairs, no one my size to call me a "doofus" or to say, "Nice shirt, Dad. Did you mug a boat person?" In fact, I see now, I had it exactly wrong. Even when he wasn't here, he was here, if you see what I mean. And now he is not here at all.

It takes only the simplest things — a wadded-up sweatshirt found behind the backseat of the car, some used chewing gum left in a patently inappropriate place — to make me want to blubber helplessly. Mrs. Bryson, meanwhile, doesn't need any kind of prod. She just blubbers helplessly.

For the past week I have found myself spending a lot of time wandering aimlessly through the house looking at the oddest things — a basketball, his running trophies, an old holiday snapshot — and thinking about all the carelessly discarded yesterdays they represent. The hard and unexpected part is the realization not just that my son is not here but that the boy he was is gone forever. I would give anything to have them both back. But of course that cannot be. Life moves on. Kids grow up and move away, and if you don't know this already, believe me, it happens faster than you can imagine.

Which is why, if you will excuse me, I am going to finish here and go off and play a little baseball on the front lawn while the chance is still there.

Highway Diversions

My father, who like all dads sometimes seemed to be practicing for a World's Most Boring Man competition, used to have the habit, when I was a boy, of identifying and commenting on the state of origin of all the other cars on any highway we happened to be traveling along.

"Hey, there's another one from Oregon," he would say. "That's three this morning." Or: "Hey, Mississippi. Now what do you suppose he's doing way up here?" Then he would look around hopefully to see if anyone wanted to elaborate or offer speculation, but no one ever did. He could go on like that all day, and sometimes did.

I once wrote a book called *The Lost Continent* in which my father featured for his many interesting and unusual talents when behind the wheel — the unerring ability to get lost in any community larger than, say, a small golf course; to pay repeated inadvertent visits to a set of tollbooths on a bridge to some distant offshore archipelago; to drive the wrong way down a one-way street so many times that eventually merchants would come and watch from their doorways. One of my teenaged children recently read that book for the first time and came with it into the kitchen where my wife was cooking and said in a tone of amazed discovery, "But this is Dad," meaning, of course, me.

I have to admit it. I have become my father. I even read license plates, though my particular interest is the slogans — "Land of Lincoln" for Illinois, "Vacationland" for Maine, the zippily inane "Shore Thing" for New Jersey. I enjoy making quips and comments on these, so when, for instance, we see "You've Got a Friend in Pennsylvania," I like to turn to the other passengers and say in a wounded tone, "Then why doesn't he call?" However, I am the only one who finds this an amusing way to pass a long journey.

It's interesting — well, perhaps not interesting exactly, but certainly a fact — that many states append slogans that are pretty well meaningless. I have never understood what Ohio was thinking when it called itself the "Buckeye State" or Indiana the "Hoosier State," and I haven't the remotest idea what New York means by dubbing itself the "Empire State." As far as I am aware, New York's many undoubted glories do not include overseas possessions.

Still, I can't criticize because I live in the state with the most demented of all license plate slogans, the strange and pugnacious "Live Free or Die." Perhaps I take these things too literally, but I really don't like driving around with an explicit written vow to expire if things don't go right. Frankly, I would prefer something a little more equivocal and less terminal — "Live Free or Pout" perhaps, or maybe "Live Free or Bitch Mightily to Anyone Who'll Listen."

All this is a somewhat circuitous way of introducing our important topic — namely, how boring it is to make a long car journey these days. If you have been following this space closely (and if not, why not?) you will recall that last week I discussed how we recently drove from New Hampshire to Ohio in order to deliver my eldest son to a university that had offered to house and educate him for the next four years in return for a sum of money not unadjacent to the cost of a moon launch.

What I didn't tell you then, because I didn't want to upset you on my first week back from vacation, is what a nightmare experience it was. Now please understand, I am as fond of my wife and children as the next man, no matter how much they cost me per annum in footwear and Nintendo games (which is, frankly, a lot), but that isn't to say that I wish to pass a week with them ever again in a sealed metal chamber on an American highway.

The trouble is not my family, I hasten to add, but the American highway. Boy, are highways dull. Part of the problem is that they are so very long — it is 850 miles from New Hampshire to central Ohio and, I can now personally attest, just as far back — but mostly it is because there is so little to get excited about along the way.

It didn't used to be like this. When I was a boy, the highways of America were scattered with diversions. They weren't always very good diversions, but that didn't matter at all. What mattered was that they were there.

At some point on every day, you could count on seeing a billboard that would say something like: "Visit World-Famous Atomic Rock — It Really Glows!" A few miles farther on there would be another billboard saying: "See the Rock That Has Baffled Science! Only 65 Miles!" This one would have a picture of a grave-looking scientist with a cartoon bubble beside his head confiding: "It Is Truly a Marvel of Nature!" or "I Am Quite Baffled!"

A few miles beyond that would be: "Experience the Atomic Rock Force Field — *If You Dare!* Just 44 Miles!" This one would show a man, interestingly not unlike one's own father, being violently flung back by some strange radiant force. In smaller letters would be the warning: "Caution: May Not Be Suitable for Small Children."

Well, that would be it. My big brother and sister, squeezed in to the backseat with me and having exhausted all the possibilities for diversion that came with holding me down and drawing vivid geometric patterns on my face, arms, and stomach with a felt marking pen, would set up a clamor to see this world-famous attraction, and I would weakly chime in.

The people who put up these billboards were brilliant, among the greatest marketing geniuses of our age. They knew precisely — to the mile, I would guess — how long it would take a carful of children to wear down a father's profound and inevitable opposition to visiting something that was going to waste time and cost money.

219

The upshot, in any case, is that we always went.

The world-famous Atomic Rock would of course be nothing like the advertised attraction. It would be almost comically smaller than illustrated and wouldn't glow at all. It would be fenced off, ostensibly for the safety of onlookers, and the fence would be covered with warnings saying: "Caution: Dangerous Force Field! Approach No Farther!" But there would always be some kid who would crawl under the fence and go up and touch it, indeed clamber all over it, without being flung aside or suffering any other evident consequences. As a rule, my extravagant felt-pen tattoos would draw more interest from the crowd.

So in exasperation my father would pile us all back into the car vowing never to be duped like this again, and we would drive on until, some hours later, we would pass a billboard that said: "Visit World-Famous Singing Sands! Only 97 Miles!" and the cycle would start again.

Out west, in really boring states like Nebraska and Kansas, people could put up signs saying pretty much anything — "See the Dead Cow! Hours of Fun for the Whole Family!" or "Plank of Wood! Just

132 Miles!" Over the years, I recall, we visited a dinosaur footprint, a painted desert, a petrified frog, a hole in the ground that claimed to be the world's deepest well, and a house made entirely of beer bottles. In fact, from some of our vacations that is all I can remember.

These things were always disappointing, but that wasn't the point. You weren't paying seventy-five cents for the experience. You were paying seventy-five cents as a kind of tribute, a thanks to the imaginative person who had helped you to pass 127 miles of uneventful highway in a state of genuine excitement, and, in my case, without being drawn on. My father never understood this. Now, I regret to say, my children don't understand it either. On this trip as we drove across Pennsylvania, a state so ludicrously vast that it takes a whole day to traverse, we passed a sign that said: "Visit World-Famous Roadside America! Just 79 Miles!"

I had no idea what Roadside America was, and it wasn't even on our route, but I insisted that we make a detour to go there. These things simply don't exist any longer. Nowadays the most exciting thing you can hope to get along the highway is a McDonald's Happy Meal. So something like

Roadside America, whatever it might be, is to be devoutly cherished. The great irony is that I was the only one in the car, and by a considerable margin, who wanted to see it.

Roadside America turned out to be a large model railway, with little towns and tunnels, farms with miniature cows and sheep, and lots of trains going around in endless circles. It was a little dusty and ill-lit but charming in a not-touched-since-1957 sort of way. We were the only customers that day, possibly the only customers for many days. I loved it.

"Isn't this great?" I said to my youngest daughter.

"Dad, you are, like, *so* pathetic," she said sadly and went out.

I turned hopefully to her little brother, but he just shook his head and followed.

I was disappointed, naturally, that they weren't moved by the experience. But I think I know what to do next time. I'll hold them down for two hours beforehand and draw all over them with a felt marking pen. Then, believe me, they'll appreciate any kind of highway diversion.

Fall in New England

Ah, autumn!

Every year about this time, for a tantalizingly short while — a week or two at most — an amazing thing happens here. The whole of New England explodes in color. All those trees that for months have formed a somber green backdrop suddenly burst into a million glowing tints and the countryside, as Frances Trollope put it, "goes to glory."

Yesterday, under the pretense of doing vital research, I drove over to Vermont and treated my startled feet to a hike up Killington Peak, 4,235 feet of sturdy splendor in the heart of the Green Mountains. It was one of those sumptuous days when the world is full of autumn muskiness and tangy, crisp perfection: vivid blue sky, deep green fields, leaves in a thousand luminous hues. It is a truly astounding sight when every tree in a landscape becomes individual, when each winding back highway and plump hillside is suddenly and infinitely splashed with every sharp shade that nature can bestow — flaming scarlet, lustrous gold, throbbing vermilion, fiery orange.

Forgive me if I seem a tad effusive, but it is impossible to describe a spectacle this grand without babbling. Even the great naturalist Donald Culross Peattie, a man whose prose is so dry you could use it to mop spills, totally lost his head when he tried to convey the wonder of a New England autumn.

In his classic *Natural History of Trees of Eastern and Central North America*, Peattie drones on for 434 pages in language that can most generously be called workmanlike (typical passage: "Oaks are usually ponderous and heavy-wooded trees, with scaly or furrowed bark, and more or less five-angled twigs and, consequently, five-ranked leaves"), but when at last he turns his attention to the New England sugar maple and its vivid autumnal regalia, it is as if someone has spiked his cocoa. In a tumble of breathless metaphors he describes the maple's colors as "like the shout of a great army . . . like tongues of flame . . . like the mighty, marching melody that rides upon the crest of some symphonic weltering sea and, with its crying song, gives meaning to all the calculated dissonance of the orchestra."

"Yes, Donald," you can just about hear his wife saying, "now take your medication, dear."

For two fevered paragraphs, he goes on like this and then abruptly returns to talking about drooping leaf axils, scaly buds, and pendulous branchlets. I understand completely. When I reached the preternaturally clear air of Killington's summit, with views to every horizon soaked in autumn luster, I found it was all I could do not to fling open my arms and burst forth with a medley of John Denver tunes. (For this reason it is a good idea to hike with an experienced companion and to carry a well-stocked first aid kit.)

Occasionally you read about some academic who has gone out with the scientific equivalent of a paint chart and announced with a grave air of discovery that the maples of Michigan or the oaks of the Ozarks achieve even deeper tints, but this is to completely miss the special qualities that make New England's fall display unique.

For one thing, the New England landscape provides a setting that no other area of North America can rival. Its sunny, white churches, covered bridges, tidy farms, and clustered villages are an ideal complement to the rich, earthy colors of nature. Moreover, there is a variety in its trees that few other areas achieve: oaks, beeches, aspens, sumacs, four varieties of maples, and others almost beyond counting provide a contrast that dazzles the senses. Finally, and above all, there is the brief, perfect balance of its climate in fall, with crisp, chilly nights and warm, sunny days, which help to bring all the deciduous trees to a coordinated climax. So make no mistake. For a few glorious days each October, New England is unquestionably the loveliest place on earth.

What is all the more remarkable about this is that no one knows quite why it all happens.

In autumn, as you will recall from your school biology classes (or, failing that, from "Mr. Wizard"), trees prepare for their long winter's slumber by ceasing to manufacture chlorophyll, the chemical that makes their leaves green. The absence of chlorophyll allows other pigments, called carotenoids, which have been present in the leaves all along, to show off a bit. The carotenoids are what account for the yellow and gold of birches, hickories, beeches, and some oaks, among others. Now here is where it gets interesting. To allow these golden colors to thrive, the trees must continue to feed the leaves even though the leaves are not actually doing anything useful except hanging there looking pretty. Just at a time when a tree ought to be storing up all its energy for use the following spring, it is instead expending a great deal of effort feeding a pigment that brings joy to the hearts of simple folk like me but doesn't do anything for the tree.

What is even more mysterious is that some species of trees go a step further and, at considerable cost to themselves, manufacture another type of chemical called anthocycanins, which result in the spectacular oranges and scarlets that are so characteristic of New England. It isn't that the trees of New England manufacture more of these anthocyanins, but rather that the New England climate and soil provide exactly the right conditions for these colors to bloom in style. In climates that are wetter or warmer, the trees still go to all this trouble — have done for years — but it doesn't come to anything. No one knows why the trees make this immense effort when they get nothing evident in return.

But here is the greatest mystery of all. Every year literally millions of people, genially and collectively known to locals as "leaf peepers," get in their cars, drive great distances to New England, and spend a succession of weekends shuffling around craft shops and places with names like Norm's Antiques and Collectibles. I would estimate that no more than 0.05 percent of them stray more than 150 feet from their cars. What a strange, inexplicable misfortune that is, to come to the edge of perfection and then turn your back on it.

They miss not only the heady joys of the out-of-doors — the fresh air, the rich, organic smells, the ineffable delight of shuffling through drifts of paper-dry leaves — but the singular pleasure of hearing the hills ringing with "Take Me Home, Country Road" sung in a loud voice in a pleasingly distinctive Anglo-Iowa twang. And that, if I say so myself, is definitely worth getting out of your car for.

The Best American Holiday

If I am looking a little bloated and sluggish today, it is because Thanksgiving has just finished, and I haven't quite recovered yet.

I have a special fondness for Thanksgiving because, apart from anything else, when I was growing up it was the one time of year we ate in our house. All the other days of the year we just kind of put food into our mouths. My mother was not a great cook, you see.

Now please don't misunderstand me. My mother is a wonderful person — kindly, saintly, ever cheerful — and when she dies she will go straight to heaven. But believe me, no one is ever going to say, "Oh, thank goodness you're here, Mrs. Bryson. Can you fix us a little something to eat?"

To be perfectly fair to her, my mother had several strikes against her in the kitchen department. To begin with, she couldn't have been a great cook even if she had wanted to. She had a career, you see — she worked for the local newspaper, which meant that she was always flying in the door two minutes before it was time to put dinner on the table.

On top of this, she was a trifle absent-minded. Her particular specialty was to cook things while they were still in the packaging. I was almost full-grown before I realized that Saran Wrap wasn't a sort of chewy glaze. A combination of haste, forgetfulness, and a charming incompetence where household appliances were concerned meant that most of her cooking experiences were punctuated with billows of smoke and occasional small explosions. In our house, as a rule of thumb, you knew it was time to eat when the firemen departed.

Strangely, all this suited my father, who had what might charitably be called rudimentary tastes in food. His palate really only responded to three flavors — salt, ketchup, and burnt. His idea of a truly outstanding meal was a plate that contained something brown and unidentifiable, something green and unidentifiable, and something charred. I am quite sure that if you slow-baked, say, an oven glove and covered it sufficiently with ketchup, he would have declared, after a ruminative moment's chewing, "Hey, this is very tasty." Good food, in short, was something that was wasted on him, and my mother labored diligently for years to see that he was never disappointed.

But on Thanksgiving, by some kind of miracle, she pulled out all the stops and outdid herself. She would call us to the table and there we would find, awaiting our unaccustomed delectation, a sumptuous array of food — an enormous golden turkey, baskets of cornbread and Parker House rolls, glistening vegetables that you could actually recognize, tureens of gravy and cranberry sauce, exquisitely fluffed mashed potatoes in a bowl so vast it took two hands to lift, two kinds of stuffing, and much else.

We would eat as if we had not eaten for a year (as, in effect, we had not) and then she would present the pièce de résistance — a plump, flaky-crusted pumpkin pie surmounted by a Matterhorn of whipped cream. It was perfect. It was heaven.

And it has left me with the profoundest joy and gratitude for this most wonderful of holidays — for Thanksgiving is the most splendid of occasions, make no mistake.

Most Americans, I believe, think that

Thanksgiving has always been held on the fourth Thursday of November and that it has been going on forever — or at least as near forever as anything gets in America.

In fact, although the Mayflower Pilgrims did indeed hold a famous feast in 1621 to thank the local Indians for their help in getting them through their first difficult year and showing them how to make popcorn and so on (for which I am grateful even yet), there is no record of when that feast was held. Given the climate of New England, it was unlikely to have been late November. In any case, for the next 242 years Thanksgiving as an event was hardly noted. The first official celebration wasn't held until 1863 — and then in August, of all months. The next year President Abraham Lincoln moved it arbitrarily to the fourth Thursday in November — no one seems to recall now why a Thursday, or why so late in the year — and there it has stayed ever since.

Thanksgiving is wonderful and for all kinds of reasons. To begin with, it has the commendable effect of staving off Christmas. Whereas in Britain the Christmas shopping season seems nowadays to kick off around about the August bank holiday, Christmas mania doesn't traditionally

232

begin in America until the last weekend in November.

Moreover, Thanksgiving remains a pure holiday, largely unsullied by commercialization. It involves no greeting cards, no trees to trim, no perplexed hunt through drawers and cupboards for decorations. I love the fact that at Thanksgiving all you do is sit at a table and try to get your stomach into the approximate shape of a beach ball and then go and watch a game of football on TV. This is my kind of holiday.

But perhaps the nicest, and certainly the noblest, aspect of Thanksgiving is that it gives you a formal, official occasion to give thanks for all those things for which you should be grateful. I think this is a wonderful idea, and I can't believe that it hasn't been picked up by more countries. Speaking personally, I have a great deal to be thankful for. I have a wife and children I am crazy about. I have my health and retain full command of most of my faculties (albeit not always simultaneously). I live in a time of peace and prosperity. Ronald Reagan will never be president again. These are all things for which I am grateful, and I am pleased to let the record show it.

The only downside is that the passage of Thanksgiving marks the inescapable onset of Christmas. Any day now — any moment — my dear wife will appear beside me and announce that the time has come to shift my distended stomach and get out the festive decorations. This is a dread moment for me and with good reason since it involves physical exertion, wobbly ladders, live electricity, hammers and nails, and the collaborative direction of said dear spouse — all things with the power to do me a serious and permanent injury. I have a terrible feeling that today may be that day.

Still, it hasn't happened yet — and for that, of course, I give my sincerest thanks of all.

Deck the Halls

When I left you last time, I was expressing a certain queasy foreboding at the thought that at any moment my wife would step into the room and announce that the time has come to get out the Christmas decorations.

Well, here we are, another week gone and just eighteen fleeting days till Christmas, and still not a peep from her. I don't know how much more of this I can take.

I hate doing the Christmas decorations because, for a start, it means going up into the attic. Attics are, of course, dirty, dark, disagreeable places. You always find things up there you don't want to find — lengths of ominously gnawed wiring, gaps in the roof through which you can see daylight and sometimes even poke your head, boxes full of useless odds and ends that you must have been out of your mind ever to have hauled up there. Three things alone are certain when you venture into the attic: that you will crack your head on a beam at least twice, that you will get cobwebs draped lavishly over your face, and that you will not find what you went looking for.

When I was growing up, my friend Bobby Hansen had a secret stairway in a closet leading up to the attic, which I thought was the classiest thing ever. I still do, come to think of it, particularly as our house in New Hampshire, like all the other houses I have ever lived in, offers access to the attic only through a hatch in the ceiling, which means you have to get a stepladder out each time you want to go up there. Now the thing about putting a stepladder directly beneath an open attic hatch, I find, is that when it comes time to go back down you discover that the ladder has mysteriously moved about four feet toward the top of the hall stairs. I don't know how this happens, but it always does.

In consequence, you have to lower your legs through the hatch and blindly grope for the ladder with your feet. If you stretch your right leg to its farthest extremity, you can just about get a toe to it, but no more. Eventually, you discover that if you swing your legs back and forth, rather like a gymnast on parallel bars, you can get one foot on top of the ladder, and then both feet on.

This, however, does not represent a great breakthrough because you are now lying at an angle of about sixty degrees and unable to make any further progress. Grunting softly, you try to drag the ladder nearer with your feet but succeed only in knocking it over with an alarming crash.

Now you really are stuck. You try to wriggle back up into the attic, but you haven't the strength, so you hang by your armpits. Plaintively, you call to your wife, but she doesn't hear you, which is not just discouraging but inexplicable. Normally, your wife can hear things no one else on earth can hear. She can hear a dab of strawberry jam fall onto a white carpet two rooms away. She can hear spilled coffee being furtively mopped up with a good bath towel. She can hear dirt being tracked across a clean floor. She can hear you just *thinking* about doing something you shouldn't do. But get yourself stuck in an attic hatch and suddenly it is as if she has been placed in a soundproof chamber.

So when eventually, an hour or so later, she passes through the upstairs hallway and sees your legs dangling there, it takes her by surprise. "What are you doing?" she says at length.

You squint down at her. "Hatch aerobics," you reply with just a hint of sarcasm.

"Do you want the ladder?"

"Oh, now there's an idea. Do you know, I've been hanging here for hours trying to think what it is I'm missing, and here you've figured it out straight off."

"Do you want it or not?"

"Of course I do."

"Then say please."

"Don't be ridiculous."

"Say please."

You hesitate, sizing up your position — which is not, in all candor, terribly strong — and say please.

"And who is the loveliest person in the universe?"

"Oh, don't do this to me," you beg. "I've been hanging here so long my armpits have a wood grain."

"And who is the loveliest person in the universe?"

"You are."

"Infinitely lovelier than you?"

"Infinitely."

You hear the sound of the ladder being righted and feel your feet being guided to the top step. The hanging has evidently done you good because suddenly you

238

remember that the Christmas decorations are not in the attic — never were in the attic — but in the basement, in a cardboard box. Of course! How silly not to have recalled! Off you dash.

Two hours later you find the decorations hidden behind some old tires and a broken baby carriage. You lug the box upstairs and devote two hours more to untangling strings of lights. When you plug the lights in, naturally they do not work, except for one string that startlingly, and in a really big way, goes WHOOOOMP! and hurls you backward into a wall with a lively jolt and a shower of sparks, and then does not work.

You decide to leave the lights and get the tree in from the car. The tree is immense and lethally prickly and impossible to grasp in any way that does not result in deep pain, loss of forward vision, and tottering imbalance. As branches poke your eyes, needles puncture your cheeks and gums, and sap manages somehow to run backward up your nose, you manhandle it to the back door, fall into the house, get up and press on, fall over, get up and press on. And so you proceed through the house, knocking pictures from walls, clearing tabletops of knicknacks, knocking over unseen chairs. Your wife, so recently missing and unaccounted for, now seems to be everywhere, shouting confused and lively instructions: "Mind the thingy! Not *that* thingy — *that* thingy! Oh, look out! Go left! Left! Not *your* left — *my* left!" Then eventually, in a softer voice, "Are you all right, honey? Didn't you see those steps?"

By the time you reach the living room the tree looks as if it has been defoliated by acid rain, and so do you.

It is at this point that you realize you have no idea where the Christmas tree stand is. So, sighing, you hike up to town to the hardware store to buy another, knowing that for the next three weeks all the Christmas tree stands you have ever purchased — twenty five in all, one for each Christmas of your adulthood — will spontaneously reappear, mostly by dropping onto your head from a high shelf when you are rooting in the bottom of a closet, but occasionally taking up positions in the middle of darkened rooms or near the top of the hall stairs. If you don't know it already, know it now: Christmas tree stands are the work of the devil and they want you dead.

While you are at the hardware store, you

buy two additional strings of lights. These will not work either.

Eventually, exhausted in both mind and body, you manage to get the tree up, lit, and covered with ornaments. You stand in the posture of Quasimodo, regarding it with a kind of weak loathing.

"Oh, isn't it *lovely!*" your wife cries, clasping her hands ecstatically beneath her chin. "Now let's do the outside decorations," she announces suddenly. "I bought a special surprise for you this year — a life-size Santa Claus that goes on the roof. You fetch the forty-foot ladder and I'll open the crate. Oh, isn't this fun!" And off she skips.

Now you might reasonably say to me: "Why put yourself through this annual living hell? Why go up to the attic when you know the decorations won't be there? Why untangle the lights when you know from decades of experience that they have not the slightest chance of working?" And my answer to you is that you just have to. It is part of the ritual. Christmas wouldn't be Christmas without it.

Which is why I've decided to make a start now even though Mrs. Bryson hasn't ordered me to. There are some things in life that just have to be faced up to, whether you want to or not.

If you need me for anything, I'll be hanging from the hatch.

Fun in the Snow

For reasons I cannot begin to understand, when I was about eight years old my parents gave me a pair of skis for Christmas. I went outside, strapped them on, and stood in a racing crouch, but nothing happened. This is because there are no hills in Iowa.

Casting around for something with a slope, I decided to ski down our back porch steps. There were only five steps, but on skis the angle of descent was surprisingly steep. I went down the steps at about, I would guess, 110 miles an hour, and hit the bottom with such force that the skis jammed solid, whereas I continued onward and outward across the patio in a graceful, rising arc. About twelve feet away loomed the back wall of our garage. Instinctively adopting a spread-eagled posture for maximum impact, I smacked into it somewhere near the roof and slid down its vertical face in the manner of food flung against a wall.

It was at this point I decided that winter

sports were not for me. I put away the skis and for the next thirty-five years thought no more about the matter. Then we moved to New England, where people actually look forward to winter. At the first fall of snow they cry out with joy and root in closets for sleds and ski poles. They become suffused with a strange vitality — an eagerness to get out into all that white stuff and schuss about on something fast and reckless.

With so many active people about, including every member of my own family, I began to feel left out. So a few weeks ago, in an attempt to find a winter pastime, I borrowed some ice skates and went with my two youngest to Occum Pond, a popular local spot for skating.

"Are you sure you know how to skate?" my daughter asked uneasily.

"Of course I do, my petal," I assured her. "I have been mistaken many times for Peggy Fleming, on the ice and off."

And I do know how to skate, honestly. It's just that my legs, after years of inactivity, got a little overexcited to be confronted with so much slipperiness. As soon as I stepped onto the ice, they decided they wanted to visit every corner of Occum Pond at once, from lots of different directions. They went this way and that, scissoring and splaying, sometimes getting as much as twelve feet apart, but constantly gathering momentum, until at last they flew out from under me and I landed on my butt with such a wallop that my coccyx hit the roof of my mouth and I had to push my esophagus back in with my fingers.

"*Wow!*" said my startled butt as I clambered heavily back to my feet. "That ice is *hard*."

"Hey, let ME see," cried my head and instantly down I went again.

And so it went for the next thirty minutes, with various extremities of my body — shoulders, chin, nose, one or two of the more adventurous internal organs — hurling themselves at the ice in a spirit of investigation. From a distance I suppose I must have looked like someone being worked over by an invisible gladiator. Eventually, when I had nothing left to bruise, I crawled to shore and asked to be covered with a blanket. And that was it for my attempt at ice skating.

Next I tried sledding, which I don't even want to talk about, except to say that the man was very understanding about his dog, all things considered, and that that lady across the road would have saved us all a lot of trouble if she had just left her garage door open.

It was at about this juncture that my friend Danny Blanchflower stepped into the picture. Danny is a professor of economics at Dartmouth and a very brainy fellow. He writes books with sentences like "When entered contemporaneously in the full specifications of column 5.7, profit-per-employee has a coefficient of 0.00022 with a t-statistic of 2.3" and isn't even joking. For all I know, it may even mean something. As I say, he's a real smart guy, except for one thing. He is crazy about snowmobiling.

Now, a snowmobile, as far as I am concerned, is a rocket ship designed by Satan to run on snow. It travels at speeds up to seventy miles an hour, which — call me chicken, I don't care — seems to me a trifle fleet on narrow, winding paths through boulder-strewn woods.

For weeks Danny pestered me to join him in a bout of this al fresco madness. I tried to explain that I had certain problems with outdoor activities vis-à-vis the snowy season, and that somehow I didn't think a powerful, dangerous machine was likely to provide my salvation.

"Nonsense!" he cried. Well, to make a

long story short, the next thing I knew I was on the edge of the New Hampshire woods, wearing a snug, heavy helmet that robbed me of all my senses except terror, sitting nervously astride a sleek, beastlike conveyance, its engine throbbing in anticipation of all the trees against which it might soon dash me. Danny gave me a rundown on the machine's operation, which for all I understood might have been a passage from one of his books, and jumped onto his own machine.

"Ready?" he shouted over the roar of his engine.

"No."

"Great!" he called and took off with a flare of afterburners. Within two seconds he was a noisy dot in the distance.

Sighing, I gently engaged the throttle and, with a startled cry and a brief wheelie, took off with a velocity seldom seen outside a Tom and Jerry cartoon. Shrieking hysterically and jettisoning weight via my bladder with every lively bump, I flew through the woods as if on an Exocet missile. Branches slapped my helmet. Moose reared and fled. The landscape flashed past as if in some hallucinogen-induced delirium.

Eventually, Danny stopped at a crossroad, beaming all over, engine purring. "So what do you think?"

I moved my lips but no sound emerged. Danny took this as assent.

"Well, now that you've got the hang of it, shall we bang up the pace a bit?"

I formed the words "Please, Danny, I want to go home. I want to see my mom," but again no sound emerged.

And off he went. For hours we raced at lunatic speeds through the endless woods, bouncing through streams, swerving past boulders, launching into flight over fallen logs. When at length this waking nightmare concluded, I stepped from my machine on legs made of water.

Afterward, to celebrate our miraculous intactness, we repaired to Murphy's, our convivial local hostelry, for a beer. When the barmaid put the glasses down in front of us it occurred to me, with a flash of inspiration, that here at last was something I could do: winter drinking.

I had found my calling. I'm not as good at it yet as I hope to be — my legs still tend to go after about three hours — but I'm doing a lot of stamina training and am looking to have a very good season next year.

The Mysteries of Christmas

One of the many small mysteries I hoped to resolve when I first moved to England was this: When British people sang "A-Wassailing We'll Go," where was it they went and what exactly did they do when they got there?

Throughout an American upbringing I heard this song every Christmas without ever finding anyone who had the faintest idea of how to go about the obscure and enigmatic business of wassailing. Given the perky lilt of the carol and the party spirit in which it was always sung, it suggested to my youthful imagination rosy-cheeked wenches bearing flagons of ale in a scene of general merriment and abandon before a blazing yule log in a hall decked with holly, and with this in mind I looked forward to my first English Christmas with a certain frank anticipation. In my house, the most exciting thing you could hope for in the way of seasonal recklessness was being offered a cookie shaped like a Christmas tree.

So you may conceive of my disappointment when my first Christmas in England came and went and not only was there no wassailing to be seen but no one I quizzed was any the wiser as to its arcane and venerable secrets. In fact, in twenty years in England I never did find anyone who had ever gone a-wassailing, at least not knowingly. Nor, while we are at it, did I encounter any mumming, still less any hodening (a kind of organized group begging for coins with a view to buying drinks at the nearest pub, which I think is an outstanding idea), or many of the other traditions of an English Christmas that were expressly promised in the lyrics of carols and the novels of authors like Jane Austen and Charles Dickens.

It wasn't until I happened on a copy of T. G. Crippen's scholarly and ageless *Christmas and Christmas Lore*, published in London in 1923, that I finally found that *wassail* was originally a salutation. From the Old Norse *ves heil*, it means "in good health." In Anglo-Saxon times, according to Crippen, it was customary for someone offering a drink to say, "Wassail!" and for the recipient to respond "Drinkhail!" and for the participants to repeat the exercise until comfortably horizontal.

It is clear from Crippen's tome that in 1923 this and many other ancient and agreeable Christmas customs were still commonly encountered in Britain. Now, alas, they appear to be gone for good.

Even so, Christmas is something that the British still do exceptionally well, and for all kinds of reasons. To begin with, the British still pack all their festive excesses (eating, drinking, gift-giving, more eating, more drinking) into this one single occasion, whereas we in America spread ours out over three separate holidays.

In America, the big eating holiday is, of course, Thanksgiving. Thanksgiving is a great holiday — probably the very best holiday in America, if you ask me. (For the benefit of those unacquainted with its provenance, Thanksgiving commemorates the first harvest feast at which the pilgrims sat down with the Indians to thank them for all their help and to tell them, "Oh, and by the way, we've decided we want the *whole* country.") It is a great holiday because you don't have to give gifts or send cards or do anything but eat until you begin to look like a balloon that has been left on a helium machine too long.

The trouble is that it comes less than a month before Christmas. So when on December 25 Mom brings out another turkey, you don't go, "Turkey! YIPPEEE!" but rather, "Ah, turkey again is it, Mother?" Under such an arrangement Christmas dinner is bound to come as an anticlimax.

Also, Americans don't drink much at Christmas, as a rule. Indeed, I suspect most people in America would think it faintly unseemly to imbibe anything more than, say, a small sherry before lunch on Christmas Day. We save our large-scale drinking for New Year's Eve, whereas the British think they are doing exceptionally well if they save it till, say, lunchtime of Christmas eve.

But the big difference — the thing that makes a British Christmas incomparable — is Boxing Day, as December 26 is known.

Curiously, for all its venerated glory, no one knows quite how Boxing Day came to be or why it is so called. It appears to be a relatively recent phenomenon — the great and majestic *Oxford English Dictionary* can trace the term back no further than 1849 — though, like so many Christmas traditions, its roots lie much deeper. Its origins may have something to do with church alms boxes, which were opened at Christmas and their contents distributed to the poor. What is certain is that at least as far back as the 1500s, and possibly earlier, it was customary for servants, apprentices, shopkeepers, and others in a subservient position to receive year-end gifts of money from those they had served all year. These small gratuities were put in an earthenware container, called a "box," which was broken open at Christmastime and the proceeds used to fund a bit of high living.

Since most servants had to wait upon their masters on Christmas Day, their own Christmas celebrations were deferred to the day after. Hence December 26 became the day on which their boxes were opened, and hence Boxing Day.

Whatever the origins, Boxing Day is very nearly as dear to British hearts as the day that precedes it. Indeed, there are those of us who think it is altogether superior since it doesn't involve long, perplexed hours spent on the floor trying to assemble dollhouses and tricycles from instructions written in Taiwan, or the uttering of false professions of gratitude and delight to Auntie Joan for the gift of a hand-knitted sweater bearing the sort of patterns you get when you rub your eyes too hard. It is a day, in short, that has most of the advantages of Christmas (lots of good food, general goodwill toward all, a chance to doze in an armchair during daylight hours) without any of the attendant drawbacks.

We as a family still preserve an English Christmas even though we are no longer in England. We have crackers and plum pudding with brandy butter and mince pies and a yule log and we drink to excess and, above all, we observe Boxing Day.

It's quite wonderful really. But I do still wish I could find someone to wassail with.

Life in
a Cold Climate

Something rather daring that I like to do at this time of year is to go out without putting on my coat or gloves or any other protection against the elements and walk the thirty or so yards to the bottom of our driveway to bring in the morning paper from a little box on a post.

Now you might say that that doesn't sound very daring at all, and in a sense you would be right because it only takes about twenty seconds there and back, but here is the thing that makes it special: Sometimes I hang around out there just to see how long I can stand the cold.

I don't wish to sound smug or boastful, but I have devoted much of my life to testing the tolerance to extremes of the human body, often with very little regard to the potential peril to myself — for instance, allowing a leg to go fast asleep in a movie theater and then seeing what happens if I try suddenly to rise and go for popcorn, or wrapping a rubber band around my index finger to see if I can make it explode. It is through this work that I have made some important breakthroughs, notably the discovery that very hot surfaces don't necessarily look hot, and that temporary amnesia can be reliably induced by placing the head immediately beneath an open drawer or cupboard door.

I expect your instinct is to regard such behavior as foolhardy, but let me remind you of all those occasions when you yourself have stuck a finger into a small flame just to see what would happen (and what exactly *did* happen, eh?), or stood first on one leg and then on the other in a scalding bath waiting for an inflow of cold water to moderate the temperature, or sat at a kitchen table quietly absorbed with letting melted candle wax drip onto your fingers, or a great deal else I could mention.

At least when I engage in these matters, it is in a spirit of serious scientific inquiry. Which is why, as I say, I like to go for the morning paper in the least encumbering apparel that decency and Mrs. Bryson will allow.

This morning when I set off it was −19°F out there — cold enough to reconfigure the anatomy of a brass monkey, as I believe the saying has it. Unless you come from a really cold place yourself, or are reading this in a chest freezer, you may find such extreme chilliness difficult to conceive of. So let me tell you just how cold it is: *very*.

When you step outside in such weather, for the first instant it is startlingly invigorating — not unlike the experience of diving into cold water, a sort of wake-up call to every corpuscle. But that phase passes quickly. Before you have trudged a few yards, your face feels as it would after a sharp slap, your extremities are aching, and every breath you take hurts. By the time you return to the house your fingers and toes are throbbing with a gentle but insistent pain and you notice with interest that your cheeks yield no sensation at all. The little residual heat you brought from the house is long gone, and your clothes have ceased to have any insulating value. It is decidedly uncomfortable.

Nineteen degrees below zero is unusually cold even for northern New England, so I was interested to see how long I could bear such an exposure, and the answer was thirty-nine seconds. I don't mean that's how long it took for me to get bored with the idea, or to think, "Gracious, it *is* rather chilly; I guess I'll go in now." I mean that's how long it took me to be so cold that I would have climbed over my mother to get inside first.

New Hampshire is famous for its harsh winters, but in fact there are plenty of places much worse. The coldest temperature ever recorded here was −46°F, back in 1925, but twenty other states have had lower lows than that. The bleakest thermometer reading yet seen in the United States was at Prospect Creek, Alaska, in 1971 when the temperature fell to −79.8°F.

Of course, almost any place can have a cold snap. The real test of a winter is in its duration. In International Falls, Minnesota, the winters are so long and ferocious that the mean annual temperature is just 36.5°F, which is very mean indeed. Nearby there is a town called (honestly) Frigid, where I suspect the situation is even worse but they are just too depressed to report.

However, the record for most wretched inhabited place ever must surely go to Langdon, North Dakota, which in the winter of 1935–1936 recorded 176 consecutive days of below freezing temperatures, including 67 consecutive days in which the temperature fell below 0°F (i.e., into the shrieking brass monkey zone) for at least part of the day and 41 consecutive days when the temperature did not rise above 0°F.

Just to put that in perspective, 176 days is the span of time that lies between Christmas and midsummer. Personally, I would find it very hard to spend 176 consecutive days in North Dakota at any time, but I guess that is another matter.

In any case, I have all I can handle right here in New Hampshire. I was dreading the long, cruel winters in New England, but to my surprise they delight me. Partly it is because they are so shocking. There really is something exhilarating about the sharpness of the cold, the cleanness of the air. And winters here are stunningly pretty. Every rooftop and mailbox wears a jaunty cap of snow for months on end. Nearly every day the sun shines, so there is none of the oppressive gray gloom that characterizes winter in so many other places. And when the snow begins to get trampled or dirty, there is generally a big new fall that fluffs it up again.

People here actually get excited about winter. There is skiing and ice skating and sledding on the local golf course. One of our neighbors floods his backyard and turns it into a skating pond for the kids on our street. Dartmouth has a winter carnival, with ice sculptures on the college green. It is all very cheery.

Best of all, you know that winter is just one in an endless cycle of reliable, well-defined seasons. When the cold starts to get to you, there is the reassurance of knowing that a good, hot summer is just around the corner. Apart from anything else, it means a whole new set of interesting experimental challenges involving sunburn, poison ivy, infectious deer ticks, electric hedge clippers, and — this goes without saying — barbecue lighter fluid. I can't wait.

Hail to the Chief

It's Presidents Day tomorrow. I know. I can hardly stand the excitement either.

Presidents Day is a new holiday to me. When I was growing up, we had two presidential holidays in February — Lincoln's Birthday on February 12 and Washington's Birthday on February 22. I may not be exactly right on those dates, or indeed even very close, because frankly it's been a long time since I was growing up and anyway they weren't very interesting holidays. You didn't receive presents or get to go on a picnic or anything.

The obvious shortcoming with having a holiday on a date like February 12 or February 22 is that it can fall on any day of the week, whereas most people like to have their public holidays on Mondays, which gives them a long weekend. So for a while America celebrated Washington's Birthday and Lincoln's Birthday on the Mondays nearest the appropriate dates. However, this bothered some people of a particular nature, so it was decided to have a single holiday on the third Monday of February and to call it Presidents Day.

The idea now is to honor all the presidents, whether they were good or bad, which I think is swell because it gives us an opportunity to commemorate the more obscure or peculiar presidents — people like Grover Cleveland, who reportedly had the interesting habit of relieving himself out of the Oval Office window, or Zachary Taylor, who never voted in an election and didn't even vote for himself.

As everyone knows, America has produced quite a few great presidents — Washington, Lincoln, Jefferson, Franklin and Teddy Roosevelt, Woodrow Wilson, John F. Kennedy. More interestingly, it has also produced several great men who incidentally became president, among them James Madison, Ulysses S. Grant, and — you may be surprised to hear me say this — Herbert Hoover.

I have a certain regard for Hoover — *fondness* would be much too strong a word — because he was from Iowa, and so am I. Besides, you have to feel a little sorry for the poor man. He was the only person in American history for whom attaining the White House was a retrograde career move. Nowadays when people think of Hoover at all, it is as the man who gave the world the Great Depression. Hardly anyone remembers the half century of remarkable, even heroic, achievements that preceded it.

Consider his curriculum vitae: Orphaned at eight, he put himself through college (he was in the first graduating class from Stanford University) and became a successful mining engineer in the western United States. He then went off to Australia, where he more or less started the mining industry in Western Australia — still one of the most productive regions in the world — and eventually ended up in London, where he became a vastly wealthy and influential pillar of the business community.

Such was his stature that at the outbreak of the First World War he was invited to join the British Cabinet — a signal honor, to say the least, for an American citizen — but declined and instead took on the job of directing famine relief throughout Europe, an undertaking that he managed with such thoroughness and distinction that it is estimated he saved ten million lives. By the end of the war he was one of the most admired and respected men in the world, known everywhere as the Great Humanitarian.

Returning to America, he became a trusted adviser to Woodrow Wilson, then served as secretary of commerce under Harding and Coolidge, where he oversaw a 58 percent rise in American exports in eight years. When he ran for president in 1928, he was elected in a record landslide.

In March 1929 he was inaugurated. Seven months later Wall Street crashed and the economy went into freefall. Contrary to common belief, Hoover responded at once. He spent more money on public works and unemployment relief than all his predecessors combined, provided $500 million in assistance to troubled banks, even donated his own salary to charity. But he lacked the common touch and alienated the electorate by insisting repeatedly that recovery was just around the corner. In 1932, he was defeated as resoundingly as he had been elected four years before and has been remembered ever since as an abject failure.

Still, at least he is remembered for something, which is more than can be said for many of our chief executives. Of the forty-one men who have risen to the office of president, at least half served with such lack of eminence as to be almost totally forgotten now, which I think is deserving of the warmest approbation. To be president of the United States and not accomplish anything is, after all, a kind of accomplishment in itself.

By almost universal agreement, the most vague and ineffectual of all our leaders was Millard Fillmore, who succeeded to the office in 1850 upon the death of Zachary Taylor and spent the next three years demonstrating how the country would have been run if they had just propped Taylor up in a chair with cushions. However, Fillmore has become so celebrated for his obscurity that he is no longer actually obscure, which rather disqualifies him from serious consideration.

Far more noteworthy to my mind is the great Chester A. Arthur, who was sworn in as president in 1881, posed for an official photograph, and then, as far as I can make out, was never heard from again. If Arthur's goal in life was to grow rather splendid facial hair and leave plenty of room in the history books for the achievements of other men, then his presidency can be ranked a sterling success.

Also admirable in their way were Rutherford B. Hayes, who was president from 1877 to 1881 and whose principal devotions were the advocacy of "hard money" and the repeal of the Bland-Allison Act, preoccupations so pointless and abstruse that no one can remember now what they were, and Franklin Pierce, whose term of office from 1853 to 1857 was an interlude of indistinction between two longer periods of anonymity. He spent virtually the whole of his incumbency hopelessly intoxicated, prompting the affectionate slogan "Franklin Pierce, the Hero of Many a Well-Fought Bottle."

My favorites, however, are the two presidents Harrison. The first was William Henry Harrison, who heroically refused to don an overcoat for his inaugural ceremony in 1841, consequently caught pneumonia, and with engaging swiftness expired. He was president for just thirty days, nearly all of it spent unconscious. Forty years later his grandson, Benjamin Harrison, was elected president and succeeded in the challenging ambition of achieving as little in four years as his grandfather had in a month.

As far as I am concerned, all these men deserve public holidays of their own. So you may conceive my dismay at news that moves are afoot in Congress to abolish

Presidents Day and return to observing Lincoln's and Washington's birthdays separately, on the grounds that Lincoln and Washington were truly great men and, moreover, didn't pee out the window. Can you believe that? Some people have no sense of history.

Lost in Cyberland

When we moved to America, the change in electrical systems meant I needed all new stuff for my office — computer, fax machine, answering machine, and so on. I am not good at shopping or parting with large sums of money at the best of times, and the prospect of trailing around a succession of shops listening to sales assistants touting the wonders of various office products filled me with foreboding.

So imagine my delight when in the first computer store I went to I found a machine that had everything built into it — fax, answering machine, electronic address book, Internet capability, you name it. Advertised as "The Complete Home Office Solution," this computer promised to do everything but make the coffee.

So I took it home and set it up, flexed my fingers, and wrote a perky fax to a friend in London. I typed his fax number in the appropriate box as directed and pushed "Send." Almost at once, noises of international dialing came out of the computer's built-in speakers. Then there was a ringing tone, and finally an unfamiliar voice that said: *"Allo? Allo?"*

"Hello?" I said in return, and realized that there was no way I could talk to this person, whoever he was.

My computer began to make shrill fax noises. *"Allo? Allo?"* the voice said again, with a touch of puzzlement and alarm. After a moment, he hung up. Instantly, my computer redialed his number.

And so it went for much of the morning, with my computer repeatedly pestering some unknown person in an unknown place while I searched frantically through the manual for a way to abort the operation. Eventually, in desperation, I unplugged the computer, which shut down with a series of "Big Mistake!" and "Crisis in the Hard Drive!" noises.

Three weeks later — this is true — we received a phone bill with $68 in charges for calls to Algiers. Subsequent inquiries revealed that the people who had written the software for the fax program had not considered the possibility of overseas transmissions. The program was designed to read seven-digit phone numbers with three-digit area codes. Confronted with any other combination of numbers, it went into a sort of dial-a-bedouin default mode.

I also discovered that the electronic address book had a similar aversion to addresses without standard U.S. zip codes, rendering it all but useless for my purposes, and that the answering machine function had a habit of coming on in the middle of conversations.

For a long time it puzzled me how something so expensive, so leading edge, could be so useless, and then it occurred to me that a computer is a stupid machine with the ability to do incredibly smart things, while computer programmers are smart people with the ability to do incredibly stupid things. They are, in short, a dangerously perfect match.

You will have read about the millennium bug. You know then that at the stroke of midnight on January 1, 2000, all the computers in the world will for some reason go through a thought process something like this: "Well, here we are in a new year that ends in '00. I expect it's 1900. But wait — if it's 1900, computers haven't been invented yet. Therefore I don't exist. Guess I had better shut myself down and wipe my memory clean." The estimated cost to put this right is $200 trillion gazillion or some such preposterous sum. A computer, you see, can calculate pi to twenty thousand places but can't work out that time always moves forward. Programmers, meanwhile, can write eighty thousand lines of complex code but fail to note that every hundred years you get a new century. It's a disastrous combination.

When I first read that the computer industry had created a problem for itself so basic, so immense, and so foolish, I suddenly understood why my fax facility and other digital toys are worthless. But this still doesn't adequately explain the wondrous — the towering — uselessness of my computer's spell checker.

Like nearly everything else to do with computers, a spell checker is marvelous in principle. When you have done a piece of work, you activate it and it goes through the text looking for words that are misspelled. Actually, since a computer doesn't understand what words are, it looks for letter clusters it isn't familiar with, and here is where the disappointment begins.

First, it doesn't recognize any proper nouns — names of people, places, corporations, and so on — or nonstandard spellings like *kerb* and *colour*. Nor does it recog-

271

nize many plurals or other variant forms (like *steps* or *stepped*), or abbreviations or acronyms. Nor, evidently, any word coined since Eisenhower was president. Thus, it recognizes *sputnik* and *beatnik* but not *Internet, fax, cyberspace,* or *butthead,* among many others.

But the really distinctive feature of my spell checker — and here is the part that can provide hours of entertainment for anyone who doesn't have anything approaching a real life — is that it has been programmed to suggest alternatives. These are seldom less than memorable. For this column, for instance, for *Internet* it suggested *internat* (a word that I cannot find in any dictionary, American or British), *internode, interknit,* and *underneath. Fax* prompted no fewer than thirty-three suggested alternatives, including *fab, fays, feats, fuzz, feaze, phase,* and at least two more that are unknown to lexicography: *falx* and *phose. Cyberspace* drew a blank, but for *cyber* it came up with *chubbier* and *scabbier.*

I have tried without success to discern the logic by which a computer and programmer working in tandem could decide that someone who typed *f-a-x* would really have intended to write *p-h-a-s-e,* or why *cyber* might suggest *chubbier* and *scabbier* but not, say, *watermelon* or *full-service gas station,* to name two equally random alternatives. Still less can I explain how nonexistent words like *phose* and *internat* would get into the program. Call me exacting, but I would submit that a computer program that wants to discard a real word in favor of one that does not exist is not ready to be offered for public use.

Not only does the system suggest imbecilic alternatives, it positively aches to put them in. You have to all but order the program not to insert the wrong word. If you accidentally accept its prompt, it automatically changes that word throughout the text. Thus, to my weary despair, I have in recent months produced work in which "woolens" was changed throughout to "wesleyans," "Minneapolis" to "monopolists," and — this is a particular favorite — "Renoir" to "rainware." If there is a simple way to unpick these involuntary transformations, then I have not found it.

Now I read in *U.S. News & World Report* that the same computer industry that failed to notice the coming of a new millennium has equally failed for years to realize that the materials on which it stores information — magnetic tapes and so forth — irremediably degrade in a not-very-long time. NASA scientists who recently tried to access material on the 1976 Viking mission to Mars discovered that 20 percent of it has simply vanished and that the rest is going fast.

So it looks as if computer programmers will be putting in some late nights over the next couple of years. To which, frankly, I say hooray. Or *haywire, heroin,* and *hoopskirt,* as my computer would prefer it.

Your Tax Form Explained

Enclosed is your 1998 United States Internal Revenue Service Tax Form 1040-ES OCR: "Estimated Tax for Self-Employed Individuals." You may use this form to estimate your 1998 fiscal year tax IF:

1. You are the head of a household AND the sum of the ages of your spouse and dependents, minus the ages of qualifying pets (see Schedule 12G), is divisible by a whole number. (Use Supplementary Schedule 142C if pets are deceased but buried on your property.)

2. Your Gross Adjusted Income does not exceed your Adjusted Gross Income (except where applicable) AND you did not pay taxable interest on dividend income prior to 1903.

3. You are not claiming a foreign tax credit, except as a "foreign" tax credit. (Warning: Claiming a foreign tax credit for a foreign "tax" credit, except where a foreign "tax credit" is involved, may result in a fine of $125,000 and 25 years' imprisonment.)

4. You are one of the following: married and filing jointly; married and not filing jointly; not married and not filing jointly; jointed but not filing; other.

Instructions

Type all answers in ink with a number two lead pencil. Do not cross anything out. Do not use abbreviations or ditto marks. Do not misspell "miscellaneous." Write your name, address, and social security number, and the name, address, and social security numbers of your spouse and dependents, in full on each page twice. Do not put a check mark in a box marked "cross" or a cross in a box marked "check mark" unless it is your express wish to do the whole thing again. Do not write "Search me" in any blank spaces. Do not make anything up.

Complete Sections 47 to 52 first, then proceed to even-numbered sections and complete in reverse order. Do NOT use this form if your total pensions and annuities disbursements were greater than your advanced earned income credits OR vice versa.

Under "Income," list all wages, salaries, net foreign source taxable income, royalties, tips, gratuities, taxable interest, capital gains, air miles, and money found down the back of the sofa. If your earnings are derived wholly, or partially but not primarily, or wholly AND partially but not primarily, from countries other than the United States (if uncertain, see USIA Leaflet 212W, "Countries That Are Not the United States") OR your rotated gross income from Schedule H was greater than your earned income credit on nontaxable net disbursements, you MUST include a Grantor/Transferor Waiver Voucher. Failure to do so may result in a fine of $1,500,000 and seizure of a child.

Under Section 890f, list total farm income (if none, give details). If you were born after January 1, 1897, and are NOT a widow(er), include excess casualty losses and provide carryover figures for depreciation on line 27iii. You MUST list number of turkeys slaughtered for export. Subtract, but do not deduct, net gross dividends from pro rata interest payments, multiply by the total number of steps in your home, and enter on line 356d.

On Schedule F1001, line c, list the contents of your garage. Include all electrical and nonelectrical items on Schedule 295D, but DO NOT include electrical OR nonelectrical items not listed on Supplementary Form 243d.

Under "Personal Expenditures," itemize all cash expenditures of more than $1, and include verification. If you have had dental work and you are not claiming a refund on the federal oil spill allowance, enter your shoe sizes since birth and enclose specimen shoes (right foot only). Multiply by 1.5 or 1,319, whichever is larger, and divide line 3f by 3d. Under Section 912g, enter federal income support grants for the production of alfalfa, barley (but not sorghum, unless for home consumption), and okra WHETHER OR NOT you received any. Failure to do so may result in a fine of $3,750,000 and death by lethal injection.

If your children are dependent but not living at home, or living at home but not dependent, or dependent and living at home but hardly ever there AND you are not claiming exemption for leases of maritime vessels in excess of 12,000 tons deadweight (15,000 tons if you were born in Guam), you MUST complete and include a Maritime Vessel Exemption Form. Failure to do so may result in a fine of $111,000,000 and a nuclear attack on a small, neutral country.

On pages 924–926, Schedule D, enter the names of people you know personally who are Communists or use drugs. (Use extra pages if necessary.)

If you have interest earnings from savings accounts, securities, bearer bonds, certificates of deposit, or other fiduciary instruments but DO NOT know your hat size, complete Supplementary Schedules 112d and 112f and enclose with all relevant tables. (Do not send chairs at this time.) Include, but do not collate, ongoing losses from mining investments, commodities transactions, and organ transplants, divide by the total number of motel visits you made in 1996, and enter in any remaining spaces. If you have unreimbursed employee expenses, tough.

To compute your estimated tax, add lines 27 through 964, deduct lines 45a and 699f from Schedule 2F (if greater or less than 2.2% of average alternative minimum estimated tax for last five years), multiply by the number of RPMs your car registers when stuck on ice, and add 2. If line 997 is smaller than line 998, start again. In the space marked "Tax Due," write a very large figure.

Make your check payable to "Internal

Revenue Service of the United States of America and to the Republic for Which It Stands," and mark for the attention of Patty. On the back of your check write your social security number, Taxpayer Identification Number, IRS Tax Code Audit Number(s), IRS Regional Office Sub-Unit Zone Number (UNLESS you are filing a T/45 Sub-Unit Zone Exclusion Notice), sexual orientation, and smoking preference, and send to:

Internal Revenue Service of the United States of America
Tax Reception and Orientation Center
Building D/Annex G78
Suite 900
Subduction Zone 12
Box 132677-02
Drawer 2, About Halfway Back
Federal City
Maryland 10001

If you have any questions about filing, or require assistance with your return, phone 1-800-BUSY SIGNAL. Thank you and have a prosperous 1999. Failure to do so may result in a fine of $125,000 and a long walk to the cooler.

Book Tours

Ten years ago this month, I got a phone call from an American publisher telling me that he had just bought one of my books and was going to send me on a three-week, sixteen-city publicity tour.

"We're going to make you a media star," he said brightly.

"But I've never been on TV," I protested in mild panic.

"Oh, it's easy. You'll love it," he said with the blithe assurance of someone who doesn't have to do it himself.

"No, I'll be terrible," I insisted. "I have no personality."

"Don't worry, we'll *give* you a personality. We're going to fly you to New York for a course in media training."

My heart sank. All this had a bad feeling about it. For the first time since I accidentally set fire to a neighbor's garage in 1961, I began to think seriously about the possibility of plastic surgery and a new life in Central America.

So I flew to New York and, as it turned out, the media training was less of an ordeal than I had feared. I was put in the hands of a kindly, patient man named Bill Parkhurst, who sat with me for two days in a windowless studio somewhere in Manhattan and put me through an endless series of mock interviews.

He would say things like: "OK, now we're going to do a three-minute interview with a guy who hasn't looked at your book until ten seconds ago and doesn't know whether it's a cookbook or a book on prison reform. Also, this guy is a tad stupid and will interrupt you frequently. OK, let's go."

He would click his stopwatch and we would do a three-minute interview. Then we would do it again. And again. And so it went for two days. By the afternoon of the second day I was having to push my tongue back in my mouth with my fingers.

"Now you know what you'll feel like by the second day of your tour," Parkhurst observed cheerfully.

"What's it like after twenty-one days?" I asked.

Parkhurst smiled. "You'll love it."

Amazingly he was nearly right. Book tours are actually kind of fun. You get to stay in nice hotels, you are driven every-where in big silver cars, you are treated as if you are much more important than you actually are, you can eat steak three times a day at someone else's expense, and you get to talk endlessly about yourself for weeks at a stretch. Is this a dream come true or what?

It was an entirely new world for me. As you will recall if you have been committing these pieces to memory, when I was growing up my father always took us to the cheapest motels imaginable — the sort of places that made the Bates Motel in *Psycho* look sophisticated and well appointed — so this was a gratifyingly novel experience. I had never before stayed in a really fancy hotel, never ordered from room service, never called on the services of a concierge or valet, never tipped a doorman. (Still haven't!)

The great revelation to me was room service. I grew up thinking that ordering from the room service menu was the pin-nacle of graciousness — something that happened in Cary Grant movies but not in the world I knew — so when a publicity person suggested I make free use of it, I jumped at the chance. In doing so I discov-ered something you doubtless knew already: Room service is *terrible*.

I ordered room service meals at least a dozen times in hotels all over the country, and it was always dire. The food would take hours to arrive and it was invariably cold and leathery. I was always fascinated by how much effort went into the presentation — the white tablecloth, the vase with a rose in it, the ostentatious removal of a domed silver lid from each plate — and how little went into keeping the food warm and tasty.

At the Huntington Hotel in San Francisco, I particularly remember, the waiter whipped away a silver lid to reveal a bowl of white goo.

"What's that?" I asked.

"Vanilla ice cream, I believe, sir," he replied.

"But it's melted," I said.

"Yes it has," he agreed. "Enjoy," he added with a bow, pocketing a large tip and withdrawing.

Of course, on book tours it's not all lounging around in swank hotel rooms, watching TV, and eating melted ice cream. You also have to give interviews — lots and lots of them, more than you can imagine, often from before dawn until after midnight — and do a positively ludicrous amount of traveling in between. Because there are so many authors out there pushing their books — as many as two hundred at busy periods, I was told — and only so many radio and TV programs to appear on, you tend to be dispatched to wherever there is an available slot. In one five-day period, I flew from San Francisco to Atlanta to Chicago to Boston and back to San Francisco. I once flew from Denver to Colorado Springs in order to do a thirty-second interview that — I swear — went approximately like this:

Interviewer: "Our guest today is Bill Bryson. So you've got a new book out, do you, Bill?"

Me: "That's right."

Interviewer: "Well, that's wonderful. Thanks so much for coming. Our guest tomorrow is Dr. Milton Greenberg, who has written a book about bedwetting called *Tears at Bedtime*."

The whole point, as Bill Parkhurst taught me, is to sell yourself shamelessly, and believe me, you soon learn to do it. Since that initial experience I have done six other book tours in America, four in Canada, three in Australia and New Zealand, two in South Africa, one in continental Europe, and eight in Britain. That's not to mention all the literary festivals and other such events that become part of your life if you write for a living and would kind of like people to buy your stuff.

I suppose all this is on my mind because by the time you read this I will be in the middle of a three-week promotional tour in Britain. Now I don't want you to think I am sucking up, but touring in Britain is a dream compared with nearly every other country. To begin with, distances are shorter than in a country like America, which helps a lot, and there is a lot less very early and very late radio and TV to get through. That helps a lot, too. Above all, members of the British reading public are unusually intelligent and discerning, not to mention enormously good-looking and generous in their purchasing habits. Why, I have even known people to throw down a Sunday newspaper and say, "I think I'll go out and buy that book of old Bill's this very minute. I might even buy several copies as Christmas presents."

It's a crazy way to make a living, but it's one of those things you've got to do. I just thank God it hasn't affected my sincerity.

(*This was written for a British audience, of*

course, but I would just like to say here that American book buyers are also unusually intelligent and discerning, not to mention enormously good-looking and generous.)

The Waste Generation

One of the most arresting statistics that I have seen in a good while is that 5 percent of all the energy used in the United States is consumed by computers that have been left on all night.

I can't confirm this personally, but I can certainly tell you that on numerous occasions I have glanced out hotel room windows late at night, in a variety of cities, and been struck by the fact that lots of lights in lots of office buildings are still burning, and that computer screens are indeed flickering.

Why don't we turn these things off? For the same reason, I suppose, that so many people leave their car engines running when they pop into a friend's house, or keep lights blazing in unoccupied rooms, or have the central heating cranked up to a level that would scandalize a Finnish sauna housekeeper — because, in short, electricity, gasoline, and other energy sources are so relatively cheap, and have been for so long, that it doesn't occur to behave otherwise.

Why, after all, go through the irksome annoyance of waiting twenty seconds for your computer to warm up each morning when you can have it at your immediate beck by leaving it on all night?

We are terribly — no, we are ludicrously — wasteful of resources in this country. The average American uses twice as much energy to get through life as the average European. With just 5 percent of the world's population, we consume 20 percent of its resources. These are not statistics to be proud of.

In 1992 at the Earth Summit in Rio de Janeiro, the United States, along with other developed nations, agreed to reduce the emission of greenhouse gases to 1990 levels by 2000. This wasn't a promise to think about it. It was a promise to do it.

In the event, greenhouse emissions in the United States have continued relentlessly to rise — by 8 percent overall since the Rio summit, by 3.4 percent in 1996 alone. In short, we haven't done what we promised. We haven't tried to do it. We haven't even pretended to try to do it. Frankly, I'm not sure that we are even capable of trying to pretend to try to do it.

Consider this: In 1992, Congress decreed that before the end of the decade half of all government vehicles should be able to run on alternative fuels. To comply with this directive, the Postal Service bought ten thousand new trucks and, at a cost of $4,000 each, modified them to run on ethanol as well as gasoline. In May 1998, the first of 350 such trucks ordered for the New York City area began to be delivered. Unfortunately, none of these vehicles is ever likely to use ethanol for the simple reason that the nearest ethanol station is in Indianapolis. When asked by a reporter for the *New York Times* whether anyone anywhere at any level of government had any intention of doing anything about this, the answer was no. Meanwhile, the Postal Service, along with all other federal agencies, will continue to spend $4,000 a pop of taxpayers' money modifying trucks to run on a fuel on which almost none of them will ever run.

What the administration *has* done in terms of greenhouse emissions is introduce a set of voluntary compliance standards that industries are entirely free to ignore if they wish, and mostly of course they so wish. Now President Clinton wants another fifteen or sixteen years before rolling back emissions to 1990 levels.

Perhaps I am misreading the national mood, but it is hard to find anyone who seems much exercised about this. Increasingly there is even a kind of antagonism to the idea of conservation, particularly if there is a cost attached. A recent survey of twenty-seven thousand people around the globe by a Canadian group called Environics International found that in virtually every advanced nation people were willing to sacrifice at least a small measure of economic growth for cleaner air and a healthier environment. The one exception: the United States. It seems madness to think that a society would rate marginal economic growth above a livable earth, but there you are. I had always assumed that the reason to build a bigger economy was to make the world a better place. In fact, it appears, the reason to build a bigger economy is, well, to build a bigger economy.

Even President Clinton's cautiously inventive proposals to transfer the problem to a successor four terms down the road have met with fervent opposition. A coalition of industrialists and other interested parties called the Global Climate Information Project has raised $13 million to fight pretty much any initiative that gets in the way of their smokestacks. It has been running national radio ads grimly warning that if the president's new energy plans are implemented gasoline prices could go up by fifty cents a gallon.

Never mind that that figure is probably inflated. Never mind that even if it were true we would still be paying but a fraction for gasoline what people in other rich nations pay. Never mind that it would bring benefits that everyone could enjoy. Never mind any of that. Mention an increase in gas prices for any purpose at all and — however small the amount, however sound the reason — most people will instinctively resist.

What is saddest about all this is that a good part of these goals to cut greenhouse emissions could be met without any cost at all if we merely modified our extravagance. It has been estimated that the nation as a whole wastes about $300 billion of energy a year. We are not talking here about energy that could be saved by investing in new technologies. We are talking about energy that could be saved just by switching things off or turning things down.

Take hot water. Nearly every household

in Europe has a timer device on its hot water system. Since people clearly don't need hot water when they are at work or fast asleep, there isn't any need to keep the tank heated, so the system shuts down. Here in America I don't know how to switch off my hot water tank. I don't know that it is possible. There is piping hot water in our house twenty-four hours a day, even when we are far away on vacation. Doesn't seem to make much sense.

According to *U.S. News & World Report*, the United States must maintain the equivalent of five nuclear power plants just to power equipment and appliances that are on but not being used — lights burning in rooms that are unoccupied, computers left on when people go to lunch or home for the night, all those mute, wall-mounted TVs that flicker unwatched in the corners of bars.

In England, we had something called an off-peak energy plan. The idea was to encourage users to shift some of their electricity consumption to nighttime hours, thus spreading demand. So we bought timer devices and ran our washing machine, dryer, and dishwasher in the middle of the night and were rewarded for this small inconvenience with big savings on the electricity consumed during those hours. I would be pleased to continue the practice now, if only some utility would offer it to me.

I am not suggesting that the British are outstandingly virtuous with regard to conservation — in some areas like recycling and insulation their behavior is nothing to write home about — merely that these are simple ideas that could be easily embraced here.

It would be really nice, of course, to see a wholesale change in direction. I would dearly love, for instance, to be able to take a train to Boston. Every time I travel to Boston now, I have either to drive myself or sit in a cramped minibus with up to nine other hapless souls for two and a half hours. How nice it would be to speed across the New England landscape in the club car of a nicely appointed train, like Cary Grant and Eva Marie Saint in an Alfred Hitchcock movie. Once, not so long ago, it was possible to travel all over New England by train. According to a body called the Conservation Law Foundation, the whole of the rail system in northern New England could be restored for $500 million. That's a lot of money, of course, but consider this: As I write, Burlington,

Vermont, is spending $100 million on a single twelve-mile loop road.

I don't know how worrying global warming is. No one does. I don't know how much we are imperiling our futures by being so singularly casual in our consumption. But I can tell you this. Last year I spent a good deal of time hiking the Appalachian Trail. In Virginia, where the trail runs through Shenandoah National Park, it was still possible when I was a teenager to see Washington, D.C., seventy-five miles away, on clear days. Now, in even the most favorable conditions, visibility is less than half that. In hot, smoggy weather, it can be as little as two miles.

The forest that covers the Appalachian Mountains is one of the richest and loveliest on Earth. A single valley in the Great Smoky Mountains National Park can contain more species of native trees than the whole of western Europe. A lot of those trees are in trouble. The stress of dealing with acid rain and other airborne pollutants leaves them helplessly vulnerable to diseases and pests. Oaks, hickories, and maples are dying in unsettling numbers. The flowering dogwood — one of the most beautiful trees in the American South, and once one of the most abundant — is on the brink of extinction. The American hemlock seems poised to follow.

This may be only a modest prelude. If global temperatures rise by four degrees Centigrade over the next half century, as some scientists confidently predict, then all of the trees of Shenandoah National Park and the Smokies, and for hundreds of miles beyond, will die. In two generations one of the last great forests of the temperate world will turn into featureless grassland.

I think that's worth turning off a few computers for, don't you?

A Slight
Inconvenience

Our subject today is convenience in modern life, and how the more convenient things supposedly get the more inconvenient they actually become.

I was thinking about this the other day (I'm always thinking, you know — it's amazing) when I took my younger children to a Burger King for lunch, and there was a line of about a dozen cars at the drive-through window.

We parked, went in, ordered and ate, and came out again — all in about ten minutes. As we departed, I noticed that a white pickup truck that had been last in line when we arrived was still four or five vehicles back from collecting its food. It would have been much quicker if the driver had parked like us and gone in and gotten his food himself, but he would never have thought that way because the drive-through window is *supposed* to be speedier and more convenient.

You see my point, of course. We have become so attached to the idea of convenience that we will put up with almost any inconvenience to achieve it. It's crazy, I know, but there you are. The things that are supposed to speed up and simplify our lives more often than not actually have the opposite effect, and this set me to thinking (see, there I go again) why this should be.

Americans have always had a strange devotion to the idea of assisted ease. It is an interesting fact that nearly all the everyday inventions that take the struggle out of life — escalators, automatic doors, elevators, refrigerators, washing machines, frozen food, fast food, microwaves, fax machines — were invented here or at least first widely embraced here. Americans grew so used to a steady stream of labor-saving advances, in fact, that by the 1960s they had come to expect machines to do pretty much everything for them.

The moment I first realized that this was not necessarily a good idea was at Christmas of 1961 or '62 when my father was given an electric carving knife. It was an early model and, like most prototypes, was both bulky and rather formidable. Perhaps my memory is playing tricks on me, but I have a clear impression of him donning goggles and heavy rubber gloves before plugging it in. What is certainly true is that when he sank it into the turkey, it didn't so much carve the bird as send pieces of it flying everywhere in a kind of fleshy white spray, before the blade struck the plate with a shower of blue sparks, and the whole thing flew out of his hands, and skittered across the table and out of the room, like a creature from a *Gremlins* movie. We never saw it again, though we used to sometimes hear it thumping against table legs late at night.

Like most patriotic Americans, my father was forever buying gizmos that proved to be disastrous — clothes steamers that failed to take the wrinkles out of suits but had wallpaper falling off the walls in whole sheets, an electric pencil sharpener that could consume an entire pencil (including the metal ferrule and the tips of your fingers if you weren't real quick) in less than a second, a water pick that was so lively it required two people to hold and left the bathroom looking like the inside of a car wash, and much else.

But all of this was nothing compared with the situation today. We are now surrounded with items that do things for us to an almost absurd degree — automatic cat food dispensers, electric juicers and can openers, refrigerators that make their own ice cubes, automatic car windows, disposable toothbrushes that come with the toothpaste already loaded. People are so addicted to convenience that they have become trapped in a vicious circle: The more labor-saving appliances they acquire, the harder they need to work; the harder they work, the more labor-saving appliances they feel they need to acquire.

There is almost nothing, no matter how ridiculous, that won't find a receptive audience so long as it promises to provide some kind of relief from effort. I recently saw advertised, for $39.95, a "lighted, revolving tie rack." You push a button and it parades each of your ties before you, saving you the exhausting ordeal of making your selection by hand.

Our house in New Hampshire came replete with contraptions installed by earlier owners, all of them designed to make life that little bit easier. Up to a point, a few actually do, but most are just kind of wondrously useless. One of our rooms, for instance, came equipped with automatic curtains. You flick a switch on the wall and four pairs of curtains effortlessly open or close. That, at any rate, is the idea. In practice what happens is that one curtain opens, one closes, one opens and closes repeatedly, and one does nothing at all for five minutes and then starts to emit smoke. We haven't gone anywhere near them since the first week.

Something else we inherited was an automatic garage door. In theory, this sounds wonderful and even rather classy. You sweep into the driveway, push a button on a remote control device, and then, depending on your sense of timing, pull into the garage smoothly or take the bottom panel off the door. Then you flick the button again and the door shuts behind you, and anyone walking past thinks: "Wow! Classy guy!"

In reality, I have found, our garage door will close only when it is certain of crushing a tricycle or mangling a rake and, once closed, will not open again until I get up on a chair and do something temperamental to the control box with a screwdriver and hammer, and eventually call in the garage door repairman, a fellow named Jake who has been taking his vacations in the Maldives since we became his clients. I have given Jake more money than I earned in my first four years out of college, and still I don't have a garage door I can count on.

You see my point again. Automatic curtains and garage doors, electric cat food dispensers and revolving tie racks only *seem* to make life easier. In fact, all they do is add expense and complication to your existence.

And therein lie our two important lessons of the day. First, never forget that the first syllable of convenience is *con*. And second, send your children to garage door-repair school.

At the Drive-In

Sometime in the early 1930s, Richard Hollingshead of New Jersey bolted a motion picture projector to the roof of his car, climbed into the front seat, and began watching movies that he projected onto the door of his garage.

Goodness knows what he was thinking or where the idea came from, but the sight of flickering images on his garage door intrigued people on his street and they came over to have a look. Soon people from all over the neighborhood were dropping in to watch movies on Hollingshead's garage door.

In 1933, Hollingshead patented the idea and later that year opened America's first drive-in movie theater in the nearby town of Camden. It was not an immediate success. For years the concept languished, but in the 1950s, as Americans became increasingly mobilized, the idea suddenly took off in a big way. From virtually nothing in 1950, the number of drive-in movie theaters grew to six thousand by late in the decade.

At their peak, they were almost as numerous and popular as conventional movie theaters. Teenagers could do things in cars they could not with propriety do in a normal theater. Parents with young children were spared the expense of engaging a baby-sitter because they could put the kids in the back in their pajamas. Moms could nurse babies. Some drive-ins even offered special services like laundering. You would drop off a bag of dirty clothes as you entered and pick it up washed, dried, and folded when you left.

And then, almost as quickly as they arose, America's drive-ins began to fade away. Today they have largely vanished from the American landscape. Drive down almost any two-lane highway in the country and one thing you can almost certainly count on seeing at some point in the day is a derelict drive-in movie theater.

Not far from us, just over the Connecticut River in Vermont, is one of the last remaining drive-ins. It is open just on Friday and Saturday nights in summer, and I daresay that when the current owner retires it will go altogether. Impetuously, a few nights ago I suggested that we go for the evening.

"Why?" said my youngest daughter with great dubiousness.

"Because it will be fun," I explained.

I was astonished to realize that not only had no one in the family been to a drive-in movie, but they weren't even clear on the principle behind it.

"It's simple," I explained. "You drive into a field with a big screen, park beside a metal post with a speaker on it on a length of wire, and hang the speaker on the inside of your car door for the sound."

"And then?"

"Then you watch the movie."

"Is it air-conditioned?" asked my youngest son.

"Of course it's not air-conditioned. You're outdoors."

"Why not just go to a real movie theater where there's air-conditioning and comfy seats?"

I tried to think of a compelling answer, but the reasons that leapt to mind — because you can smoke and drink beer and smooch extravagantly — didn't seem to apply here. "Because it will be fun," I repeated again, but with less conviction.

Our two teenagers excused themselves at

once, arguing that they would sooner have a disfiguring skin disease than be seen at a public entertainment with their parents, but my wife, two younger children, and my son's friend Bradley — a precocious eight-year-old whom I would happily leave at a turnout in the Nevada desert if the opportunity ever presented itself — reluctantly agreed to give it a try.

And so we drove over the river to our venerable drive-in. Almost at once I began to remember why drive-ins went into such a precipitate decline. To begin with, it is not remotely comfortable to sit in a car to watch a movie. If you are in the driver's seat, you have a steering wheel in your lap the whole time. If you are in the back, you can't really see at all. Unless you had the foresight to clean the windshield before you set off, you will be watching the picture through a smear of squashed bugs and road dirt. The sound quality from the little speakers is always appalling and tinny and makes every character sound as if he is speaking from the inside of a gym locker. In a place like New England, the evenings invariably turn cool, so you shut the car windows to keep warm and then spend the rest of the evening wiping condensation from the inside of the windshield with the back of your arm. Often it rains. Above all, daylight saving time means that it isn't dark enough to see the movies until about 10 P.M.

So we sat for ages, one of only about half a dozen cars in a field large enough for 250, and squinted at vague, shadowy images on a distant screen.

"I can't see the picture," came a voice from the back.

"That's because it's not quite dark yet," I said.

"Then why are they showing it?"

"Because otherwise they wouldn't be able to start it until after 10 P.M., and nobody would come."

"But nobody has come."

"Who wants a treat?" I said, cannily changing the subject.

I took the children to the refreshment booth and bought enough food to feed a medium-size community for six months. By the time we returned to the car, it was almost dark enough to make out the images on the screen. However, our speaker kept cutting out. So we moved to another position. In the process, Bradley spilled his popcorn, a 24-ounce soda, and a box of malted milk balls.

So I got out and mopped him down with

an old blanket I found in the trunk. Then my son announced that he needed to go to the bathroom.

"Would you like to come too, Bradley?" I inquired sweetly.

"Nope."

"Are you quite sure?"

"Yup."

"You're not going to tell me you need to go as soon as I get back?"

"Nope."

I took my son to the toilet. When we returned, Bradley announced that he needed to go now. "Real bad," he added for emphasis.

So I took Bradley. By the time we completed our toilet rounds, the film was half over and no one knew what was going on. It also turned out that the new speaker was even worse than the previous one had been.

So I started the engine again, instructed the kids to hold tight to their drinks and popcorn, and backed out of our position. There was a horrible wrenching noise.

"You should probably put the speaker back on the post before you drive off," observed Bradley sagely.

"You're quite right, Bradley," I agreed. "Still, this cord might come in handy if I need to garotte anyone."

Bradley announced that he had spilled his drink again and needed to go to the bathroom. So I gave Bradley yet another wipe-down and took the kids for more refreshments. By the time we got back, the movie was finishing. Between us, we had watched seventeen minutes of it, about eight minutes with sound.

"Next time you want to waste twenty-two dollars on some harebrained notion, let me know and I'll send a check in the post, and then we can stay at home and watch TV," my wife suggested.

"Excellent idea," I agreed.

Drowning
in Red Tape

I'm not even going to begin to tell you about the frustration of trying to get a foreign-born spouse or other loved one registered as a legal resident in the United States because I haven't the space, and anyway it is much too boring. Also, I can't talk about it without weeping copiously. Also, you would think I was making most of it up.

You would scoff, I am quite sure, if I told you that an acquaintance of ours — an English academic of high standing — sat open-mouthed while his daughter was asked such questions as "Have you ever engaged in any unlawful commercial vice, including, but not limited to, illegal gambling?" and "Have you ever been a member of, or in any way affiliated with, the Communist Party or any other totalitarian party?" and — my particular favorite — "Do you plan to practice polygamy in the U.S.?" His daughter, I should point out, was five years old.

You see, I am weeping already.

There is something seriously wrong with a government that asks such questions of any person, not merely because the questions are intrusive and irrelevant, and not merely because inquiries into one's political affinities fly in the face of our treasured Constitution, but because they are such a preposterous and monumental waste of everyone's time. Who, after all, when asked if he intends to engage in genocide, espionage, multiple marriages, or any other of an extremely long and interestingly paranoid list of undesirable activities, is going to say: "I certainly do! Say, will this harm my chances of getting in?"

If all that was involved was answering a list of pointless questions under oath, then I would just sigh and let it be. But it is infinitely more than that. Acquiring legal status in America involves fingerprints, medical examinations, blood tests, letters of affidavit, birth and marriage certificates, employment records, proof of financial standing, and much else — and all of it must be assembled, validated, presented, and paid for in very specific ways. My wife recently had to make a 250-mile round trip to give a blood sample at a clinic recognized by the U.S. Immigration and Naturalization Service even though one of the finest university-affiliated hospitals in America is here in the town in which we live.

There are endless forms to fill out, each with pages of instructions, which often contradict other instructions and almost always lead to the need for more forms. Here, exactly as written, is a typical fragment of instructions regarding the presentation of fingerprints:

> *Submit a complete set of fingerprints on Form FD-258. . . . Complete the information on the top of the chart and write your A# (if any) in the space marked "Your no. OCA" or "Miscellaneous no. MNU."*

If you don't have form FD-258 (and you don't) or aren't sure which is your MNU number (and you aren't), you can spend days repeatedly dialing a phone number that is forever busy, only to be told by a weary, overworked-sounding voice when you finally do get through that you must call another number, which the person tells you once in a mumble and you don't quite catch, so that you have to go through the entire process again. After a while you begin to understand why flinty-eyed cow-pokes in places like Montana turn their ranches into fortresses and threaten to shoot any government officer fool enough to walk into the crosshairs.

And it's no good just filling in the forms to the best of your ability, because if anything is even a jot out of order, it is all sent back. My wife had her file returned once because the distance between her chin and hairline on a passport-sized photograph was out by one-eighth of an inch.

This has been going on for two years for us. Understand, my wife does not want to practice brain surgery, engage in espionage, assist or collude in the trafficking of drugs, participate in the overthrow of the American government (though, frankly, I would not stand in her way), or take part in any other proscribed activity. She just wants to do a little shopping and be legally resident with her family. Doesn't seem too much to ask.

Goodness knows what the holdup is. Occasionally we get a request for some additional document. Every few months I write to ask what is happening, occasionally imploring to be put in touch with a real person, some actual human who will surely see that it is a ridiculous waste of government money and everyone's time to infinitely prolong a process that ought to be routine, but I never get a response.

Three weeks ago, we received a letter from the INS office in London, which we thought must be the official approval at last. Good joke! It was a computer-generated letter saying that because her application had been inactive for twelve months it was being canceled. Inactive! Canceled! Show me to the gun cabinet, please.

All this is a very roundabout way of getting to a story concerning some British friends of ours here in Hanover. The husband is a professor at Dartmouth. Eighteen months ago, he and his family went back to England for a year's sabbatical. When they arrived at Heathrow airport, excited to be back home, the immigration officer asked them how long they were staying.

"A year," my friend answered brightly.

"And what about the American child?" the officer asked with a cocked eyebrow.

Their youngest, you see, had been born in America, and they had never bothered to register him as British. He was only four, so it wasn't as if he would be looking for work or anything.

They explained the situation. The immigration man listened gravely, then went off to consult a supervisor.

It had been eight years since my friends had left Britain, and they weren't sure just how much more like America it might have grown in that period. So they waited uneasily. After a minute the immigration man returned, followed by his supervisor, and said to them in a low voice, "My supervisor is going to ask you how long you intend to stay in Britain. Say, 'Two weeks.' "

So the supervisor asked them how long they intended to stay, and they said, "Two weeks."

"Good," said the supervisor, then added as if by way of an afterthought, "It might be an idea to register your child as British within the next day or two, in case you should decide to extend your stay."

"Of course," said my friend.

And they were in. And that was that. And would that it were one-tenth — nay, one-thousandth — as simple as that here. It is a source of continuing wonder and dismay to me that in a country as devoted to friendliness and helpfulness as America that doesn't extend to government agencies.

Now if you will excuse me, I am going to go off and stock up on ammo.

Life's Mysteries

I don't understand most things. I really don't. I am full of admiration for people who can talk knowledgeably about household wiring or torque ratios on their car engines, but that's not me, I'm afraid. I remember years ago, after buying my first car, being asked how big the engine was. "Oh, I don't know," I said, quite sincerely. "About this big, I suppose," and I spread my arms to the appropriate dimensions. It was about then I realized I was not cut out for technical discourse.

So when I say I don't understand most things, I am quite sincere. I don't understand chemistry, anatomy and physiology, mathematics beyond what is necessary to make small change, geophysics, astrophysics, particle physics, molecular biology, or newspaper weather maps, among much else. I don't know what an enzyme is, or an electron or proton or quark. Don't have the faintest idea. I don't even know my own body. I couldn't begin to tell you what my spleen does or where you would look to find it. I wouldn't know my own endocrine glands if they reached out and goosed me.

Nearly every technological marvel of our age is a source of mystery and wonder to me. Take the mobile telephone. I cannot for the life of me conceive of how these things work. Imagine for the sake of argument that you are in New York and I am in a wheat field in Nebraska and you call me up on my mobile phone. How does the signal that you have generated in New York know to come beaming down to me in a wheat field in Nebraska? And where exactly are our voices when they are traveling back and forth between the two phones? And why don't we have to shout to be heard? And if modern science can get a voice to travel through thin air and come out clearly thousands of miles away, why can't they deliver pizza in the same way? And what am I doing in a wheat field in Nebraska anyway?

You see what I mean? I just don't understand most things. Here are some other things I have never been able to figure out:

What did insects do at night before there were electric lights?

Why is it that the more hair I lose off the

top of my head the more grows in my nostrils?

When the phone rings, why does someone always say, "Is that the phone?"

How do aquarium fish get so much energy out of a few little flakes of food? And what are those flakes made out of, precisely? And how did anyone ever determine that that is what they want to eat?

Why do elevators have signs that say "Maximum load 1,200 lbs" or something similar? And why do they always put the signs inside where it's too late to do anything about it? And what are you expected to do with this information anyway? Are you supposed to turn to the other occupants and say, "I believe I'm about 210 pounds. How much do the rest of you weigh?" Do you ask the heavier people to step off until you have completed your calculations?

Is it actually possible that there are people who can eat I Can't Believe It's Not Butter and not believe it's not butter?

Why is it that the less leather there is in a woman's shoe the more it costs?

How did anyone ever invent solitaire? This has been bothering me for years. You could give me a pack of cards and all the time in the world, and still it would never occur to me to lay them out in seven unequal piles, and to turn the remaining cards over three at a time, and to array those cards in descending order by alternate color, and to make four additional piles up on top and put cards there in ascending order by suit, and all the rest of it. That would just never occur to me. Never.

Why do we thank someone from the bottom of our heart? Why not the middle of our heart? Why not, indeed, the whole heart? Why not the heart, lungs, brains, spleen, etc.?

Why couldn't Dick Vitale have found something quieter to do for a living?

Why, when we do something foolish, do we say, "That will teach you to do such and such," when what we mean is, "That will teach you not to do such and such"?

Why is it that phone calls in the middle of the night are always wrong numbers?

Why are planes, trains, and buses on time when you are late and late when you are on time?

How is it that no matter how carefully you examine potted plants before purchasing you always choose the one that has a terminal illness?

How can my computer know when the

clocks change between normal time and daylight saving time every spring and fall, and yet can't figure out that when I want to italicize one little word I mean just that one little word and not everything that follows? Also, why is it that every time I switch it on, it is as if it has never been switched on before? Why can't it come on instantly like a radio or stereo system and just do its business? Why does it have to check its innards and announce everyone who has ever had a copyright interest in it? Why, above all, when I try to switch it off, does it put up a little window that says: "Are you sure you want to switch off?"

Why do we foot a bill rather than, say, head it? Why do we say that we are head over heels about something when our head normally is over our heels? Why can you slow up but not speed down? Why do we say that something that is in rapid motion is moving fast, but something that is not moving at all is stuck fast? Why do we say our nose is running? (Mine slides.)

How is it that we live in a world in which we can measure the farthest stars, travel at twice the speed of sound, and probe the ocean's depths, and yet they still can't make a pencil sharpener that isn't completely useless?

Finally, and above all, why would anyone in a free society choose to become a dentist?

So Sue Me

I have a friend in Britain, an academic, who was recently approached by the lawyers for an American company to be an expert witness in a case they were handling. They told him they wanted to fly the lead attorney and two assistants to London to meet him.

"Wouldn't it be simpler and cheaper if I flew to New York instead?" my friend suggested.

"Yes," he was told without hesitation, "but this way we can bill the client for the cost of three trips."

And there you have the American legal mind at work.

Now I have no doubt that a large number of American lawyers — well, two anyway — do wonderfully worthwhile things that fully justify charging their clients $150 an hour, which I gather is the going rate now. But the trouble is that there are just too many of them. In fact — and here is a truly sobering statistic — the United States has more lawyers than all the rest of the world put together: almost 800,000 of them, up from an already abundant 260,000 in 1960. We now boast 300 lawyers for every 100,000 citizens. Britain, by contrast, has 82; Japan a mere 11.

And of course all those lawyers need work. Most states now allow lawyers to advertise, and many of them most enthusiastically do. You cannot watch TV for half an hour without encountering at least one commercial showing a sincere-looking lawyer saying: "Hi, I'm Vinny Slick of Bent and Oily Law Associates. If you've suffered an injury at work, or been in a vehicular accident, or just feel like having some extra money, come to me and we'll find someone to sue."

Americans, as is well known, will sue at the drop of a hat. In fact, I daresay someone somewhere has sued over a dropped hat, and won $20 million for the pain and suffering it caused. There really is a sense that if something goes wrong for whatever reason and you are anywhere in the vicinity, then you ought to collect a pile of cash.

This was neatly illustrated a couple of years ago when a chemical plant in Richmond, California, suffered an explosion that spewed fumes over the town. Within hours, some two hundred lawyers and their representatives had descended on the excited community, handing out business cards and advising people to present themselves at the local hospital. Twenty thousand residents eagerly did so.

News footage of the event makes it look like some kind of open-air party. Of the twenty thousand happy, smiling, seemingly very healthy people who lined up for examination at the hospital's emergency room, just twenty were actually admitted. Although the number of proven injuries was slight, to say the least, seventy thousand townspeople — virtually all of them — submitted claims. The company agreed to a $180 million settlement. Of this, the lawyers got $40 million.

Every year over ninety million lawsuits are filed in this extravagantly litigious country — that's one for every two and a half people — and many of these are what might charitably be called ambitious. As I write, two parents in Texas are suing a high school baseball coach for benching their son during a game, claiming humiliation and extreme mental anguish. In Washington State, meanwhile, a man with heart problems is suing local dairies "because their milk cartons did not warn him about cholesterol." I am sure you read recently about the woman in California who sued the Walt Disney Company after she and her family were mugged in a parking lot at Disneyland. A central part of the suit was that her grandchildren suffered shock and trauma when they were taken behind the scenes to be comforted and they saw Disney characters taking off their costumes. The discovery that Mickey Mouse and Goofy were in fact real people inside costumes was apparently too much for the poor tykes.

That case was dismissed, but elsewhere people have won fortunes out of all proportion to any pain or loss they might actually have suffered. Recently there was a much-publicized case in which an executive at a Milwaukee brewery recounted the racy plot of an episode of *Seinfeld* to a female colleague, who took offense and reported him for sexual harassment. The brewery responded by firing the man, and he responded by suing the brewery. Now I don't know who deserved what in this case — it sounds to me like they all wanted a good, sound spanking — but the upshot is that the dismissed executive was awarded $26.6 million, roughly four hundred thousand times his annual salary, by a sympathetic (i.e., demented) jury.

This sort of thing goes to the highest level. As I write, the estate of Richard M. Nixon is suing the government for $210 million — let me just repeat that sum: $210 million — to compensate the Nixon family for lost earnings from papers and other documents that the government seized as evidence in the Watergate case. You understand what I am saying, of course. A president of the United States, after acting with the crassest illegality, is driven from office in disgrace, and twenty-four years later his family is asking for $210 million of the nation's money. The day cannot be far off when Bill Clinton will be suing for the mental trauma suffered from having oral sex while trying simultaneously to run a nation. That must be worth at least a couple of billion, surely.

Allied with the idea that lawsuits are a quick way to a fortune, whether deserved or not, is the interesting and uniquely American notion that no matter what happens, someone else must be responsible. So if, say, you smoke eighty cigarettes a day for fifty years and eventually get cancer, then it must be everyone else's fault but your own, and you sue not only the manufacturer of your cigarettes, but the wholesaler, the retailers, the delivery company that delivered the cigarettes to the retailer, and so on. One of the most extraordinary features of the American legal system is that it allows plaintiffs to sue people and enterprises only tangentially connected to the alleged complaint.

Because of the way the system works (or, more accurately, doesn't work) it is often less expensive for a company or institution to settle out of court than to let the matter proceed to trial. I know a woman who slipped and fell while entering a department store on a rainy day and, to her astonishment and gratification, was offered a more or less instant settlement of $2,500 if she would sign a piece of paper agreeing not to sue. She signed.

The cost of all this to society is enormous — several billion dollars a year at least. New York City alone spends $200 million a year settling "slip and fall" claims — people tripping over curbs and the like. According to a recent ABC television documentary on America's runaway legal system, because of inflated product liability costs consumers in the United States pay $500 more than they need to for every car they buy, $100 more for football helmets, and $3,000 more for heart pacemakers. According to the documentary, they even pay a little on top (as it were) for haircuts because one or two distressed customers successfully sued their barbers after being given the sort of embarrassing trims that I receive as a matter of routine.

All of which, naturally, has given me an idea. I am going to go and smoke eighty cigarettes, then slip and fall while drinking high-cholesterol milk and relating the plot of a *Seinfeld* show to a passing female in the Disneyland parking lot, and then I'll call Vinny Slick and see if we can strike a deal. I don't expect to settle for less than $2.5 billion — and that's before we've even started talking about my latest haircut.

The Great Indoors

I was out for a walk the other day and I was struck by an odd thing. It was a glorious day — as good as a day can get, and very probably the last of its type that we shall see for many a long wintry month around here — yet almost every car that passed had its windows up.

All these drivers had adjusted their temperature controls to create a climate inside their sealed vehicles that was identical to the climate already existing in the larger world outside, and it occurred to me that where fresh air is concerned we have rather lost our minds, or sense of proportion, or something.

Remarkable as it may seem, we have grown so reflexively habituated to the idea of passing the bulk of our lives in a series of controlled environments that the possibility of an alternative no longer occurs to most of us. So we shop in enclosed malls, and drive to those malls with the car windows up and the air-conditioning on, even when the weather is flawless, as it was on this day. We work in office buildings where we cannot open the windows even if we wanted to — not, of course, that anyone would want to. When we go on vacation, it is often in an outsized motor-home that allows us to view the great outdoors without actually exposing ourselves to it. Increasingly, when we go to a sporting event it is in an indoor stadium. And almost all those Dick and Jane things we did as kids — ride bikes up and down the street, run to the park, play hide 'n' seek or some game of ball — have pretty much vanished. Walk through almost any American neighborhood now in summer and you won't see children doing any of this stuff because they are all inside. All you will hear is the uniform hum of air-conditioning units.

Cities across the nation have taken to building what are called skywalks — enclosed pedestrian flyovers, climate controlled of course — connecting all the buildings in their downtowns. In Des Moines, Iowa, where I grew up, the first skywalk was erected between a hotel and parking ramp about twenty-five years ago and was such a hit that soon other downtown businesses were getting in on the act.

Now it is possible to walk halfway to Omaha without ever experiencing fresh air. All the stores that used to be at street level have moved up to the second floor, where the pedestrian traffic now is. Now the only people you ever see at street level in Des Moines are winos and office workers standing around having a smoke. The outdoors, you see, has become a kind of purgatory, a place to which you are banished.

There are even clubs composed of office workers who change into sweatsuits and spend their lunch hours taking brisk, healthful hikes along a measured course through the skywalks. Similar clubs, typically composed of retired people, can be found at nearly every shopping mall in the nation. These are people, you understand, who meet at malls not to shop but to get their daily exercise.

The last time I was in Des Moines, I ran into an old friend of the family. He was dressed in a sweatsuit and flushed with that glow that denotes recent healthful activity. He told me that he had just come from a session with the Valley West Mall Hiking Club. It was a splendid April day, and I asked him why the club didn't use any of the city's several large and handsome parks.

"No rain, no cold, no hills, no muggers," he replied without hesitation.

"But there are no muggers in Des Moines," I pointed out.

"That's right," he agreed at once, "and do you know why? Because there's nobody outside to mug." He nodded his head emphatically, as if I hadn't thought of that, as indeed I had not.

The apotheosis of this strange movement may be the Opryland Hotel in Nashville, Tennessee, where I went not long ago on an assignment for a magazine. The Opryland Hotel is a most extraordinary institution. To begin with, it is immense — essentially, it is a self-contained city — and almost gorgeously ugly, a sort of Graceland meets *Gone with the Wind* meets Mall of America.

But what really sets the Opryland apart is that it is a Total Indoor Environment. At its heart are three stupendously commodious glass-roofed atriums, five or six stories high and extending to nine acres overall, which offer all the benefits of the out-of-doors without any of the inconveniences. These "interiorscapes," as the hotel fondly calls them, are replete with tropical foliage, full-sized trees, waterfalls, streams, "open-air" restaurants and cafés, and multilevel walkways. The effect is strikingly reminiscent of those illustrations you used to get in *Popular Science* magazine in the 1950s showing what life would be like in a space colony on Venus (or at least what it would be like if all the space colonists were overweight middle-aged people in Nike sneakers and baseball caps who spent their lives walking around eating handheld food). It is, in short, a flawless, aseptic, self-contained world, with a perfect unvarying climate and an absence of messy birds, annoying insects, irksome and unpredictable weather, or indeed any kind of reality.

On my first evening, anxious to escape the hordes of shuffling grazers and curious to see what the weather was like back on Planet Earth, I stepped outside with a view to having a stroll through the grounds. And guess what? There were no grounds — just acres and acres of parking lot, stretching away to an unseen horizon like a great inland sea. A couple of hundred yards away was the perimeter fence of the Opryland Amusement Park, but there was no foot access to the park from the hotel. The only way of getting there, I discovered by inquiring, was to purchase a $3 ticket and board an air-conditioned bus for a forty-five-second ride to the front gate.

Unless you wanted to walk around among thousands and thousands of parked cars, there was no place to take the air or stretch your legs. At Opryland, the out-doors is indoors, and that, I realized with a shiver, is precisely the way many millions of people would have the whole world if it were possible.

As I stood there, a bird dropped onto the toe of my left shoe the sort of thing you don't normally appreciate a bird's drop-ping (to coin a phrase). I looked from the sky to my shoe and back to the sky again.

"Thank you," I said, and I believe I nearly meant it.

Death Watch

The last time it occurred to me, in a serious way, that Death is out there — you know, really out there, just hovering — and that my name is in his book, was on a short flight from Boston to Lebanon, New Hampshire, when we got in a little trouble.

The flight is only fifty minutes, over the old industrial towns of northern Massachusetts and southern New Hampshire, and on toward the Connecticut River, where the plump hills of the Green and White Mountains lazily merge. It was a late October afternoon, just after the clocks had changed for winter, and I had rather hoped I might enjoy the last russety blush of autumn color on the hills before the daylight went, but within five minutes of takeoff our little sixteen-seater plane was enveloped in bouncy clouds, and it was obvious that there would be no spectacular panoramas this day.

So I read a book and tried not to notice the turbulence or to let my thoughts preoccupy themselves with unhappy fantasies involving splintering wings and a long, shrill, vertical plunge to earth.

I hate little planes. I don't like most planes much, but little planes I dread because they are cold and bouncy and make odd noises, and they carry too few passengers to attract more than passing attention when they crash, as they seem to do quite regularly. Almost every day in any newspaper you will see an article like this:

Dribbleville, Indiana — All nine passengers and crew died today when a 16-seat commuter plane operated by Bounce Airlines crashed in a ball of flames shortly after takeoff from Dribbleville Regional Airport. Witnesses said the plane did four figure eights in the sky, then fell for, oh gosh, a really long time before slamming into the ground at 1,892 miles an hour. It was the eleventh little-noted crash by a commuter airline since Sunday.

These things really do go down all the time. In 1997, a commuter plane crashed on a flight from Cincinnati to Detroit. One of the passengers who died was on her way to a memorial service for her brother, who had been killed in a crash in West Virginia two weeks before.

So I tried to read my book, but I kept glancing out the window into the impenetrable murk. Something over an hour into the flight — later than usual — we descended through the bumpy clouds and popped out into clear air. We were only a few hundred feet over a dusky landscape. There were one or two farmhouses visible in the last traces of daylight, but no towns. Mountains, severe and muscular, loomed up around us on all sides.

We rose back up into the clouds, flew around for a few minutes, and dropped down again. There was still no sign of Lebanon or any other community, which was perplexing because the Connecticut River Valley is full of little towns. Here there was nothing but darkening forest stretching to every horizon.

We rose again, and repeated the exercise twice more. After a few minutes, the pilot came on and in that calm, unflappable voice of airline pilots said: "I don't know if you folks have noticed, but we're, ah, having a little trouble eyeballing the airport on account of the, ah, inclement weather. There's no radar at Lebanon, so we have to do all of this visually, which makes it a little, ah, tricky. The whole of the eastern seaboard is socked in with fog, so there's no point in trying another airport. Anyway, we're gonna keep trying because if there is one thing for certain it's that sooner or later this baby is going to have to come down *somewhere!*"

Actually, I just made that last line up, but that was the gist of it. We were blundering around in clouds and dying light looking for an airport tucked among mountains. We had been in the air for almost ninety minutes by now. I didn't know how long these things could fly, but at some point clearly we would run out of fuel. Meanwhile, at any moment we could, in the course of our blundering drops through the clouds, slam into the side of a mountain.

This didn't seem fair. I was on my way home from a long trip. Scrubbed little children, smelling of soap and fresh towels, would be waiting. There was steak for dinner, possibly with onion rings. Extra wine had been laid in. I had gifts to disburse. This was not a convenient time to be flying into mountains. So I shut my eyes and said in a very sincere inner voice: "Please oh please oh please oh please get this thing down safely, and I will be exceptionally good forever, and I really

338

mean it. Thank you."

And miraculously it worked. On about the sixth occasion that we popped from the clouds, there below us were the flat roofs, illuminated signs, and gorgeously tubby customers of the Kmart Shopping Plaza, and just across the road from it was the perimeter fence of the airport. We were aimed slightly the wrong way, but the pilot banked sharply and brought the plane in on a glidepath that would, in any other circumstance, have had me shrieking.

We landed with a lovely smooth squeal. I have never been so happy. My wife was waiting for me in the car outside the airport entrance, and on the way home I told her all about my gripping adventure in the sky. The trouble with believing that you are about to die in a crash, as opposed to actually dying in a crash, is that it doesn't make nearly as good a story.

"You poor sweetie," my wife said soothingly, but just a little distractedly, and patted my leg. "Well, you'll be home in a minute and there's a lovely cauliflower supreme in the oven for you."

I looked at her. "Cauliflower supreme? What the —" I cleared my throat and put on a new voice. "And what is cauliflower supreme exactly, dear? I understood we

339

were having steak."

"We were, but this is much healthier for you. Maggie Higgins gave me the recipe."

I sighed. Maggie Higgins was a health-conscious busybody whose assertive views on diet were forever being translated into dishes like cauliflower supreme for me. She was fast becoming the bane of my life, or at least of my stomach.

Life's a funny thing, isn't it? One minute you're praying to be allowed to live, vowing to face any hardship without complaint, and the next you are mentally banging your head on the dashboard and thinking: "I wanted steak, I wanted steak, I wanted steak."

"Did I tell you, by the way," my wife went on, "that Maggie fell asleep with hair coloring on the other day and her hair turned bright green?"

"Really?" I said, perking up a little. This was good news indeed. "Bright green, you say?"

"Well, everyone told her it was lemony, but really, you know, it looked like Astro-turf."

"Amazing," I said — and it was. I mean to say, two prayers answered in one day.

In Praise of Diners

A couple of years ago, when I was sent ahead of the rest of the family to scout out a place for us to live, I included the town of Adams, Massachusetts, as a possibility because it had a wonderful old-fashioned diner on Main Street.

Unfortunately, I was compelled to remove Adams from the short list when I was unable to recall a single other virtue in the town, possibly because it didn't have any. Still, I believe I would have been happy there. Diners tend to take you like that.

Diners were once immensely popular, but like so much else they have become increasingly rare. Their heyday was the years between the wars, when Prohibition shut the taverns and people needed some place else to go for lunch. From a business point of view, diners were an appealing proposition. They were cheap to buy and maintain and, because they were factory built, they came virtually complete. Having acquired one, all you had to do was set it on a level piece of ground, hook up water and electricity, and you were in business. If trade didn't materialize, you simply loaded it onto a flatbed truck and tried your luck elsewhere. By the late 1920s, about a score of companies were mass-producing diners, nearly all in a stream-lined art deco style known as moderne, with gleaming stainless-steel exteriors, and insides of polished dark wood and more shiny metal.

Diner enthusiasts are a somewhat obsessive breed. They can tell you whether a particular diner is a 1947 Kullman Blue Comet or a 1932 Worcester Semi-Streamliner. They appreciate the design details that mark out a Ralph Musi from a Starlite or an O'Mahoney, and will drive long distances to visit a rare and well-preserved Sterling, of which only seventy-three were made between 1935 and 1941.

The one thing they don't talk about much is food. This is because diner food is generally much the same wherever you go — which is to say, not very good. My wife and children refuse to accompany me to diners for this very reason. What they fail to appreciate is that going to diners is not about eating; it's about saving a crucial part of America's heritage.

We didn't have diners in Iowa when I was growing up. They were mostly an East Coast phenomenon, just as restaurants built in the shape of things (pigs, doughnuts, derby hats) were a West Coast phenomenon. The closest thing we had to a diner was a place down by the Raccoon River called Ernie's Grill. Everything about it was squalid and greasy, including Ernie, and the food was appalling, but it did have many of the features of a diner, notably a long counter with twirly stools, a wall of booths, patrons who looked as if they had just come in from killing big animals in the woods, possibly with their teeth, and a fondness for diner-style lingo. When you ordered, the waitress would call out to the kitchen in some indecipherable code, "Two spots on a dot — easy on the Brylcreem. Dribble on the griddle and cough twice in a bucket," or something similarly alarming and mystifying.

But Ernie's was in a square, squat, anonymous brick building, which patently lacked the streamlined glamour of a classic diner. So when, decades later, I was sent to look for a livable community in New England, a diner was one of the things high on my shopping list. Alas, they are getting harder and harder to find.

Hanover, where we eventually settled, does have a venerable eating establishment called Lou's, which celebrated its fiftieth anniversary last year. It has the decor and superficial ambience of a diner — booths and a long counter and an air of busyness — but it is really a restaurant. The menu features items like quiches and quesadillas, and it prides itself on the freshness of its lettuce. The customers are generally well-heeled and yuppie-ish. You can't imagine any of them climbing into a car with a deer lashed to the hood.

So you may conceive of my joy when, about six months after we moved to Hanover, I was driving one day through the nearby community of White River Junction and passed an establishment called the Four Aces. Impulsively, I went in and found an early postwar Worcester in nearly mint condition. It was wonderful. Even the food was pretty good, which was disappointing, but I have learned to live with it.

No one knows how many diners like this remain. Partly it is a problem of definition. A diner is essentially any place that serves food and calls itself a diner. Under the broadest definition, there are about twenty-five hundred diners in the United States. But no more than a thousand of these, at the outside, are what could be called "classic" diners, and the number of those diminishes yearly. Recently Phil's, the oldest diner in California, closed. It had been in business in north Los Angeles since 1926, making it, by California standards, about as venerable as Stonehenge, but its passing was hardly noted.

Most diners can't compete with the big fast-food chains. A traditional diner is small, with perhaps eight booths and a dozen or so counter spaces, and because they provide waitress service and individually cooked meals their operating costs are higher. Most diners are also old, and we live in an age in which it is almost always much cheaper to replace than to preserve. An enthusiast who bought an old diner in Jersey City, New Jersey, discovered to his horror that it would cost $900,000 — perhaps twenty years' worth of potential profits — to bring it back to its original condition. Much cheaper to tear it down and turn the site over to a Taco Bell or a McDonald's.

What you get a lot of instead these days are ersatz diners. The last time I was in

Chicago I was taken to a place called Ed Debevic's, where the waitresses wore badges giving their names as Bubbles and Blondie and where the walls were lined with Ed's bowling trophies. But, there never was an Ed Debevic. He was just the creative figment of a marketing man. No matter. Ed's was humming. A dining public that had disdained genuine diners when they stood on every corner was now standing in line to get into a make-believe one. If there is one thing that mystifies me about modern life it is this impulse to celebrate things we couldn't wait to get rid of.

You find it at Disneyland, where people flock to stroll up and down a Main Street just like the ones they abandoned wholesale in the 1950s. It happens at restored colonial villages like Williamsburg, Virginia, and Mystic, Connecticut, where visitors drive long distances and pay good money to savor the sort of compact and tranquil atmosphere that they long ago fled for the accommodating sprawl of suburbs. I can't begin to account for it, but it appears that in this country these days we really only want something when it isn't really real.

But that is another subject. Meanwhile, I

am off to the Four Aces while the chance is still there. There aren't any waitresses called Bubbles, but the bowling trophies are real.

Shopping Madness

I went into a Toys "Я" Us the other day with my youngest so that he could spend some loot he had come into. (He had gone short on Anaconda Copper against his broker's advice, the little scamp.) And entirely by the way, isn't Toys "Я" Us the most mystifying name of a commercial concern you have ever heard of? What does it *mean?* I have never understood it. Are they saying they believe themselves to be toys? Do their executives carry business cards saying "Dick "Я" Me"? And why is the R backward in the title? Surely not in the hope or expectation that it will enhance our admiration? Why, above all, is it that even though there are thirty-seven checkout lanes at every Toys "Я" Us in the world, only one of them is ever open?

These are important questions, but sadly this is not our theme today, at least not specifically. No, our theme today is shopping. To say that shopping is an important part of American life is like saying that fish appreciate water.

Apart from working, sleeping, watching TV, and accumulating fatty tissue, we devote more time in this country to shopping than to any other pastime. Indeed, according to the Travel Industry Association of America, shopping is now the number one holiday activity of Americans. People actually plan their vacations around shopping trips. Hundreds of thousands of people a year travel to Niagara Falls, it transpires, not to see the falls but to wander through its two megamalls. Soon, if developers in Arizona get their way, vacationers will be able to travel to the Grand Canyon and not see it either, for there are plans, if you can believe it, to build a 450,000-square-foot shopping complex by its main entrance.

Shopping these days is not so much a business as a science. There is even now an academic discipline called retail anthropology whose proponents can tell you exactly where, how, and why people shop the way they do. They know which proportion of customers will turn right upon entering a store (87 percent) and how long on average those people will browse before wandering out again (two minutes and thirty-six seconds). They know the best ways to lure shoppers into the magic, high-margin depths of the shop (an area known in the trade as "Zone 4") and the layouts, color schemes, and background music that will most effectively hypnotize the unassuming browser into becoming a helpless purchaser. They know everything.

So here is my question. Why then is it that I cannot go shopping these days without wanting either to burst into tears or kill someone? For all its science, you see, shopping in this country is no longer a fun experience, if it ever was.

A big part of the problem is the stores. They come in three types, all disagreeable.

First, there are the stores where you can never find anyone to help you. Then there are the stores where you don't want any help, but you are pestered to the brink of madness by a persistent sales assistant, probably working on commission. Finally, there are the stores where, when you ask where anything is, the answer is always, "Aisle seven." I don't know why, but that is what they always tell you.

"Where's women's lingerie?" you ask.
"Aisle seven."
"Where's pet food?"
"Aisle seven."
"Where's aisle six?"

"Aisle seven."

My least favorite of all store types is the one where you can't get rid of the salesperson. Usually these are department stores at big malls. The salesperson is always a white-haired lady working in the men's wear department.

"Can I help you find anything?" she says.

"No thank you, I'm just browsing," you tell her.

"OK," she replies, and gives you a smarmy smile that says: "I don't really like you; I'm just required to smile at everyone."

So you wander round the department and at some point you idly finger a sweater. You don't know why because you don't like it, but you touch it anyway.

In an instant, the sales assistant is with you. "That's one of our most popular lines," she says. "Would you like to try it on?"

"No thank you."

"Go ahead, try it on. It's you."

"No, I really don't think so."

"The changing rooms are just there."

"I really don't want to try it on."

"What's your size?"

"Please understand, I don't want to try it

351

on. I'm just browsing."

She gives you another smile — her withdrawing smile — but thirty seconds later she is back, bearing another sweater. "We have it in peach," she announces.

"I don't want that sweater. In any color."

"How about a nice necktie then?"

"I don't want a tie. I don't want a sweater. I don't want anything. My wife is having her legs waxed and told me to wait for her here. I wish she hadn't, but she did. She could be hours and I still won't want anything, so please don't ask me any more questions. Please."

"Then how are you set for pants?"

Do you see what I mean? It becomes a choice between tears and manslaughter. The irony is that when you actually require assistance there is never anyone around.

At Toys "Я" Us my son wanted a Star Troopers Intergalactic Cosmic Death Blaster, or some such piece of plastic mayhem. We couldn't find one anywhere, nor could we find anyone to guide us. The store appeared to be in the sole charge of a sixteen-year-old boy at the single active cash register. He had a queue of about two dozen people, which he was processing very slowly and methodically.

Standing in line is not one of my advanced social skills, particularly when I am standing there simply to acquire information. The line moved with painful slowness. At one point, the young man took ten minutes to change the receipt roll, and I nearly killed him then.

At last my turn came. "Where's the Star Troopers Intergalactic Cosmic Death Blasters?" I said.

"Aisle seven," he replied without looking up.

I stared at the top of his head. "Don't trifle with me," I said.

He looked up. "Excuse me?"

"You people always say 'Aisle seven.' "

There must have been something in my look because his answer came out as a kind of whimper. "But, mister, it is aisle seven — Toys of Violence and Aggression."

"It'd better be," I said darkly and departed.

Ninety minutes later we found the Death Blasters in aisle two, but by the time I got back to the register the young man had gone off duty.

The Death Blaster is wonderful, by the way. It fires those rubber-cupped darts that stick to the victim's forehead — not painful, but certainly startling. My son was disappointed, of course, that I wouldn't let him have it, but you see, I need it for when I go shopping.

The Fat of the Land

I have been thinking a lot about food lately. This is because I am not getting any. My wife, you see, recently put me on a diet. It is an interesting diet of her own devising that essentially allows me to eat anything I want so long as it contains no fat, cholesterol, sodium, or calories and isn't tasty. In order to keep me from starving altogether, she went to the grocery store and bought everything that had "bran" in its title. I am not sure, but I believe I had bran cutlets for dinner last night. I am very depressed.

Obesity is a serious problem in America (well, serious for fat people anyway). Half of all adult Americans are overweight and more than a third are defined as obese (i.e., big enough to make you think twice before getting in an elevator with them).

Now that hardly anyone smokes, it has taken over as the number one health fret in the country. About three hundred thousand Americans die every year from diseases related to obesity, and the nation spends $100 billion treating illnesses arising from overeating — diabetes, heart disease, high blood pressure, cancer, and so on. (I hadn't realized it, but being overweight can increase your chance of getting colon cancer — and this is a disease you really, really don't want to get — by as much as 50 percent. Ever since I read that, I keep imagining a proctologist examining me and saying: "*Wow!* Just how many cheeseburgers have you *had* in your life, Mr. Bryson?") Being overweight also substantially reduces your chances of surviving surgery, not to mention getting a decent date.

Above all, it means that people who are theoretically dear to you will call you "Mr. Blimpy" and ask you what you think you are doing every time you open a cupboard door and, entirely by accident, remove a large bag of Cheez Doodles.

The wonder to me is how anyone can be thin in this country. We went to an Applebee's Restaurant the other night where they were promoting something called "Skillet Sensations." Here, verbatim, is the menu's description of the Chili Cheese Tater Skillet:

We start this incredible combination with

crispy, crunchy waffle fries. On top of those we generously ladle spicy chili, melted Monterey jack and cheddar cheeses, and pile high with tomatoes, green onions, and sour cream.

You see what I am up against? And this was one of the more modest offerings. The most depressing thing is that my wife and children can eat this stuff and not put on an ounce. When the waitress came, my wife said: "The children and I will have the De Luxe Supreme Goo Skillet Feast, with extra cheese and sour cream, and a side order of nachos with hot fudge sauce and biscuit gravy."

"And for Mr. Blimpy here?"

"Just bring him some dried bran and a glass of water."

When, the following morning over a breakfast of oat flakes and chaff, I expressed to my wife the opinion that this was, with all respect, the most stupid diet I had ever come across, she told me to find a better one, so I went to the library. There were at least 150 books on diet and nutrition — *Dr. Berger's Immune Power Diet, Straight Talk About Weight Control, The Rotation Diet* — but they were all a little earnest and bran-obsessed for my tastes.

Then I saw one that was precisely of the type I was looking for. By Dale M. Atrens, Ph.D., it was called *Don't Diet.* Now here was a title I could work with.

Relaxing my customary aversion to consulting a book by anyone so immensely preposterous as to put "Ph.D." after his name (I don't put Ph.D. after my name on my books, after all — and not just because I don't have one), I took the book to that reading area that libraries put aside for people who are strange and have nowhere to go in the afternoons but nonetheless are not quite ready to be institutionalized, and devoted myself to an hour's reflective study.

The premise of the book, if I understood it correctly (and forgive me if I am a little sketchy on some details, but I was distracted by the man opposite me, who was having a quiet chat with a person from the next dimension), is that the human body has been programmed by eons of evolution to pack on adipose tissue for insulating warmth in periods of cold, padding for comfort, and energy reserves in times of crop failures.

The human body — mine in particular evidently — is extremely good at doing this. Tree shrews can't do it at all. They must spend every waking moment eating. "This may be why tree shrews have produced so little great art or music," Atrens quips. Ha! Ha! Ha! Then again, it may be because the tree shrew eats leaves, whereas I eat Ben and Jerry's double chocolate fudge ice cream.

The other interesting thing Atrens points out is that fat is exceedingly stubborn. Even when you starve yourself half to death, the body shows the greatest reluctance to relinquish its fat reserves.

Consider that each pound of fat represents 5,000 calories — about what the average person eats in total in two days. That means that if you starved yourself for a week — ate nothing at all — you would lose no more than three and a half pounds of fat, and, let's face it, still wouldn't look a picture in your swimsuit.

Having tortured yourself in this way for seven days, naturally you would then slip into the pantry when no one was looking and eat everything in there but a bag of chickpeas, thereby gaining back all the loss, plus — and here's the crux — a little something extra, because now your body knows that you have been trying to starve it and are not to be trusted, so it had better lay in a little extra wobble in case you get any more foolish notions.

This is why dieting is so frustrating and hard. The more you try to get rid of your fat, the more ferociously your body holds on to it.

So I have come up with an ingenious alternative diet. I call it the Fool-Your-Body-Twenty-Hours-a-Day Diet. The idea is that for twenty hours in each twenty-four you ruthlessly starve yourself, but at four selected intervals during the day — for convenience we'll call them breakfast, lunch, dinner, and midnight snack — you feed your body something like an 18-ounce sirloin steak with a baked potato and extra sour cream, or a large bowl of double chocolate fudge ice cream, so that it doesn't *realize* that you are actually starving it. Brilliant, eh?

I don't know why this didn't occur to me years ago. I think it may be that all this bran has cleared my head. Or something.

Your New Computer

Congratulations. You have purchased an Anthrax/2000 Multimedia 615X Personal Computer with Digital Doo-Dah Enhancer. It will give years of faithful service, if you ever get it up and running. Also included with your PC is a bonus pack of preinstalled software — Lawn Mowing Planner, Mr. Arty-Farty, Blank Screen Saver, and Antarctica Route Finder — which will provide hours of pointless diversion while using up most of your computer's spare memory.

So turn the page and let's get started!

Getting Ready

Congratulations. You have successfully turned the page and are ready to proceed.

Important meaningless note: The Anthrax/2000 is configured to use 80386, 214J10, or higher processors running at 2472 Herz on variable speed spin cycle. Check your electrical installations and insurance policies before proceeding. Do not machine wash.

To prevent internal heat build-up, select a cool, dry environment for your computer. The bottom shelf of a refrigerator is ideal.

Unpack the box and examine its contents. (Warning: Do not open box if contents are missing or faulty, as this will invalidate your warranty. Return all missing contents in their original packaging with a note explaining where they have gone and a replacement will be sent within twelve working months.)

The contents of the box should include some of the following: monitor with mysterious De Gauss button; keyboard; computer unit; miscellaneous wires and cables not necessarily designed for this model; 2,000-page Owner's Manual; Short Guide to the Owner's Manual; Quick Guide to the Short Guide to the Owner's Manual; Laminated Super-Kwik Set-Up Guide for People Who Are Exceptionally Impatient or Stupid; 1,167 pages of warranties, vouchers, notices in Spanish, and other loose pieces of paper; 292 cubic feet of Styrofoam packing material.

Something They Didn't Tell You at the Store

Because of the additional power needs of the preinstalled bonus software, you will need to acquire an Anthrax/2000 auxiliary software upgrade pack, a 900-volt memory capacitator for the auxiliary software pack, a 50-megaherz oscillator unit for the memory capacitator, 2,500 mega-gigabytes of additional memory for the oscillator, and an electrical substation.

Setting Up

Congratulations. You are ready to set up. If you have not yet acquired a degree in electrical engineering, now is the time to do so.

Connect the monitor cable (A) to the portside outlet unit (D); attach power offload unit suborbiter (Xii) to the coaxial AC/DC servo channel (G); plug three-pin mouse cable into keyboard housing unit (make extra hole if necessary); connect modem (B2) to offside parallel audio/video lineout jack. Alternatively, plug the cables into the most likely looking holes, switch on, and see what happens.

Additional important meaningless note: The wires in the ampule modulator unit are marked as follows according to international convention: blue = neutral or live; yellow = live or blue; blue and live = neutral and green; black = instant death. (Except where prohibited by law.)

Switch the computer on. Your hard drive will automatically download. (Allow three to five days.) When downloading is complete, your screen will say: "Yeah, what?"

Now it is time to install your software. Insert Disc A (marked "Disc D" or "Disc G") into Drive Slot B or J, and type: "Hello! Anybody home?" At the DOS command prompt, enter your License Verification Number. Your License Verification Number can be found by entering your Certified User Number, which can be found by entering your License Verification Number. If you are unable to find your License Verification or Certified User numbers, call the Software Support Line for assistance. (Please have your License Verification and Certified User numbers handy as the support staff cannot otherwise assist you.)

If you have not yet committed suicide, then insert Installation Diskette 1 in drive slot 2 (or vice versa) and follow the instructions on your screen. (Note: Owing to a software modification, some instructions will appear in Turkish.) At each prompt, reconfigure the specified file path, double-click on the button launch icon, select a single equation default file from the macro selection register, insert the VGA graphics card in the rear aerofoil, and type "C:\>" followed by the birthdates of all the people you have ever known.

Your screen will now say: "Invalid file path. Whoa! Abort or continue?" Warning: Selecting "Continue" may result in irreversible file compression and a default overload in the hard drive. Selecting "Abort," on the other hand, will require you to start the installation process all over again. Your choice.

When the smoke has cleared, insert disc A2 (marked "Disc A1") and repeat as directed with each of the 187 other discs.

When installation is complete, return to file path, and type your name, address, and credit card numbers and press "SEND." This will automatically register you for our free software prize, "Blank Screensaver IV: Nighttime in Deep Space," and allow us to pass your name to lots and lots of computer magazines, online services, and other commercial enterprises, who will be getting in touch shortly.

Congratulations. You are now ready to

use your computer. Here are some simple exercises to get you off to a flying start.

Writing a Letter

Type "Dear — —" and follow it with a name of someone you know. Write a few lines about yourself, and then write, "Sincerely yours" followed by your own name. Congratulations.

Saving a File

To save your letter, select File Menu. Choose Retrieve from Sub-Directory A, enter a backup file number, and place an insertion point beside the macro dialogue button. Select secondary text box from the merge menu, and double-click on the supplementary cleared document window. Assign the tile cascade to a merge file and insert in a text equation box. Alternatively, write the letter out longhand and put it in a drawer.

Advice on Using the Spreadsheet Facility

Don't.

Troubleshooting Section

You will have many, many problems with your computer. Here are some common problems and their solutions.

Problem: My computer won't turn on.

Solution: Check to make sure the computer is plugged in; check to make sure the power button is in the ON position; check the cables for damage; dig up underground cables in your yard and check for damage; drive out into country and check electricity pylons for signs of fallen wires; call hotline.

Problem: My keyboard doesn't seem to have any keys.

Solution: Turn the keyboard the right way up.

Problem: My mouse won't drink its water or go on the spinning wheel.

Solution: Try a high-protein diet or call your pet shop support line.

Problem: I keep getting a message saying: "Non-System General Protection Fault."

Solution: This is probably because you are trying to use the computer. Switch the computer to OFF mode and any annoying messages will disappear.

Problem: My computer is a piece of useless junk.

Correct — and congratulations. You are now ready to upgrade to an Anthrax/3000 Turbo model, or go back to pen and paper.

How to Rent a Car

We've been back in the States for nearly two and a half years now, if you can believe it (and even, come to that, if you can't), so you would think I would be getting the hang of things by now, but no. The intricacies of modern American life still often leave me muddled. Things are so awfully complicated here, you see.

I had occasion to reflect on this the other week when I went to pick up a rental car at the airport in Boston, and the clerk, after logging every number that has ever been associated with me and taking imprints from several credit cards, said: "Do you want Third-Party Liability Waiver Damage Exclusion Coverage?"

"I don't know," I said uncertainly. "What is it?"

"It provides coverage in the event of a Second-Party Waiver Indemnification Claim being made against you, or a First- or Second-Party Exclusion Claim being made by you on behalf of a fourth party

369

twice removed."

"Unless you're claiming a First-Party Residual Cross-Over Exemption," added a man in the line behind me, causing me to spin my head.

"No, that's only in New York," corrected the rental car man. "In Massachusetts you can't claim cross-over exemption unless you have only one leg and are not normally resident in North America for tax purposes."

"You're thinking of Second-Party Disallowance Invalidity Coverage," said the second man in the line to the first. "Are you from Rhode Island?"

"Why, yes I am," said the first man.

"Then that explains it. You have Variable Double Negative Split-Weighting down there."

"I don't understand any of this," I cried in a small whimper.

"Look," said the car rental agent, "suppose you crash into a person who has Second-Party Disallowance Invalidity Coverage but not First- and Third-Party Accident Indemnification. If you've got Third-Party Waiver Damage Exclusion Coverage, you don't have to claim on your own policy under the Single-Digit Reverse Liability Waiver. How much Personal Loss

Rollover do you carry?"

"I have no idea," I said.

He stared at me. "You don't know?" he said.

Out of the corner of my eye I could see the other people in the line exchanging amused glances.

"Mrs. Bryson deals with these things," I explained a trifle inadequately.

"Well, what's your Baseline Double Footfault Level?"

I gave a small, helpless, please-don't-hit-me look. "I don't know."

He drew in breath in a way that suggested that perhaps I should consider taking a Greyhound. "It sounds to me like you need the Universal Full-Coverage Double Top-Loaded Comprehensive Switchback Plan."

"With Graduated Death Benefit," suggested the second person in the line.

"What's all that?" I asked unhappily.

"It's all here in the leaflet," said the clerk. He passed one to me. "Basically, it gives you $100 million of coverage for theft, fire, accident, earthquake, nuclear war, swamp gas explosions, derailment leading to hair loss, meteor impact, and intentional death — so long as they occur simultaneously and providing you give twenty-four hours' notice in writing and file an Incident Intention Report."

"How much is it?"

"One hundred and seventy-two dollars a day. But it comes with a set of steak knives."

I looked to the other people in the line. They nodded.

"OK, I'll take it," I said in exhausted resignation.

"Now do you want the Worry-Free Fuel Top-Up Option," the clerk went on, "or the Fill-It-Yourself Cheap Person's Option?"

"What's that?" I asked, dismayed to realize that this hell wasn't yet over.

"Well, with the Worry-Free Fuel Top-Up Option, you can bring the car back on empty and we will refill the tank for a one-time charge of $32.95. Under the other plan, you fill the tank yourself before returning the car and we put the $32.95 elsewhere on the bill under 'Miscellaneous Unexplained Charges.' "

I consulted with my advisers and took the Worry-Free plan.

The clerk checked the appropriate box. "And do you want the Car Locator Option?"

"What's that?"

"We tell you where the car is parked."

"*Take it*," urged the man nearest me with feeling. "I didn't take it once in Chicago and spent two and a half days wandering around the airport looking for the damned thing. Turned out it was under a tarpaulin in a cornfield near Peoria."

And so it went. Eventually, when we had worked our way through two hundred or so pages of complexly tiered options, the clerk passed the contract to me.

"Just sign here, here, and here," he said. "And initial here, here, here, and here — and over here. And here, here, and here."

"What am I initialing?" I asked warily.

"Well, this one gives us the right to come to your home and seize one of your children or a nice piece of electronic equipment if you don't bring the car back on time. This one is your agreement to take a truth serum in the event of a dispute. This one waives your right to sue. This one avows that any damage to the car now or at any time in the future is your responsibility. And this one is a twenty-five dollar donation to Bernice Kowalksi's leaving party."

Before I could respond, he whipped away the contract and replaced it on the counter with a map of the airport.

"Now to get to the car," he continued, drawing on the map as if doing one of those maze puzzles that you find in children's coloring books, "you follow the red signs through Terminal A to Terminal D2. Then you follow the yellow signs, including the green ones, through the parking ramp to the Sector R escalators. Take the down escalator up to Passenger Assembly Point Q, get on the shuttle marked "Satellite Parking/Mississippi Valley," and take it to Parking Lot A427-West. Get off there, follow the white arrows under the harbor tunnel, through the quarantine exclusion zone, and past the water filtration plant. Cross runway 22-Left, climb the fence at the far side, go down the embankment, and you'll find your vehicle parked in bay number 12,604. It's a red Toro. You can't miss it."

He passed me my keys and a large box filled with documents, insurance policies, and other related items.

"And good luck to you," he called after me.

I never did find the car, of course, and I was hours late for my appointment, but in fairness I have to say that we have had a lot of pleasure from the steak knives.

The Wasteland

I have been watching a movie called *Magnificent Obsession* lately. Made in 1954 and starring Rock Hudson and Jane Wyman, it is one of those gorgeously mediocre movies they made in abundance in the early 1950s when people would still watch almost anything (as opposed to now when you have to put in lots of fiery explosions and at least one scene involving the hero rappeling down an elevator shaft).

Anyway, if I've got it right, *Magnificent Obsession* involves a handsome young racing car driver played by Rock who carelessly causes Ms. Wyman to go blind in a car crash. Rock is so consumed with guilt at this that he goes off and studies eye medicine at the "University of Oxford, England," or some place, then comes back to Perfectville under an assumed name and dedicates his life to restoring Jane's sight. Only of course she doesn't know it's him on account of she is blind, as well as apparently a little slow with regard to recognizing the voices of people who have left her permanently maimed.

Needless to say, they fall in love and she gets her sight back. The best scene is when Rock removes her bandages and she sputters, "Why, it's . . . *you!*" and slumps into an extravagant but comely swoon, but unfortunately does not strike her head on the coffee table and lose her vision again, which would have improved the story considerably, if you ask me. Also, Jane has a ten-year-old daughter played by one of those pigtailed, revoltingly precocious child actors of the fifties that you just ache to push out a high window. I expect also Lloyd Nolan is in there somewhere because Lloyd Nolan is always in 1950s movies with parts for doctors.

I may not have all the details right because I have not been watching this movie in order, or even on purpose. I have been watching it because one of our cable channels has shown it at least fifty-four times in the last two months, and I keep coming across it while trawling around looking for something actual to watch.

We get about fifty channels in our house — it is possible on some systems now to get up to two hundred, I believe — so you think at first that you are going to be spoiled for choice, but gradually you come to the conclusion that the idea of the bulk of TV these days is simply to fill up the air with any old junk. I have watched "current affairs" investigations that were ten years old. I have seen Barbara Walters interviewing people who died years ago, and weren't that interesting to begin with. On this very evening, under the category of "drama," my cable channel magazine lists as its most sublime and compelling offerings *Matlock* and *Little House on the Prairie*. Tomorrow it recommends *The Waltons* and *Dallas*. The next day it is *Dallas* again and *Murder, She Wrote*.

You begin to wonder who watches it all. One of our channels is a twenty-four-hour cartoon network. That there are people out there who wish to watch cartoons through the night is remarkable enough, but what is truly astounding to me is that the channel carries commercials. What could you possibly sell to people who voluntarily watch *Deputy Dawg* at 2:30 A.M.? Bibs?

But perhaps the most mind-numbing feature is that the same programs are shown over and over at the same times each night. Tonight at 9:30 P.M. on Channel 20 we can watch *The Munsters*. Last night at 9:30 P.M. on Channel 20 it was *The Munsters.* Tomorrow night at 9:30 P.M. on Channel 20 it will be — did you guess correctly? — *The Munsters.* Each *Munsters* showing is preceded by an episode of *Happy Days* and followed by an episode of *The Mary Tyler Moore Show.* It has been like this for years, as far as I can tell, and will stay like this forever.

And it is like this on virtually every channel for every time slot. If you turn on the Discovery Channel and find a program on Hollywood stunts (and you will), you can be certain that the next time you turn to the Discovery Channel at the same hour, it will be a program on Hollywood stunts. Probably it will be the same episode.

I have the fondest memories of programs from my childhood that I would adore to see again in small, measured doses — a little *Burns and Allen,* perhaps some *Jack Benny,* a discriminating selection of *Leave It to Beaver* and *Sgt. Bilko,* maybe a little *77 Sunset Strip* and *Wagon Train* for nostalgia's sake — but I don't want to watch any of them over and over and over, at the same time each night, and in any case I won't because the best of the old programs seem curiously forgotten and unavailable. I just don't understand it.

No doubt the fault is mine. When I left

America I had never lived in a household that received more than four channels. In England, for the next twenty years, it was four channels again. So it may be simply that I have not developed the skills necessary to deal with such a multiplicity of choice. Then again it may be that it's just all crap.

What I can tell you is that with so many channels to choose from, and nearly all of them interrupted every few minutes by commercials, you don't actually watch anything. As a friend recently explained to me, you don't watch television here to see what is on, you watch it to see what else is on. And the one thing to be said for American TV is that there is always something else on. You can trawl infinitely. By the time you have reached the fiftieth channel you have forgotten what was on the first, so you start the cycle again in the forlorn hope that you might find something absorbing this time through.

I'd love to go on, but I must leave you now. I notice that *Magnificent Obsession* is about to start, and I really would like to see Jane Wyman lose her sight. It's the best part. Besides, I keep thinking that if I watch long enough Lloyd Nolan will shove that little girl out an upstairs window.

The Flying Nightmare

My father was a sportswriter who flew a lot for his work in the days before it was common to do so, and occasionally he would take me on one of his trips with him. It was exciting, of course, just to go away for a weekend with my dad, but at the heart of the experience was the thrill of getting on a plane and going somewhere.

Everything about the process felt special and privileged. Checking in, you would be one of a small group of well-dressed people (for in those days people actually dressed up to fly). When the flight was called, you would stroll across a broad tarmac to a gleaming silver plane, and up one of those wheeled staircases. Entering the plane was like being admitted to some special club. Just stepping aboard, you became a little more stylish and sophisticated. The seats were comfy and, for a small boy, commodious. A smiling stewardess would come and give you a little winged badge that said "Assistant Pilot" or something similarly responsible sounding.

All that romance has long since vanished, I'm afraid. Today commercial planes are little more than winged buses, and the airlines, without detectable exception, regard passengers as irksome pieces of bulk freight that they consented, at some time in the remote past, to carry from place to place and now wish they hadn't.

I cannot begin to describe in a space this modest all the spirit-sapping features of modern air travel — the routinely overbooked flights, the endless standing in lines, the delays, the discovery that your "direct" flight to Dallas actually involves stops in Scranton and Nashville and involves layovers of ninety minutes and two changes of planes, the near-impossibility of finding a friendly face among the gate agents, the being treated like an idiot and a cipher.

Yet in the oddest ways airlines continue to act as if it is still 1955. Take the safety demonstration. Why after all these years do the flight attendants still put a life vest over their heads and show you how to pull the little cord that inflates it? In the entire history of commercial aviation no life has been saved by the provision of a life vest. I am especially fascinated by the way they include a little plastic whistle on each vest. I always imagine myself plunging vertically toward the ocean at 1,200 miles an hour and thinking: "Well, thank gosh I've got this whistle."

It is no good asking what they are thinking because they are not thinking anything. I recently boarded a flight from Boston to Denver. When I opened the overhead storage compartment, I found an inflated dinghy entirely filling the space.

"There's a boat in here," I breathed in amazement to a passing flight attendant.

"Yes, sir," said the flight attendant snappily. "This plane meets FAA specifications for overwater flights."

I stared at him in small wonder. "And which body of water do we cross between Boston and Denver?"

"The plane meets FAA specifications for overwater flights whether or not overwater flights are scheduledly anticipated," was his crisp reply, or something similarly inane and mangled.

"Are you telling me that if we go down in water, 150 passengers are supposed to get into a two-man dinghy?"

"No, sir, there's another flotation craft in here." He indicated the bin on the opposite side.

"So two boats for 150 people? Does that strike you as just a little absurd?"

"Sir, I don't make the rules, and you are blocking the aisle."

He talked to me like this because all airline employees eventually talk to you like this if you press them a little bit, and sometimes even if you don't. I feel safe in saying that there is not an industry anywhere in which the notions of service and customer satisfaction are less regarded. All too often the most innocuous move — stepping up to a counter before the check-in clerk is ready to receive you, inquiring why a flight is delayed, ending up with no place to stow your coat because your overhead locker contains an inflated boat — can lead to snappishness and rebuke.

Mind you, with the notable exception of me and a few other meek souls who feel a certain commitment to orderliness, most passengers these days deserve what they get. This is because they take on bulging suit bags and wheeled carry-ons that are at least twice the officially permitted size, so that the overhead bins fill up long before the flight is fully boarded. To make sure they get a bin to themselves, they board before their row is called. On any flight now you will find perhaps 20 percent of the seats filled by people whose row numbers have not been called. I have watched this process with weary exasperation for some years, and I can tell you that it takes roughly half as long again for an American plane to get boarded and airborne as it does anywhere else in the developed world.

The result of this is a kind of war between airline employees and passengers, which all too often redounds on the innocent in a way that cries out for justice.

I particularly recall an experience of a few years ago when my wife, children, and I boarded a flight in Minneapolis to fly to London and discovered that we had been allocated seats in six different parts of the aircraft, up to twenty rows apart. Bemused, my wife pointed this out to a passing stewardess.

The stewardess looked at the boarding passes. "That's correct," she said and started to move away.

"But we'd like some seats together please," said my wife.

The stewardess looked at her, then gave a small, hollow laugh. "Well, it's a little late *now*," she said. "We're boarding. Didn't you check your boarding passes?"

"Only the top one. The check-in clerk"

— who was, let me interject here, a disagreeable specimen herself — "didn't tell us she was scattering us all over the plane."

"Well, there's nothing I can do now."

"But we have small children."

"I'm sorry, you'll just have to make do."

"Are you telling me to put a two-year-old and a four-year-old off by themselves for an eight-hour flight across the Atlantic?" my wife asked. (This was an idea that I believed I could warm to, but I made a grave face, in solidarity.)

The stewardess gave an elaborate, put-upon sigh and, with an air of undisguised resentment, asked a kindly white-haired couple to exchange seats, which allowed my wife and the two youngest to sit together. The rest of us would remain separated.

"Next time look at your boarding passes before you leave the terminal," the attendant snapped at my wife in parting.

"No, next time we will fly with someone else," my wife replied, and indeed ever since we have.

"And one day, I'll have a column in a newspaper and I'll write about this," I called after her in a haughty voice. Of course, I didn't say any such thing, and it would be a terrible abuse of my position to tell you that it was Northwest Airlines that treated us in this shabby and inexcusable way, so I won't.

Enough Already

I have finally figured out what is wrong with everything. There is too much of it. I mean by that that there is too much of every single thing that one could possibly want or need except time, money, good plumbers, and people who say thank you when you hold open a door for them. (And, entirely by the way, I would like to put it on the record here that the next person who goes through a door that I've held open and doesn't say "Thank you" is going to get it in the kidneys.)

America is of course a land of bounteous variety, and for a long time after we first moved here I was dazzled and gratified by the wealth of choice everywhere. I remember going to the supermarket for the first time and being genuinely impressed to find that it stocked no fewer than eighteen varieties of incontinence diaper. Two or three I could understand. Half a dozen would seem to cover every possible incontinence contingency. But eighteen — gosh!

This *was* a land of plenty. And what a range of choice they offered. Some were scented, some were dimpled for extra comfort, and they came in a variety of strengths from, as it were, "Oops, bit of a dribble" to "Whoa! Dambusters!" Those weren't the labels they actually used, of course, but that was the gist of it. They even came in a choice of colors.

For nearly every other type of product — frozen pizzas, dog food, ice creams, cereals, cookies, potato chips — the choices were often literally in the hundreds. Every new flavor seemed to have pupped another flavor. When I was a boy shredded wheat was shredded wheat and that was it. Now you could have it coated in sugar or cinnamon, in bite-size morsels, with slices of genuine bananalike material, and goodness knows what else.

And this applies to everything. You can now choose, apparently, among thirty-five varieties of Crest toothpaste. According to *The Economist*, "The average supermarket in America devotes 20 feet of shelving to medicines for coughs and colds." (And never mind that of the 25,500 "new" consumer products launched in the United States last year, 93 percent were merely modified versions of existing products.)

After twenty years in England this copious abundance was, as you might imagine, almost intoxicating. Lately, however, I have come to suspect that perhaps you can get too much choice. I found myself edging around to this view recently when I was at the airport in Portland, Oregon, standing in a line of about fifteen people at a coffee stand. It was 5:45 A.M., not my best time of day, and I had just twenty minutes till my flight was to be called, but I really, really needed to get some caffeine into my system. You know how it is.

It used to be if you wanted a cup of coffee that's what you asked for and that's what you got. But this place, being a 1990s sort of coffee stand, offered at least twenty choices — plain latte, caramel latte, breve, macchiato, mocha, espresso, espresso mocha, black forest mocha, americano, and so on — in a range of sizes. There was also a galaxy of muffins, croissants, bagels, and pastries. All of these could be had in any number of variations, so that every order went something like this:

"I'll have a caramel latte combo with decaf mocha and a cinnamon twist, and a low-fat cream cheese sourdough bagel, but I'd like the pimento grated and on the side.

Are your poppyseeds roasted in polyunsaturated vegetable oil?"

"No, we use double-extra-lite canola extract."

"Oh, that's no good for me. In that case, I'll have a New York three-cheese pumpernickel fudge croissant. What kind of emulsifiers do you use in that?"

In my mind's eye, I saw myself taking each customer by the ears, shaking his or her head slowly eighteen or twenty times, and saying: "You're just trying to get a cup of coffee and a bread product before your flight. Now ask for something simple and scram."

Fortunately for all these people, until I have had my first cup of coffee in the morning (and this is particularly true during hours in single digits) all I can do is rise, dress myself (a bit), and ask for a cup of coffee. Anything else is beyond me. So I just stood and waited stoically while fifteen people placed complex, time-consuming, preposterously individualized orders.

When at last my turn came, I stepped up and said: "I'd like a large cup of coffee."

"What kind?"

"Hot and in a cup and very large."

"Yeah, but what kind — mocha, macchiato, what?"

"I want whichever one is a normal cup of coffee."

"You want americano?"

"If that means a normal cup of coffee, then yes."

"Well, they're all coffees."

"I want a normal cup of coffee like millions of people drink every day."

"So you want an americano?"

"Evidently."

"Do you want regular whipped cream or low-cal with that?"

"I don't want whipped cream."

"But it comes with whipped cream."

"Look," I said in a low voice, "it is 6:10 A.M. I have been standing for twenty-five minutes behind fifteen seriously selective people, and my flight is being called. If I don't get some coffee right now — and by right now I mean *right* now — I am going to have to murder someone, and I think you should know that you are on the short list." (I am not, as you will gather, a morning person.)

"So does that mean you want low-cal whipped cream or regular?"

And so it went.

This abundance of choice not only makes every transaction take ten times as long as it ought to, but in a strange way actually breeds dissatisfaction. The more there is, the more people crave, and the more they crave, the more they, well, crave more. You have a sense sometimes of being among millions and millions of people needing more and more of everything, constantly, infinitely, unquenchably. We appear to have created a society in which the principal pastime is grazing through retail establishments looking for things — textures, shapes, flavors — not before encountered.

The last time I went for breakfast, I had to choose among nine options for my eggs (poached, scrambled, sunny side up, over easy, and so on), sixteen types of pancake, six varieties of juice, two shapes of sausage, four kinds of potato, and eight varieties of toast, muffin, or bagel. I have taken out mortgages that involved less decision-making than that. I thought I had finished when the waitress said: "Do you want whipped butter, pat butter, butter-margarine blend, or butter substitute?"

"You're joking," I said.

"I don't joke about butter."

"Then pat butter," I said weakly.

"Low-sodium, no-sodium, or regular?"

"Surprise me," I answered in a whisper.

To my astonishment, my wife and children love all this. They love going into an ice cream parlor and being able to choose among seventy-five flavors of ice cream, and then seventy-five types of topping to put on that ice cream.

For my part, I find increasingly that I miss the simplicity, the almost willful paucity, of the English way of doing things. Confronted with a glass case filled with twenty-seven types of pizza or a food court stand offering 126 possible permutations of pretzel, I just wish for a nice cup of tea and a simple, virtually flavorless bun, but I'm afraid I am the only person in the house who feels that way. I trust that my wife and kids will eventually grow sated by all this, but there is no sign of it happening yet.

Still, looking on the bright side, at least I am well-fixed for incontinence diapers.

At a Loss

Of all the things I am not very good at, living in the real world is perhaps the most outstanding. I am constantly filled with wonder at the number of things that other people do without any evident difficulty that are pretty much beyond me. I cannot tell you the number of times that I have gone looking for the rest room in a movie theater, for instance, and ended up standing in an alley on the wrong side of a self-locking door. My particular specialty now is returning to hotel desks two or three times a day and asking what my room number is. I am, in short, easily confused.

I was thinking about this the last time we went *en famille* on a big trip. It was at Easter, and we were flying to England for a week. When we arrived at the airport in Boston and were checking in, I suddenly remembered that I had recently joined British Airways' frequent flyer program. I also remembered that I had put the card in the carry-on bag that was hanging around my neck. And here's where the trouble started.

The zipper on the bag was jammed. So I pulled on it and yanked at it, with grunts and frowns and increasing consternation. While Mrs. Bryson dealt with the checking-in process, I went off into a self-absorbed little world of my own, one that involved just me and a recalcitrant zipper. I pulled and tugged and fiddled, and pulled harder and harder, with more grunts and growls, until the zipper abruptly and lavishly gave way. The side of the bag flew open and everything within — newspaper clippings and other loose papers, a 14-ounce can of pipe tobacco, magazines, passport, English money, film — was ejected over an area about the size of a tennis court.

I watched dumbstruck as a hundred carefully sorted documents came raining down in a fluttery cascade, coins bounced to a variety of noisy oblivions, and the now-lidless can of tobacco rolled crazily across the concourse disgorging its contents as it went.

"My tobacco!" I cried in horror, thinking what I would have to pay for that much tobacco in England, and then changed the cry to "My finger! My finger!"

as I discovered that I had gashed my finger on the zipper and was dripping blood in a lively manner. (I am not very good around flowing blood generally, but when it's my own — well, I think hysterics are fully in order.) Confused and unable to help, my hair went into panic mode.

It was at this point that my wife looked at me with an expression of wonder — not anger or exasperation, but just simple wonder — and said: "I can't believe you do this for a living."

But I'm afraid it's so. I always have catastrophes when I travel. Once on an airplane, I leaned over to tie a shoelace just at the moment that the person in the seat ahead of me threw his seat back into full recline, and I found myself pinned helplessly in the crash position. It was only by clawing the leg of the man sitting next to me that I managed to get myself freed.

On another occasion, I knocked a soft drink onto the lap of a sweet little lady sitting beside me. The flight attendant came and cleaned her up, and brought me a replacement drink, and instantly I knocked it onto the woman again. To this day, I don't know how I did it. I just remember reaching out for the new drink and watching helplessly as my arm, like some cheap prop in one of those 1950s horror movies with a name like "The Undead Limb," violently swept the drink from its perch and onto her lap.

The lady looked at me with the stupefied expression you would expect to receive from someone whom you have repeatedly drenched, and uttered an exceptionally earnest oath that started with "Oh" and finished with "sake" and in between had some words that I have never heard uttered in public before, certainly not by a nun.

This, however, was not my worst experience on a plane flight. My worst experience was when I was writing important thoughts in a notebook ("Buy socks," "clutch drinks carefully," etc.) sucking thoughtfully on the end of my pen as you do, and fell into conversation with an attractive lady in the next seat. I amused her for perhaps twenty minutes with a scattering of urbane bons mots, then retired to the lavatory where I discovered that the pen had leaked and that my lips, tongue, teeth, and gums were now a striking, scrub-resistant navy blue, and would remain so for several days.

So you will understand, I trust, when I tell you how much I ache to be suave. I would love just once in my life to rise from a dinner table without looking as if I have just experienced an extremely localized seismic event, get in a car and close the door without leaving fourteen inches of coat outside, wear light-colored pants without discovering at the end of the day that I have at various times sat in chewing gum, ice cream, cough syrup, and motor oil. But it is not to be.

Now on planes when the food is delivered, my wife says: "Take the lids off the food for Daddy" or "Put your hoods up, children. Daddy's about to cut his meat." Of course, this is only when I am flying with my family. When I am on my own, I don't eat, drink, or lean over to tie my shoelaces, and never put a pen anywhere near my mouth. I just sit very, very quietly, sometimes on my hands to keep them from flying out unexpectedly and causing liquid mischief. It's not much fun, but it does at least cut down on the laundry bills.

I never did get my frequent flyer miles, by the way. I never do. I couldn't find the card in time. This has become a real frustration for me. Everyone I know — everyone — is forever flying off to Bali first class with their air miles. I never get to collect anything. I must fly 100,000 miles a year, yet I have accumulated only about

212 air miles divided among twenty-three airlines.

This is because either I forget to ask for the air miles when I check in or I remember to ask for them but the airline then manages not to record them or the check-in clerk informs me that I am not entitled to them. In January, on a flight to Australia — a flight for which I was going to get about a zillion frequent flyer miles — the clerk shook her head when I presented my card and told me I was not entitled to any.

"Why?"

"The ticket is in the name of B. Bryson and the card is in the name of W. Bryson."

I explained to her the venerable relationship between the names Bill and William, but she wouldn't have it.

So I didn't get my frequent flyer miles, and I won't be jetting off to Bali first class just yet. Perhaps just as well, really. I could never go that long without eating.

Old News

"Science finds the secret of aging," announced a headline in our paper the other day, which surprised me because I've never thought of it as a secret. It just happens. No secret in that.

As far as I am concerned, there are three good things about getting older. I can sleep sitting up, I can watch "Seinfeld" reruns over and over without being able to say definitively whether I have seen them already, and I can't remember the third thing. That's the problem with getting older, of course — you can't remember anything.

For me, it's getting worse. Increasingly I have telephone conversations with my wife that go like this:

"Hello, dear. I'm in town. Why am I here?"

"You've gone to get an ink cartridge for your printer."

"Thank you."

You would think that as I get older this

would get better because there is less of my mind to grow absent, but it doesn't seem to work that way. You know how as the years tick by you find yourself more and more standing in some part of the house you don't often visit — the laundry area perhaps — looking around with pursed lips and a thoughtful gaze, trying to remember why you are there? It used to be with me that if I retraced my steps back to where I began, the purpose of this curious expedition would come to me. No more. Now I can't even remember where I began. No idea at all.

So I wander through the house for twenty minutes looking for some sign of recent activity — a lifted floorboard perhaps, or a burst pipe, or maybe a telephone receiver on its side and a curious little voice squawking: *"Bill? You still there?"* — something in any case that might have prompted me to get up and go off in search of a notepad or stopcock or goodness knows what. Usually in the course of these wanderings I find some other thing that needs attending to — a lightbulb that's burned out, say — so I go off to the kitchen cupboard where the light bulbs are kept and open the door and . . . yes, that's right, have no idea why I am there. So the process starts again.

Time is my particular downfall. Once something moves into the past tense, I lose all track of it. My sincerest dread in life is to be arrested and asked: "Where were you between the hours of 8:50 A.M. and 11:02 A.M. on the morning of December 11, 1998?" When this happens, I will just hold out my wrists for the handcuffs and let them take me away because there isn't the remotest chance of my recalling. It has been like this for me for as long as I can remember, which of course is not very long.

My wife does not have this problem. She can remember everything that ever happened and when. I mean every little detail. Out of the blue she will say things to me like: "It was sixteen years ago this week your grandmother died."

"Really?" I reply, amazed. "I had a grandmother?"

The other thing that happens a lot these days is that when I am out with my wife somebody I would swear I have never seen before comes up and chats with us in a friendly and familiar fashion.

"Who was that?" I will ask when he has departed.

"That was Lottie Rhubarb's husband."

I think for a moment, but nothing comes.

"Who's Lottie Rhubarb?"

"You met her at the Talmadges' barbecue at Big Bear Lake."

"I've never been to Big Bear Lake."

"Yes you have. For the Talmadges' barbecue."

I think again for a minute. "So who are the Talmadges?"

"The people on Park Street who had the barbecue for the Skowolskis."

By now I am beginning to feel desperate. "Who are the Skowolskis?"

"The Polish couple you met at the barbecue at Big Bear Lake."

"I didn't *go* to a barbecue at Big Bear Lake."

"Of course you did. You sat on a skewer."

"I sat on a *skewer?*"

We have had conversations like this that have gone on for three days, and I have still been none the wiser at the end.

I have always been absentminded, I'm afraid. When I was a boy I had an afternoon newspaper route in the wealthiest neighborhood in Des Moines, which sounds like a plum assignment but was not because, in the first place, rich people are the biggest skinflints at Christmas (especially, let the record show, Mr. and Mrs. Arthur J. Niedermeyer of 27 St. John's Road, Dr. and Mrs. Richard Gumbel in the big brick house on Lincoln Place, and Mr. and Mrs. Samuel Drinkwater of the Drinkwater banking fortune; I hope you are all in nursing homes now) and because every house was set back a quarter of a mile from the street at the end of a long, curving drive.

Even in hypothetically ideal circumstances, it would take hours to complete such a route, but I never got to such a point. My problem was that while my legs did the route, my mind would be in that state of dozy reverie that characterizes all absentminded people.

Without fail, at the end of the route I would look into my bag and, with a long-suffering sigh, find half a dozen papers left over, each representing a house I had visited — a long drive I had trudged up, a porch I had crossed, a screened door I had opened — without actually leaving a newspaper behind. Needless to say, I would have no recollection of which of the eighty properties on my route these were, so I would sigh again and walk the route a second time. By such means did I pass my childhood. I wonder if the Neidermeyers, Gumbels, and Drinkwaters had known what hell I went through every day to get them their stupid *Des Moines Tribune* whether they would have been quite so happy to stiff me at Christmas. Probably.

Anyway, you are probably wondering about this secret of aging I alluded to in the opening paragraph. According to the newspaper account, it appears that a Dr. Gerard Schellenberg at the Seattle Veterans Administration Medical Research Center has isolated the genetic culprit behind aging. It seems that embedded in each gene is something called a helicase, which is part of a family of enzymes, and that this helicase, for no good reason, peels apart the two strands of chromosomes that make up your DNA, and the next thing you know you are standing at the kitchen cupboard trying to remember what the heck brought you there.

I can't give you any more details than that because naturally I have mislaid the article, and anyhow it hardly matters because in a week or two somebody else will come along and uncover some other secret of aging, and everyone will forget about Dr. Schellenberg and his findings — which is, of course, precisely what I have begun to do already.

So in conclusion we can see that forget-fulness is probably not such a bad thing after all. I believe that's the point I was trying to make, but to tell you the truth, I don't remember now.

Rules for Living

In order to make the world a better place, the following rules will take force with immediate effect across the planet.

1. It is no longer permitted to be stupid *and* slow. You must choose one or the other.

2. People who wear articles of clothing on which the manufacturer's name or logo is prominently displayed must also wear a badge saying: "Yes, I Am an Idiot."

3. If in the course of parking your car you are not able to maneuver the vehicle into a space in less time than it takes to undergo and recover from open heart surgery, it is not permitted to park in that space.

4. When standing in line at a retail establishment, it is a requirement that you familiarize yourself with the currency of your nation before attempting a transaction. It is not permitted to engage the sales assistant in conversation regarding the weather, the health or personal relationships of mutual acquaintances, or other matters not relevant to the purchase. When purchasing food or beverages, anyone who has to leave the line to ask his or her partner whether the partner wants a sugar cone or a plain cone, or a small, medium, or large macchiato, or anything like that, will be escorted from the premises. Anyone who reaches the front of a line and says, "Now what do I want?" and purses his lips thoughtfully or drums his fingers on his chin while studying the ordering options as if for the first time will be taken outside and shot.

5. If you are waiting for an elevator that is slow to come and you are the sort of person who pushes the call button repeatedly in the sincere belief that that will make a difference, you are no longer permitted to use elevators.

6. Martha Stewart is, with immediate effect, illegal.

7. All hotel room lights will switch off by the door, by the bed, and in an easily identifiable location on the light fixtures themselves. If a hotel patron climbs into bed and discovers that a floor lamp across the room cannot be turned off from the bed, he is entitled to a free night's stay. If he then must spend five minutes or more fig-

uring out how to turn the floor lamp off, he is entitled to help himself, gratis, to the contents of the minibar.

8. All instruction booklets that say "Attach lock washers D1 and D2 to hub seal J by means of spindle brackets H-4a and H-5," or anything remotely similar, are illegal.

9. Boxes of Christmas cards that carry messages like "May your holidays be wrapped in warmth and touched with wonder" must bear a large label on the outside of the box saying: "Do Not Purchase: Message Inside Is Embarrassing and Sentimental."

10. All cars will come equipped with gas caps on both sides and at the rear, and gas station hoses will be at least six feet longer.

11. Any electronic clock or other timing device on which the time is set by holding down a button and scrolling laboriously through the minutes and hours is illegal. Also, when you are trying to set the alarm on such a device for, say, 7:00 A.M., and the numbers get to about 6:52 and then suddenly speed up and you discover to your dismay that you have gone past the desired hour and have to start all over again, that is extremely illegal.

12a. The following are, with immediate

effect, free of charge: airport baggage carts, any kind of operator assistance involving a pay telephone, plain bottled water, airline headsets, room service, any portion of a consultation with a lawyer, doctor, or accountant that involves the lawyer, doctor, or accountant talking about his golf game or other aspect of his personal life.

12b. The price of the following will immediately be reduced by two-thirds: movie theater popcorn, alcohol in restaurants, orthodontia, airline flights of more than two hours in which no food is served, carbonated bottled water, vending machine products (especially those little packets of peanut butter crackers), college textbooks, toast as a side order, any portion of a consultation with a lawyer, doctor, or accountant not specified in 12a.

13. It is no longer permitted to pronounce *et cetera* as if it had a "k" in it, as this is beginning to annoy the author. Also, it is not permitted to use *absent* at the start of a sentence, as in "Absent a change of direction by the government . . .", to urge the author or any other living person to "have a good one," or to say in any context whatever that one is seeking closure.

14. Supermarkets henceforth are required to put everything where a middle-aged man who doesn't shop much can find it.

15. Revolving doors must go in both directions, the direction to be decided by the author. Giant revolving doors that take ten people at a time are illegal unless the occupants are known to each other and have agreed beforehand to move at the same speed.

16. Americans who intend to travel abroad in a group with other Americans must first clear their wardrobes with the author. British men must secure written permission to wear shorts outside their own country.

17. That shrill, piercing noise you get when you mistakenly dial someone's fax number is, with immediate effect, extremely illegal. Also, it is illegal to play music, commercials, or promises that an agent will be available shortly to anyone you put on hold on a telephone. On second thought, it is illegal to put anyone on hold on a telephone.

18. Photocopiers will clearly indicate where you are supposed to put the piece of paper you want copied and will provide an immediate refund and spoken apology each time they produce a horizontal photocopy when a vertical one is desired. Any user of a photocopier who instructs the machine to produce a tablecloth-sized photocopy or one hundred copies of a single document, or anything like that, and who then does not reset the machine to its normal settings will be hunted down by the photocopier police and made to drink a cup of toner.

19. In office buildings and retail premises in which entry is through double doors and one of those doors is locked for no reason, the door must bear a large sign saying: "This Door Is Locked for No Reason."

20. For an experimental period of ten years, smoking will be permitted in all those places where it is now banned and banned where it is now permitted. Nonsmokers who find smoke disagreeable will be permitted to step outside and loiter by the main entrance for ten minutes each hour.

21. Pedestrians will have the right of way at all times and in all places. Anyone who honks at a pedestrian (but especially the author) at any time for any reason will have his or her car taken away.

22. All microwave ovens will automatically recognize whatever food is placed

within them and cook accordingly. All washing machines will wash any article of attire, including neckties, business suits, and leather footwear, without shrinkage or running of colors.

23. Any symbol on any button on any automobile dashboard that involves wavy lines, a triangle, or any other depiction that means absolutely nothing to anyone is no longer permitted. On unfamiliar vehicles, such as rental cars, the lever that activates the turn signal will be whichever one the author deems it to be.

24. In a public rest room, when you have washed your face as well as your hands and then discover that there is only a hot air dryer, that is very illegal.

25. Liver and goat cheese will no longer be regarded as foods. In fancy restaurants, salads may no longer contain anything that can be found growing at the side of any public highway.

26. Until further notice it is illegal to talk with enthusiasm about any aspect of e-mail, personal organizers, cellular telephones, online shopping, or anything with the word *digital* in it.

27. All reviews of the author's work will, with immediate effect, be submitted to the author for correction and helpful revision before publication.

28. All Americans will appreciate irony. Britons will understand that two ice cubes in a drink is not nearly enough.

Thank you for helping to make the world a better place. Your cooperation is appreciated.

Our Town

I have just been reading a fascinating tome called, with engaging redundancy, "The Town of Hanover Annual Town Report," which is sent to every household in our community at this time of year. Running to 132 pages, it is packed with graphs, tables, and charts concerning matters of municipal life that I mostly don't understand — "sewer rental abatements," "vehicle reserve code administration allowances," "shared revenue block grants" — and am pretty happy not to.

But tucked away among the abstruse figures are some heartwarming nuggets of real information. I am happy to report, for instance, that of the 13,397 "incidents" the police dealt with last year, the overwhelming majority — virtually all, in fact — were in a benign and helpful role: attending to minor accidents and breakdowns, accompanying ambulances on emergency runs, rounding up lost pets, unlocking cars for the absentminded.

In much the same way, the valiant members of the fire department were mostly engaged with good works. Of the brigade's 565 call-outs last year, only 30 were for fires. The rest were concerned with flooded basements, stuck elevators, rescue calls, and "extrication" — i.e., getting cats out of trees.

All in all, the report provides a statistical confirmation of what I see every day with my own eyes — that this is a safe, well-ordered, thriving little community.

We have, for instance, the best public library I have ever seen in a town of this size. It has, the town report notes with justifiable pride, over 73,000 books, tapes, and other related items and last year checked out over 206,000 volumes — impressive numbers for a small-town library. It is open 56 hours a week, 335 days a year. Last year it offered 244 programs and other events and its public meeting room was used 815 times. These are all figures to be proud of.

Hanover is also the only town I know in which the movie theater is owned by the local civic improvement society, and the profits are used to enhance the town. There is a certain real satisfaction in knowing that if I am dragged to see

Godzilla this summer (as I most assuredly will be) and if I hate it (as I also most assuredly will) the cost of my tickets will be converted into a tub of geraniums by the Town Hall or something else esthetically pleasing.

But what I really like about Hanover is that it is just the way small towns are supposed to be. It has an agreeably yesteryear Main Street with a post office, a drugstore, a rambling bookstore, a wonderfully snug and convivial bar-cum-restaurant called Murphy's, an equally cherishable cafe called Lou's, a couple of banks, and our lovely old movie theater. The buildings are mostly unassuming brick structures, with green canvas awnings to give shade from sun and cover from rain. Together they provide a cozy ensemble that is at once welcoming and convenient. It is a scene that you have seen in the movies a million times.

You wouldn't believe how rare these places are becoming. Small towns everywhere are dying. Just since 1991 America has lost nine thousand corner drugstores. That's nearly one-third of the small, independent neighborhood drugstores in the country. That's an awful lot of drugstores in less than a decade. Most other types of locally owned businesses have been hit as hard or harder. Independent bookstores, for instance, have seen their share of book sales fall by half in less than a decade.

The principal culprits in this are big discount chains like Wal-Mart, the most successful retail group in America. Although it is moving increasingly into urban areas, Wal-Mart traditionally has specialized in erecting gargantuan warehouse-type stores just outside small and medium-size communities, offering cutthroat prices, bigger choice, and lots of free parking. Since 1980, Wal-Mart's sales have gone from $1.2 billion a year to about $120 billion a year, roughly equivalent to the gross domestic product of Greece. The bulk of that — 80 percent, according to one study — is money that was once spent in scores of different businesses in the middles of towns. According to Kenneth Stone, an Iowa State University economist who has specialized in the impact of Wal-Mart on small towns, general merchandise stores typically experience a decline in sales of 34 percent after ten years, which is of course more than many of them can bear. In lots of communities, in consequence, Wal-Mart has effectively become the new downtown.

Small-town businesses simply can't compete with the ease and cheapness of the large chains. But even those enterprises that are insulated from direct competition have been abandoning town centers in droves. The Postal Service, for instance, has been closing down old post offices all over the country and rebuilding on new sites outside town. A typical case was that of Livingston, Montana, whose residents discovered one day late last year that their post office — a lovely old building that had been at the heart of the community since 1914 — was to be shut and the business transferred to a zone of shopping malls on the periphery. There are at least four towns here in our corner of New Hampshire that have suffered this unkind fate, and all of them have downtowns that are struggling.

Hanover, miraculously, has so far managed to escape most of this. However, a new shopping mall opened a mile or so outside town recently, and I would be astonished if at least some of the local merchants don't drift out there in the coming months and years. A new Wal-Mart is about to be built in the next town down the highway, which will further erode local loyalties, and our local bookstore — which just happens to be the oldest family-run

419

bookshop in the nation — is continually and publicly worried by rumors that one of the large chains is planning a megastore nearby.

There are no plans, so far as I know, to close the post office — but then no one in Livingston, Montana, knew that their post office was to close. The postal authorities informed the town council on a Tuesday and advertised the premises for sale the next day. That's the way it goes.

It's an odd thing really because people in the United States venerate and adore small towns, at least in theory. Ask an American to conjure up an image of quintessential Americana — a Fourth of July parade, the paintings of Norman Rockwell, the movies of Jimmy Stewart — and it is as likely as not to involve a small-town scene. It is no accident that the Walt Disney Company puts a classic, picturesque Main Street at the heart of every one of its amusement parks.

Most people think they want Main Streets but won't make the small sacrifices in terms of time, cost, and footpower necessary to sustain them. The sad fact is that we have created a culture in which most people will happily — indeed, unthinkingly — drive an extra couple of miles to walk thirty less feet.

Perhaps Hanover can resist the trend. I have no idea, but I hope so. One thing is certain: If it does, it will be an exception.

Word Play

Have you ever noticed that some words sound perfect for the things they describe and other words don't sound right at all?

I had occasion to reflect on this the other morning when I passed through the kitchen and my wife asked me if I cared to join her in a bowl of muesli.

"Oh, but I don't think we could both get in," I replied, quick as anything. The joke, alas, was wasted on her, but it did set me to thinking what a curious term *muesli* is. It is not a word we use in America. When we sweep up after we have been doing woodworking and put it in a bag with mixed nuts and a little birdseed, and pretend it's a healthful breakfast product, we call it *granola,* which frankly I think is a much superior word. To my mind, *granola* sounds precisely like a crunchy cereal involving bits of grain and chaff, whereas *muesli* doesn't sound like anything at all, except perhaps a salve you would put on a cold sore (or possibly the cold sore itself).

Anyhow, it got me to thinking how some words do their job very well and others don't seem quite up to the task.

Globule, for instance, is a nearly perfect word. It just sounds right. Nobody has to tell you what *globule* means for you to know that it is not something that you want down the front of your shirt. *Scrapie* is another excellent word. Scrapie clearly couldn't be anything but a disease. (Though on reflection it might be a Scottish cut, as in "He fell down and got a wee scrapie on his knee.") *Snooze,* likewise, is also first rate, as are *chortle, clank, gasp, dribble,* and *bloat.* To hear these words is to know what they describe.

Then there is a whole group of words that are not particularly descriptive but are for some reason just very agreeable to say. *Galoshes. Pandemonium. Transubstantiation. Rudimentary. Palpitation. Kiosk. Quisling.* These are all good words.

For a truly bad word, on the other hand, I would suggest *balaclava* — a term that we in America have wisely and instinctively abjured. We use the term *ski mask,* which may not be poetic but does at least have the virtue of clarity. A balaclava, on the other hand, could be almost anything — an obscure root vegetable, a type of geological formation peculiar to the Tibetan steppe, the basic unit of currency in Albania, the sound of a large load of rocks coming off the back of a dump truck, almost anything at all. It certainly doesn't sound like something you would want to put on your head. No, the word you want for a kind of pull-down hat is *haggis.*

Haggis, you see, is not a good word for a food — too sporty, too rakish — but it would be an ideal word for a piece of knitted headwear. ("Oh, Tom, you look so handsome in your new haggis.") *Haggis* simply doesn't sound like a food (but then, as anyone who has eaten haggis will know, it doesn't taste like a food either).

Sometimes you wonder what they were thinking when they named a thing. Take the pineapple. If ever there was an object that was less like pine and less like an apple, and in nearly every respect, this surely must be it. Or grapefruit. I don't know about you, but if someone handed me an unfamiliar fruit that was yellow, sour, and the size of a cannonball, I don't believe I would say, "Well, it's rather like a grape, isn't it?"

I don't know why it is, but most foods, with the notable exceptions of mush and hash, are misnamed. Ketchup, for instance, is a splendid word, but it is quite wasted on a tomato sauce product. *Ketchup* is actually the sound of a small, half-stifled sneeze of the sort maiden aunts make after covering their mouths with a scented hankie. (For the sort of robust sneezes people like you and I make the word is, of course, *cashew*.)

A *pretzel*, meanwhile, is not a dry snack food but one of those stretcher devices into which injured people are strapped when they are being airlifted to safety from mountaintops. *Semolina* is not a pudding at all but a slow, stately dance much practiced in Spanish-speaking countries and widely used to bore tourists. (The same dance in Portugal is called a *fajita*.) *Marzipan* is, obviously, nothing you would want to put in your mouth but a kind of drip tray for collecting fat off meat roasting on a spit.

Other bad words are *anorak, spatula, tofu, pantaloons, serviette, sweetbreads,* and *settee*. Several of these, you will notice, are British. This is not because the British are bad at making up words, I hasten to add, but more a reflection of the fact that nobody is perfect. On the whole, the British are pretty good at coining terms. One of the things that impressed me a great deal when I first went to Britain was the number of excellent words they have for which we have no real equivalent in America — *gormless, skive, gobsmacked, chivvy, snog, berk, pillock, plonker, naff,* and *prat* (interesting how many of these are used for insults). The British are to be commended for every one of these.

On the other hand, they are forever abandoning very good words, which is a trifle careless to say the very least. They had a nearly perfect word in *shilling,* for example, and just let it go. *Half crown* was also very good, *guinea* better still, and *groat* practically unbeatable, and yet they just allowed them to slip away.

So here is my idea. I think we should take some of these good old words and use them to replace words that aren't good, especially those words that have multiple meanings and could cause embarrassment and confusion. As even a moment's reflection will confirm, too many words in English have too many meanings. Consider the sentence "I wonder if I might see your chest." Uttered in an antique shop this would mean one thing; on a dance floor quite another. So I think we should use the old obsolescent words to get rid of some of these confusing multiple senses. This would bring a small measure of orderliness to the language and get some fine old words back into circulation.

Anyway, that's my suggestion for the week. And now that I've got that off my groat, I think I *will* go and join my wife in that bowl of muesli.

Last Night
on the *Titanic*

On the night of the wreck our dinner tables were a picture! The huge bunches of grapes which topped the fruit baskets on every table were thrilling. The menus were wonderfully varied and tempting. I stayed at table from soup to nuts.

— *TITANIC* PASSENGER KATE BUSS,
   QUOTED IN *Last Dinner on the* Titanic:
   Menus and Recipes from the Great Liner

"Good lord, Buss, what's all the commotion?"

"Oh, hello, Smythe. Not like you to be up at this hour. Smoke?"

"Thank you, don't mind if I do. So what's the kerfuffle? I saw the captain as I came by and he looked in a dreadful stew."

"It appears we're sinking, old boy."

"Never!"

"Do you recall that iceberg we saw at dinner?"

"The one that was as big as a twenty-story building?"

"That's the one. Well, it seems we struck the deuced thing."

"Rotten luck."

"Rather."

"I suppose that explains why my cabin door was underneath the bed when I woke up. I thought it a bit odd. I say, is this a Monte Cristo?"

"H. Upmann, actually. I have a man in Gerard Street who gets them specially."

"Awfully nice."

"Yes. . . . Pity, really."

"What's that?"

"Well, I just ordered a dozen boxes at two guineas each. Still, I suppose young Bertie will be glad to get his hands on them."

"So you don't think we're going to make it?"

"Doesn't look good. Mrs. Buss asked Croaker, the quarterdeck steward, when he brought her nightcap and he said we had less than two hours. How's Mrs. Smythe, by the way? Is her stomach better?"

"Couldn't say. She's drowned, you see."

"Oh, rotten luck."

"Went out the starboard porthole when we started to list. It was her shout that woke me, as a matter of fact. Shame she's missed all the excitement. She always enjoyed a good sinking."

"Mrs. Buss is just the same."

"She didn't go over as well, did she?"

"Oh, no. She's gone to see the purser. Wanted to cable Fortnum and Mason's and cancel the order for the garden fête. Not much point now, you see."

"Quite. Still, all in all it's not been a bad voyage, wouldn't you say?"

"Couldn't agree more. The food's been top-notch. Young Kate was particularly taken with the place settings. She thought the dinner tables a picture and the grapes thrilling. She stayed from soup to nuts. You haven't seen her, by any chance?"

"No, why do you ask?"

"It's just that she rushed off in a rather odd way. Said there was something she had to do with young Lord D'Arcy before we went under. Something to do with flags, I gather."

"Flags? How odd."

"Well, she made some reference to needing a jolly roger, if I heard her right. I can't pretend I understand half the things she goes on about. And in any case I was somewhat distracted. Mrs. Buss had just spilled her nightcap down her peignoir —

in consequence of the impact, you see —
and was in a terrible temper because
Croaker wouldn't bring her another. He
told her to get it herself."

"What extraordinary insolence."

"I suppose he was a bit out of sorts
because he won't be getting his tips now,
will he? Can't say I blame him really."

"Still."

"I reported him, of course. One has to
remember one's station, even in a crisis, or
we should be in a terrible mess, don't you
agree? The quartermaster assured me he
won't get another posting on this ship."

"I should think not."

"Bit of a technicality, I suppose, but at
least it's been noted in the book."

"It's been a funny old night, when you
think about it. I mean to say, wife drowns,
ship sinks, and there was no Montrachet
'07 at dinner. I had to settle for a very mid-
dling '05."

"You think that's disappointing? Have a
look at these."

"Sorry, old boy, I can't see in this light.
What are they?"

"Return tickets."

"Oh, that is bad luck."

"Outside port cabin on the Promenade
Deck."

"Oh, very bad luck. . . . I say, what's that noise?"

"That will be the steerage passengers drowning, I expect."

"No, it sounded like a band."

"I believe you're right. Yes, you are quite right. A bit mournful, don't you think? I shouldn't want to try to dance to that."

" 'Nearer My God to Thee,' isn't it? They might have chosen something a bit more festive for our last night at sea."

"Still, I think I'll wander down and see if they've put out supper yet. Coming?"

"No, I think I'll turn in with a brandy. It's going to be a short night as it is. How long have we got, do you suppose?"

"About forty minutes, I'd say."

"Oh, dear. Perhaps I'll skip the brandy then. I don't suppose I'll be seeing you again?"

"Not in this life, old sport."

"Oh, I say, that's very good. I must remember that. Well, good night then."

"Good night."

"By the by, just a thought. The captain didn't say anything about getting into life-boats, did he?"

"Not that I recall. Shall I wake you if he makes an announcement?"

"That would be very good of you, if

you're sure it's no trouble."

"No trouble at all."

"Well, good night then. Give my regards to Mrs. Buss and young Kate."

"With the greatest pleasure. I'm sorry about Mrs. Smythe."

"Well, worse things happen at sea, as they say. I expect she'll bob up somewhere. She was awfully buoyant. Well, good night."

"Good night, old sport. Sleep well."

Property News

We recently bought a flat in London. Well, to be absolutely precise, we haven't actually bought it. We've just sort of borrowed it for the next sixty-three years. It's leasehold, you see, so, despite having paid a king's ransom, and promising to keep it in good order and wipe around the sink and so on, in February 2061 it automatically reverts to an owner whose identity I do not know and who may not even yet be born. (But here's a little secret. I don't intend to do any clearing up after Christmas 2060, so won't *he* be in for a surprise?)

Now I have owned property in Britain before so most of the process of purchasing wasn't too much of a shock. All those things peculiar to the British system, like stamp duty and solicitors' fees and surveyors' reports that cost an arm and a leg and say nothing ("A visual inspection was made of the heating system, which appeared to be in reasonable working order, though a program of regular maintenance is recommended, and for this I'm charging you £400, you chump"), were much as expected.

No, the surprise came when my wife and I flew to London with the demented idea that we would try to get it more or less furnished in a week. I'm not sure if I had forgotten or if I never knew, but it came as a surprise to me to discover that the furniture sections of London department stores don't actually sell anything. They just put out attractive items to look at.

To ensure that no one buys anything, they generally leave these sections unmanned. I believe there are whole floors at John Lewis of Oxford Street that have not seen a member of staff since just before the war. Here, and elsewhere, you can wander around for hours, waving credit cards and calling out "Hello? Hello?" in perfect confidence that no one will ever come to serve you.

If by some miracle you find an employee who is willing to attend you, it would be wrong to assume that this means you will be able to conclude a transaction. We made this discovery on the second morning when we went to Peter Jones, another large and well-known department store, to buy a breakfast table for the kitchen. There were about eight types to choose from and, after a careful look, we made a selection.

"I'm afraid that one's been discontinued," said the sales assistant.

"Then why, pray, is it on display?"

"We're waiting for the new models to come in and we didn't want to leave a blank space on the floor."

But of course.

My wife and I conferred and went for our second choice. It wasn't a particularly special table but it had a card on it saying that it was available and in stock, which meant at least we could take it away with us.

"We'll take this one," I said.

"Certainly, sir. We can have that to you by Monday of next week."

"Pardon me?"

"Or the Friday of the following week at the very latest."

"But the card says it's in stock," I sputtered.

He favored us with one of those bland, condescending smiles that you only ever see on people in the British retail trade who are dealing with foreigners. "Indeed, it is — in our warehouse in Swindon."

"So we can't have it now?"

"No, but you can certainly have it by the

436

second Wednesday of next month."

"But you just said Monday of next week or the following Friday at the very latest, or something," I said, confused.

"Precisely, sir — the third Tuesday of the month after next. That's assuming it's in stock. Shall I check for you?"

I nodded dumbly.

He made a call and came back to us looking very happy. "Yes, there's one in stock. Would you like it?"

"Yes, please."

He went off to place the order, then came back looking even happier. "I'm afraid it's just gone," he said. "I can put in a special order for you. It will take about thirty days."

"Thirty days to get a kitchen table?"

"Oh no, sir. Thirty days to process the order. The table itself will take somewhat longer."

"How long?"

He surveyed the order book thoughtfully. "Well, the table comes from Sweden. If the manufacturer has it in stock and can get it to the dock at Uppsala on the monthly shipment and it doesn't get held up in customs and the paperwork goes through at our warehouse in Middlesbrough, then I can almost certainly guarantee you a provisional delivery date by next Michaelmas. Or the one after at the very latest."

It was like this for almost everything. The longest delivery date we were quoted was fourteen weeks when we ordered a sofa.

"Fourteen weeks?" I cried, aghast. Now excuse my rough colonial edges, but fourteen weeks is a period of time an American shopper cannot conceive of. To an American shopper there are just three spans of time: now, tomorrow at the very latest, and we'll look elsewhere. The idea of waiting fourteen weeks for anything, other than perhaps a baby, is unknown.

Anyway, fourteen weeks came and went and not only was there no sofa but no word on when there might be a sofa. Meanwhile, we had returned to America, so we began a series of transatlantic phone calls, invariably resulting in our being transferred between departments or put on indefinite hold.

When eventually we would get through to a real person, we would have to acquaint them with the astounding idea that we proposed to give them some money in return for a product. This always seemed to throw them into confusion.

"And what kind of fridge was it you ordered?" a voice on the other end would ask tentatively.

"No, it's a sofa. An ordinary three-seater sofa."

"It sounds like you want the Orders Processing Division — or possibly Accounts Receivable," the voice would say. "Let me ask you this. When you placed your order, did they give you a yellow slip with a green tag or a green slip with a yellow tag?"

With a sigh, I would put the phone down and go off on a protracted hunt through drawers and boxes for the order slip.

"It's actually a light blue slip with a sort of maroon tag," I would announce when I returned.

"Ah," the voice would say in a portentous tone. "I'm afraid we don't deal with light blue and maroons. That's High Wycombe, that is."

"What's High Wycombe?"

"A town in Buckinghamshire."

"No, I mean what's High Wycombe got to do with it?"

"That's where they process light blue and maroons. We only deal with green and yellows here. But you know, sir, if you'd rather have a refrigerator we can guarantee delivery in time for the millennium celebrations."

And so it has gone. At the time of writing, we have been waiting almost eighteen weeks for our sofa. I don't have any idea when we might hope to see it. Still, to look on the bright side, if it isn't here in a little over six decades, it will be somebody else's problem.

Life's
Technicalities

If there is one thing that I trust I have made clear in these pages over the past many months, it is that I am not very good at technical stuff, even at the most basic level. For instance, I have only just learned, to my considerable astonishment, that what I had for years called "duck tape" is actually "duct tape."

In my experience, you either know these things instinctively or you don't. I don't. What's worse is that repairmen know that you don't know. I can't tell you the number of times I have taken a car to the shop because of some minor pinging noise in the engine and undergone an interview with a mechanic that has run something like this:

"What sort of revs have you been getting on your piston torsion?"

"I don't know."

"Have you experienced any slippage on the disk platter?"

"I don't know."

He nods thoughtfully, taking this in. "And what sort of flexion ratios have you been getting on your axial carriage?"

"I don't know."

Another long, thoughtful nod. "Well, I can tell you without even looking," he says, "that you've got a cracked combobulator on your manifold and a serious misalignment in your drive train."

"You know that without even looking?"

"No, but I know that *you* don't know — and boy is it going to cost you!"

Actually, they have never said that, at least not exactly, but you can see that that is what they are thinking.

So when, the other day, Mrs. Bryson announced to me that the washing machine repairman was due to call and, moreover, that I would have to deal with it because she was going out, I received the news with some foreboding.

"Please don't leave it to me," I begged.

"Why not?"

"Because he'll realize in the first five minutes that I'm an idiot and ratchet up his prices accordingly."

"Don't be silly," she said airily, but I knew in my heart that this was going to be one more in a long line of regrettable repair encounters.

When the repairman arrived, I showed him to the washing machine — I had made a special effort to find out where we keep it — and then retired to my desk, hoping that by some miracle he would make some small adjustment that would cost about fifty cents and then quietly let himself out, but secretly I knew that it wouldn't be as simple as that because it never is.

Sure enough, about thirty minutes after he arrived he came to my study holding something metallic and oily.

"Well, I found what it is," he said. "You've got a broken fly valve in your transverse adjudicator."

"Ah," I said, nodding gravely, as if that meant something to me.

"And I think you may have some seepage in your distributor sump."

"Sounds expensive," I said.

"Oh, you bet! I'm going to have to shut off the water."

"OK."

"So where's your auxiliary shut-off valve?"

I looked at him dumbly, my heart simultaneously sinking and beating faster with a sense of panic at the thought of an impending humiliation. "The auxiliary shut-off valve?" I repeated, stalling for time.

"Yes."

I cleared my throat. "I'm not entirely sure," I said.

He cocked an eyebrow in a way that indicated that this was going to make a story for the boys back at the depot. "You're not sure?" he said, a disbelieving smile tugging at his lips.

"Not entirely."

"I see." Not only would there be a story in this, but the extra charges would fund a very nice Christmas party, possibly with dancing girls.

It was clear from his expression that no householder in plumbing history had ever not known the location of his auxiliary shut-off valve. I couldn't bear to be the first.

"The thing is, actually, we don't have one," I blurted.

"You don't have one?"

I nodded with great sincerity. "Seems the builders forgot to put one in."

"You don't have an auxiliary shut-off valve?"

"Afraid not." I made an expression to show that I was as incredulous about this as he was.

I had hoped that this would lead him to

come up with some alternative way of making the repair, but this was a line of inquiry that he wouldn't drop.

"Where's your primary shut-off then?"

"They forgot that, too."

"You're joking."

"I wish I was."

"Well, what would you do if you had a burst pipe?"

Now this I knew. First, I would hop around excitedly, going "Oh my god, oh my god, oh my god!" as you might if, say, you looked down and unexpectedly found your legs on fire. Then I would try to stuff something like a sofa cushion into the leak, making it worse. Then I would hop about some more. Finally, I would dash out into the street and flag down passing vehicles. At about this point Mrs. Bryson would return home and sort everything out. That, at any rate, is how it has always been in the past when we have had a water-spraying event.

Obviously I couldn't admit this to the repairman, so I tried a new tack and said: "Wait a minute. Did you say *auxiliary* shut-off valve? I thought you said *ancillary* shut-off valve." I feigned a hearty chuckle at our comical misunderstanding. "No wonder you're looking at me like that. It's in the attic." I started to lead the way.

He didn't follow. "Are you sure? Normally they're in the basement."

"Yes, exactly — in the basement," I said, immediately changing direction. I led him down to the basement. I should have thought of that in the first place. The basement was full of mysterious things — pipes and spigots and boilers — any one of which might be a shut-off valve. I trusted that he would spy it immediately, and I would be able to say: "That's it. Yes, that's the one." But he didn't do anything. He just looked to me for guidance.

"I think that's it over there," I said uncertainly and pointed to something on the wall.

"That's the fusebox, Mr. Bryson."

The trouble with lying, as our own dear president has learned, is that it nearly always catches up with you in spades. Eventually I broke down and admitted that I didn't have the faintest idea where anything in my own house was, other than the refrigerator, television, and garage. As ever, I ended up seriously embarrassed and hundreds and hundreds of dollars out of pocket.

And the worst of it is, I didn't even get invited to the Christmas party.

An Address

TO THE GRADUATING CLASS OF
KIMBALL UNION ACADEMY, MERIDEN,
NEW HAMPSHIRE

I have a son who is about your age, who in fact will be graduating from Hanover High School in a couple of weeks. When I told him, rather proudly, that I had been asked to give the commencement address here today he looked at me with that special incredulous expression young people are so good at and said: "*You?* Dad, you don't even know how to turn off the back windshield wiper on the car."

And it's a fair point. I don't know how to turn off the back wiper on our car, and I probably never will. There are lots of things I don't know. I'm kind of an idiot and there is no sense denying it.

Nonetheless I have done one thing that neither my son nor any of you graduating seniors have yet done. I have survived twenty-eight years after high school. And,

447

like anyone who has reached my time of life, I have learned a thing or two.

I've learned that if you touch a surface to see if it is hot, it will be. I've learned that the best way to determine if a pen will leak is to stick it in the pocket of your best pants. I've learned that it is seldom a good idea to take clothing off over your head while riding a bicycle. And I have learned that nearly all small animals want to bite me and always will.

I have learned all these things through a long process of trial and error, and so I feel I have acquired a kind of wisdom — the kind that comes from doing foolish things over and over again until it hurts so much you stop. It's not perhaps the most efficient way of acquiring knowledge, but it works and it does at least give you some interesting scars to show at parties.

Now all of this is a somewhat hesitant way of coming around to my main point, which is that I am required by long tradition to give you some advice that will inspire you to go out and lead wholesome and productive lives, which I assume you were intending to do anyway. I'm very honored to have that opportunity.

With that in mind, I would like to offer ten very small, simple observations —

passing thoughts really — which I hope will be of some use to you in the years ahead. In no particular order, they are:

1. Take a moment from time to time to remember that you are alive. I know this sounds a trifle obvious, but it is amazing how little time we take to remark upon this singular and gratifying fact. By the most astounding stroke of luck an infinitesimal portion of all the matter in the universe came together to create you and for the tiniest moment in the great span of eternity you have the incomparable privilege to exist.

For endless eons there was no you. Before you know it, you will cease to be again. And in between you have this wonderful opportunity to see and feel and think and do. Whatever else you do with your life, nothing will remotely compare with the incredible accomplishment of having managed to get yourself born. Congratulations. Well done. You really are special.

2. But not that special. There are five billion other people on this planet, every one of them just as important, just as central to the great scheme of things, as you are. Don't ever make the horrible, unworthy mistake of thinking yourself more vital and significant than anyone else. Nearly all the people you encounter in life merit your consideration. Many of them will be there to help you — to deliver your pizza, bag your groceries, clean up the motel room you have made such a lavish mess of. If you are not in the habit of being extremely nice to these people, then get in the habit now.

Millions more people, most of whom you will never meet or even see, won't help you, indeed can't help you, may not even be able to help themselves. They deserve your compassion. We live in a sadly heartless age, when we seem to have less and less space in our consciences and our pocketbooks for the poor and lame and dispossessed, particularly those in far-off lands. I am making it your assignment to do something about it.

3. Don't ever do anything on principle alone. If you haven't got a better reason for doing something other than the principle of the thing, then don't do it.

4. Whatever it is you want to do in life, do it. If you aspire to be a celebrated ballerina or an Olympic swimmer or to sing at Carnegie Hall, or whatever, go for it. Even though everyone is tactfully pointing out

450

that you can't sing a note or that no one has ever won the 100-meter dash with a personal best time of seventy-four seconds, do it anyway. There is nothing worse than getting to my age and saying, "I could have played second base for the Boston Red Sox but my dad wanted me to study law." Tell your dad to study law. You go and climb Everest.

5. Don't make the extremely foolish mistake of thinking that winning is everything. If there is one person that I would really like to smack, it is the person who said, "Winning is not the main thing. It's the only thing." That's awful. Taking part is the main thing. Doing your best is the main thing. There is no shame in not winning. The shame is in not trying to win, which is of course another matter altogether. Above all, be gracious in defeat. Believe me, you'll get plenty of chances to put this into practice, so you might as well start working on it now.

6. Don't cheat. It's not worth it. Don't cheat on tests, don't cheat on your taxes, don't cheat on your partner, don't cheat at Monopoly, don't cheat at anything. It is often said that cheaters never prosper. In my experience, cheaters generally do prosper. But they also nearly always get

caught in the end. Cheating is simply not worth it. It's as simple as that.

7. Strive to be modest. It is much more becoming, believe me. People are always more impressed if they find out independently that you won the Nobel Prize than if you wear it around your neck on a ribbon.

8. Always buy my books, in hardback, as soon as they come out.

9. Be happy. It's not that hard. You have a million things to be happy about. You are bright and young and enormously good-looking — I can see that from here. You have your whole life ahead of you. But here's the thing to remember. You will *always* have your whole life ahead of you. That never stops and you shouldn't forget it.

10. Finally — and if you remember nothing else from what is said here today, remember this — if you are ever called upon to speak in public, keep your remarks brief. Thank you very much.

(And a bonus point for readers: If you write for a living, never hesitate to recycle material.)

Coming Home: Part II

Today marks the third anniversary of our move to the States. It occurs to me that I have never explained in these pages why we took this momentous step and that you might wonder how we decided on it. Me, too.

What I mean by that is that I honestly don't recall how or when we decided to transfer countries. What I can tell you is that we were living in a farming village in the comely depths of the Yorkshire Dales and, beautiful though it was and much as I enjoyed having conversations in the pub that I couldn't begin to understand ("Aye, I been tupping sheep up on Windy Poop and it were that mucky at bottom sinkhole I couldn't cross beck. Haven't known it this barmish since last back end o' wittering, and mine's a pint of Tetley's if you're thinking of offering"), it was becoming increasingly impractical, as the children grew and my work took me farther afield, for us to live in an isolated spot, however gorgeous.

So we made the decision to move somewhere a little more urban and built-up. And then — this is the part that gets hazy — somehow this simple concept evolved into the notion of settling in America for a time.

Everything seemed to move very swiftly. Some people came and bought the house, I signed a lot of papers, and a small army of removal men took everything away. I can't pretend that I didn't know what was happening, but I can clearly recall, exactly three years ago today, waking up in a strange house in New Hampshire, looking out the window, and thinking: "What on earth am I doing here?"

I felt as if we had made a terrible mistake. I had nothing against America, you understand. It's a wonderful country, splendid in every way. But this felt uncomfortably like a backward step — like moving in with one's parents in middle age. They may be perfectly delightful people, but you just don't want to live with them any longer. Your life has moved on. I felt like that about a nation.

As I stood there in a state of unfolding dismay, my wife came in from an exploratory stroll around the neighborhood. "Oh, it's *wonderful*," she cooed. "The people are so friendly, the weather is glorious, and you can walk anywhere you want without having to look out for cow pies."

"Everything you could want in a country," I remarked queasily.

"Yes," she said, and meant it.

She was smitten, and remains so, and I can understand that. There is a great deal about America that is deeply appealing. There are all the obvious things that outsiders always remark on — the ease and convenience of life, the friendliness of the people, the astoundingly abundant portions, the intoxicating sense of space, the cheerfulness of nearly everyone who serves you, the notion that almost any desire or whim can be simply and instantly gratified.

My problem was that I had grown up with all this, so it didn't fill me with quite the same sense of novelty and wonder. I failed to be enchanted, for instance, when people urged me to have a nice day.

"They don't actually care what kind of day you have," I would explain to my wife. "It's just a reflex."

"I know," she would say, "but it's still nice."

And of course she was right. It may be an essentially empty gesture, but at least it springs from the right impulse.

As time has passed, much of this has grown on me as well. As one of nature's great skinflints, I am much taken with all the free stuff in America — free parking, free book matches, free refills of coffee and soft drinks, free basket of candy by the cash register in restaurants and cafés. Buy a dinner at one of our local restaurants and you get a free ticket to the movies. At our photocopying shop there is a table along one wall that is cluttered with free things to which you can help yourself — pots of glue, stapler, Scotch tape, a guillotine for neatening edges, boxes of rubber bands and paper clips. You don't have to pay an extra fee for any of this or even be a customer. It's just there for anyone who wants to wander in and use it. In Yorkshire we sometimes went to a baker's where you had to pay an extra penny — a penny! — if you wanted your loaf of bread sliced. It's hard not to be charmed by the contrast.

Much the same could be said of the American attitude to life, which, generally speaking, is remarkably upbeat and lacking in negativity — a characteristic that I tend to take for granted when I am in the States but am reminded of not infrequently in Britain. The last time I arrived at

Heathrow Airport, for instance, the official who checked my passport looked me over and asked: "Are you that writer chap?"

I was very pleased, as you can imagine, to be recognized. "Why, yes I am," I said proudly.

"Come over here to make some more money, have you?" he said with disdain and slid back my passport.

You don't get much of that in the States. By and large, people have an almost instinctively positive attitude to life and its possibilities. If you informed an American that a massive asteroid was hurtling toward Earth at 125,000 miles an hour and that in twelve weeks the planet would be blown to smithereens, he would say: "Really? In that case, I suppose I'd better sign up for that Mediterranean cooking course now."

If you informed a Briton of the same thing, he would say: "Bloody typical, isn't it? And have you seen the weather forecast for the weekend?"

I asked my wife the other day if she would ever be ready to go back to England.

"Oh, yes," she said without hesitation.

"When?"

"One day."

I nodded, and I must say I felt exactly

the same. I miss England. I liked it there. There was something about it that just suited me. But if we were to leave America now, I would miss it, too, and a very great deal more than I would have thought possible three years ago. It's a wonderful country, and my wife was certainly right about one thing. It's nice not to have to watch out for cow pies.

Now please — and I really mean this — have a nice day.

We hope you have enjoyed this Large Print book. Other Thorndike Press or Chivers Press Large Print books are available at your library or directly from the publishers.

For more information about current and upcoming titles, please call or write, without obligation, to:

Thorndike Press
P.O. Box 159
Thorndike, Maine 04986 USA
Tel. (800) 257-5157

OR

Chivers Press Limited
Windsor Bridge Road
Bath BA2 3AX
England
Tel. (0225) 335336

All our Large Print titles are designed for easy reading, and all our books are made to last.